# Poetry, Praise
# And
# Politics

Dr. Arvil Jones

This book was printed in the United States of America.

To order additional copies of this book contact:

Dr. Arvil Jones
Cjones156@cinci.rr.com
513-907-7751
1304 Bonacker Ave.
Hamilton, Ohio 45011

FWB

# Foreword

Arvil Jones is an amazing writer who touches your heart with everything that comes from his pen. This book will bless you in so many ways, once you start reading it you won't want to put it down. You will feel Gods love all through it. I know everything I have ever read that Arvil has written has left me feeling closer to God, and wanting more.

Eva Dimel-Author, Radio Host, Speaker

## Contents

## A Celebration of Easter

His life was in constant peril, that our lives might be secure,

And we now enjoy sweet peace because of all He was made to endure,

He spent His whole life teaching His Father's Word and Will,

The common people heard Him gladly, and many hear Him still;

Although despised and rejected by many, He continued to love them all,

But thankfully many thousands more heeded the Master's call;

His life was one of great loneliness, suffering, pain, and loss,

And we can enjoy the gift of Salvation because of an Old Rugged Cross;

For three days and nights in a borrowed tomb His body lay quiet and still,

But then the tomb was found empty, that our hearts with joy He might fill;

And today the untold millions will again gather around His Word,

And celebrate the glorious Life of our Blessed Risen Lord!

© Arvil Jones

## A day in the life of...

She awakened to the sound of a siren, footsteps and breaking glass,
She hurriedly pulled her feet under her, allowing the people to pass;
The sidewalk she slept on was hard and cold, her house a cardboard box,
Her only defense against would-be attackers was a little pile of rocks;
She was once a lovely young lady, pursuing a law degree,
But one bad decision had stopped her from being what she wanted to be;
Her life once seemed so bright and clear, a young girl living the dream,
She had a plan, a destiny, and in her eyes was a gleam;
She only wanted to fit in with the rest of her fast-living crowd,
But still she loved her parents, and wanted to make them proud;
She tried so hard to juggle the two, and keep them satisfied,
While keeping up appearances, and still maintaining her pride;
Her beauty drew a lot of suitors, some whose intentions were bad,
One was another law student, a tall and handsome lad;
His plan was to seduce her by whatever devious means,
He always complimented her on her sexy, tight-fitting jeans;
But she had vowed to keep herself pure for her wedding day,
But he was patient and persistent, he'd get her in bed some way;
She knew that she should let him go, so she told him to leave her alone,
He backed off for a little while, then called her on the phone;
Seeing his number, she hesitated, just letting the phone ring,
But being young and careless she thought, what harm could it bring;
She answered the call reluctantly, listening for a while,
Too bad she couldn't see him with his cunning devilish smile;
I know it's over for us, he said, but just for old times' sake,
Would you be willing to join a party with me and Susan and Jake?
You know we're all law students, about to graduate,
It'll be just a simple affair, and we won't keep you too late;
In her heart she knew she should refuse his request,

But then again, it's Saturday night, and tomorrow she could rest;
He picked her up at 8:00 pm, in a long white limousine,
She thought to herself, he's the handsomest gentleman I have ever seen;
With his silver tongue and winsome smile he carefully laid his plan,
Tonight would be the night that he would become her first man;
A few mixed drinks, the lights down low, waltzing close and slow,
He slipped the drug into her drink, and she didn't even know;
She awakened early Sunday morning, unclothed and all alone,
Her friends, her pride, her dignity, and her purity were gone;
And now she had a craving she'd never known before,
A craving for something she knew she couldn't find at the grocery store;
Her body trembled, her heart was racing, her bed was wet with sweat,
Crying uncontrollably, she now began to regret;
Hurriedly she showered and dressed, stumbling in the dark,
In the mirror she gazed in horror, seeing the needle mark;
She'd been injected with heroin, repeatedly raped and abused,
Weeping, she told herself in the mirror – If only I had refused;
So weak she could barely manage the stairs, she stumbled onto the street,
She needed a fix, and gave herself to the first man she happened to meet;
Just enough money for another hit, in a sleazy motel room,
Night after night she trembled, lying there in the gloom;
Another man, another fix, another night of hell,
One Sunday morning, lying in an alley, she heard an old church bell;
She didn't know if she walked or crawled, but she moved toward that sound,
When a gentle loving hand reached down, lifting her from the ground;
There was an old country preacher who walked the streets each day,
Searching for those poor lost souls who somehow lost their way;
She held onto him tightly as he helped her slowly along,
When suddenly she thought she heard the words of an old gospel song;

The preacher gasped as he looked closer at her pallid face,
As from the church they heard the sound of the hymn – Amazing Grace;
His old heart pounded with purest joy as he began to recognize,
As he and his wife gazed lovingly into their daughter's eyes.
2016 Arvil Jones

# A Lady Under Attack

From the day she was born this lady was hated and scorned by multitudes,
Although she was pure, a descendant of noble birth;
Her enemies were men of every race, and men of highest learning,
And their hatred spread to the corners of the earth;
They shot their poisoned arrows at her, the slandered her with their tongues,
Their fiery darts they aimed at her very soul;
She was utterly despised, blasphemed and falsely accused,
Yet her character remains pristine and whole;
Each time she was attacked and slandered, she seemed to become more strong,
As her teaching quickly overspread the earth;
It seemed there was in unseen Spirit moving her along,
Wherever she went, she left behind new birth;
Men by the millions came to her, seeking for help and hope,
And in her they found sweet refuge, comfort and love;
Although she continues to be attacked by every weapon of man,
She thrives even more, being blessed by God above;
Pagan emperors, exalted monarchs, and peasants of lowly birth,
Have found in her a refuge for the soul;
Her doors are always open, no one is turned away,
Her teachings have been spread from pole to pole;
The gracious Lady has been attacked by devils and by men,
Who have vowed they will destroy her some way;
But she's lived for two millennia, and in spite of all their threats,
She holds her banner high this very day;
Her garments are whiter than the snow, being washed in the blood of Christ,
And no matter where on earth all men may search;
Never can they find a Lady who is more pure and noble,
Than this dear Lady whom we call the Church.

## A Letter to My Friend

What manner of words can one produce, except they come from his heart
To send to a friend whose heart and home are half a world apart
No more can I do but be honest and true, as these words now come to mind
When I know that you are hurting my friend, no peace at all can I find
The pain and struggles which you now endure, I will gladly make them my own
For a friend as true and faithful as you, this heart has never known
If you could somehow encase all your troubles, and send them all to me
Perhaps on the wings of an Angel, flying o'er the shining sea
And if I could receive them all into my own bosom now
Ahh, if only I could, I would endure them all somehow
If I could but relieve your heart of every burden there
'Twould be worth every moment spent for one so dear and fair
My own heart will not rest at ease while the heart of my friend doth cry
And I'll give no rest to my prayerful lips nor slumber to my eye
God grant to my friend a time of respite, mercy, peace and grace
May the pillow under her head be softer, and give a smile to her face
God take every burden that she now bears and lay them upon my soul
That her own heart may be refreshed, as your blessings like sea billows roll
I pray tonight in Your tender care, as my friend shall lie down to sleep
Your Holy Spirit will comfort her, as her life and soul Thou dost keep
And awaken her to bright sunbeams when another morning shall break
And create for my friend a blessed day, like only You can make.
For my Friend - Sylvia Lavallee
Duchess of Dorset
From Arvil Jones

## A Meeting in the Woods

Strolling along a well-beaten trail, leading through the Autumn woods,
I chanced to meet a young man, all alone;
He was sitting on a narrow bench, staring into the distance,
And I saw an empty bottle he had thrown;

His gaze was fixed, he moved not at all, no smile could I detect,
And as I looked closer his face was ashen white;
He had one hand gripping the bench, the other tucked behind him,
Holding something he desperately tried to keep out of sight;

I was really tired from all the walking, just wanting to sit down,
And enjoy the beauty of the evening Autumn sun;
When suddenly the young man quickly stirred, and without any warning,
Up to his head he placed a loaded gun;

The shock of it all made me suddenly gasp, my heart leaped into my throat,
As I desperately searched for just the right word to say,
But as he turned and looked at me with tears streaming down his face;
Immediately I knew that I must pray,

I don't know why, but I smiled at him, as my heart cried out to God,
And he looked at me as if I'd lost my mind;
Then the Holy Spirit took control of both my mind and mouth,
As I spoke to him in words so soft and kind;

I said, "young man, I don't know your name, and I don't know your case,
But this is something you don't want to do;"
He turned the gun toward me then, and pushed it into my chest,
And cursing asked, "Just who the Hell are you?"

I said, "young man, I'm a minister, a servant of Jesus Christ,
And I believe He sent me here toady;
And all I ask is that you give me only a few moments,
And listen to the words I have to say;"

At once he put the gun to my head, his tears still streaming down,
Saying, "mister, I don't need no sermon today;
And if you're going to tell me how you're going to Heaven someday,
Well, me and this gun can send you on your way;"
As I looked into his somber face, his hand began to tremble,
He lowered the gun, and I slowly bowed my head;
Then I began to pray out loud, and to my own amazement,
The young man was listening to every word I said;

In my heart I felt a sweet serenity, as I continued to pray,
As from out of somewhere there came a gentle breeze;
I saw the young man drop the gun, and then I heard him sobbing,
As he knelt beside me on his bended knees;

 By his trembling body and his quivering voice, I knew his heart was broken,
Saying, "Mister, I've lived a life of sin and shame;"
I put my arms around him, my own eyes filled with tears,
As I heard him softly call upon Jesus' name;

The Holy Spirit had done His work, a new life was created,
As looking up toward Heaven his hands he waved;
Saying, "mister, I don't know who you are, but I know who Jesus is,
And bless His holy name, I know I'm saved;"

His face was radiant, his hands were steady, his voice trembled no more,

And with gladdened hearts, two brothers could now embrace;
We strolled for miles along that trail, getting to know each other,
And thanking God for His Amazing Grace.

## A nation in mourning, a nation in shame...

Once again we bow our heads, mourning the lives we lost,
For the peace and freedoms we enjoy have come at an awful cost;
What can we say to the families whose lives are forever changed?
And all because of one whose heart and mind was so deranged,
And what can we say to the children who no longer have a Dad?
And are left with only memories of the few good times they had;
Oh, yes, we can say we're sorry, and tell them everything's alright,
But I don't believe our hollow words will help them sleep tonight;
And what can we say to the Mom and Dad whose son lies silent and still,
Who were waiting for their son to come home, but now he never will;
Yes, we do have cause for mourning, but we also have cause for shame,
For not having learned to love someone whose skin is not the same;
Our words and tears can never mend the broken heart and home,
Of the Mother who looks through the window knowing her son will never come;
No, our words are never enough, and neither all of our tears,
To comfort the father who heard the news, confirming his greatest fears;
And we ask ourselves will it ever be better, will things be brighter someday?
Will someone, somehow, keep on searching till they find a way?
To bring us all together in peace, all united as one?
The answer is No, it will not happen, till we find peace in God's Son.
2016 Arvil Jones

## A Time to Pray

Like so many of you who will read these lines,
I must sometimes search for words;
The proper words that will say all that's in my heart,

And looking at our country now,
 And the trouble that we are in;
It's hard to find a proper place to start,

I know the Bible teaches there's a time for everything,
And a season for all things under the sun;
A time to love, a time to hate, a time to live and die,
And a time to reflect upon all that we have done;

There's a time to speak, and a time to be silent, a time to hesitate,
And a time to choose the words we want to say;
A time to give, a time to get, a time to laugh or cry,
But surely there is always a time pray;

And if ever that time was upon us all, my friends that time is now,
We have no time to curse or to criticize;
We have no time to blame someone, no time at all to waste,
It's time to lift our eyes toward the skies;

It's time for every one of us to get in touch with God,
In fervent prayer for mercy and for grace;
Let the unbelievers look for worldly solutions,
It's time for us to seek the Master's face;

And even though we may not know exactly what to ask,

The Holy Spirit will help us if we try;
Our leaders need our prayers today, as they struggle with great decisions,
May God have mercy, and hear our humble cry;
Will you please join with me now, as we bow our heads and hearts,

To intercede for a world that's lost its way;
God give us grace in this time of need, and mercy for the lost,
In Jesus name your children humbly pray.
 2013 Arvil Jones

## For my Friend, Lois Puckett
## A Tribute to a Friend

I wasn't blessed like many others to know her very long,
But how blessed were the hours that we shared;
Just sitting in her living room, talking friend to friend,
She always let me know how much she cared;
But she never dwelt on minor things for very long at all,
You soon knew exactly what was on her mind;
So many times the conversation turned toward her Savior,
Or she'd ask me for a Scripture she couldn't find;
But before the day was over, you knew you were going to hear,
About her precious children she had raised;
She'd always name them one by one, Doris, Judy and Trisa,
And she didn't stop till each one had been praised;
She'd chuckle just a little, describing her three girls,
And all the mischief they used to get into;
But she never failed to say how proud she was of her son Billy,
Reminding me that he was a poet too;
She showed me his poems he'd written in a book,
Asking me if I would read a few;
And as I read her beaming smile said all that she was thinking,
And she seemed to know what I was thinking too;
She never failed to mention her beloved husband,
At the mention of his name she'd always smile;
Telling of their years together, and how they raised their family,
And how he'd been in Heaven for a while;
There was never any question about where Lois stood,
She based her life upon God's Holy Word;
And each time I would visit her, I left with calm assurance,
Her desire was to be in Heaven with her Lord;

And I know it won't be very long till I will go to see her,
Where we can talk again, friend to friend;
I'm only waiting for the call, when all my work is over,
And I, like her, have reached my journey's end.

## After Dusk

When all the work of the day is done, the calls been answered, the errands run,
I breathe a sigh and close my eyes, longing for sleep and rest;
As the dusky shadows pass into night, and now the moon is the only light,
The lingering question comes – Did I do my best?

Did I let another day go by without doing all that I could?
Did I spend the hours at what I wanted, instead of what I should?
Did I let an opportunity pass to do a kindly deed?
Did I take the time to help someone who had a special need?

Now the night is growing deeper, bringing slumber to my eyes,
And it seems that all around me I can hear the mournful cries;
One is the homeless beggar, holding his cardboard sign,
And there the hungry mother and her child waiting in line;

A Veteran in a wheelchair, without any arms or legs,
Another is a younger man who daily stands and begs;
Swiftly and ambulance passes by, its siren piercing the air,
Is it just another victim, and do I really care?

I pull the covers around me, but the question lingers on,
As the cold hard truth comes rushing in – another day is gone;
I want so much to fall asleep, but I toss till morning light,
Will tomorrow be any different, as the dusk turns

## Aging Gracefully

I feel the aches and pains in places I never thought I had,
And now I hear the title Grandpa more than I hear - Dad;
My hair that once was thick and wavy has mostly waved goodbye,
And I notice now that I can't see very well out of either eye;

And when folks talk I catch myself saying - What was that you said?
They laugh a little as I cup my ear and slightly tilt my head;
My hearing ain't what it used to be, and my teeth are the store-bought kind,
And it seems there are a lot of things that simply slip my mind;

It seems I leave things lying around, and forget where they were laid,
Like keys and watches, my store-bought teeth, my glasses and hearing aid;
My wife and I remind each other that it's time to take our pills,
And neither of us can seem to remember which one paid the bills;

I help her get up off the couch, and she helps me sit down,
And we must decide which is easier, whether to laugh or frown;
She tells me where she's hurting, I tell her I'm hurting more,
She says her feet are aching, I say my buttocks are sore;

For forty-eight years, some laughter and tears, we've managed to get by,
And during that time we've both decided, it's better to laugh than cry;
Yes, we're just aging gracefully, and God sure has been good,
We've always had a roof above us, clothes, and plenty of food;

With all our aches and pains we've gained a little wisdom too,
And one thing we have always known, our God is always true;
So we just grin and bear it all, and do the best we can,

Just loving Him, and going to church, and helping our fellow man;

For we both know that at the end of this journey here below,
There's a place of beauty, peace and rest, to which we both shall go;
A place where all our loved ones, someday we hope to see,
But until then, we'll go on trusting, and aging gracefully.
2014 Arvil Jones

## The Old Man with Alzheimer's

The elderly gentleman was walking quite slowly up an old dirt road one day,
When he sat down to rest his tired old feet, and saw a young boy at play;
He watched the boy quietly for a little while, remembering his own boyhood years,
He recalled all the bruises and skinning his knees, all the fun, and some childhood tears;
The longer he watched the little boy playing, the farther his mind went back,
To a time and place so far in the past, to a little old run-down shack;
Where he and his family lived long ago, just a poor little family of three,
He choked up a little as he quietly whispered, "There was Mama, and Papa, and me;
His mind slowly drifted away from the boy, as the tears now filled his eyes,
Then the little boy saw the old man lifting his face toward the skies;
He slowly and cautiously laid down his toys, and walked toward the old man,
Then drawing closer, he started to run, saying, "Catch me if you can;"
The old man smiled, then gently chuckled, rising slowly to his feet,
Saying, "How can I catch you little fella? I can barely get up from my seat;
The little boy knew the old man couldn't run, so he ran back toward him again,
And knowing the old man meant no harm, they both sat down in the sand;
"So what's yer name Mister, and where are ya goin, do ya live close around here?
The old man replied, "I don't really know, but I guess I must live somewhere;"
I really can't even remember my name, and as for where I'm gonna go,
One thing's for sure, I'm going to Heaven, and that's all I really know;

Then the little boy knew there was something wrong with the elderly gentleman's mind,
And looking into the old man's face, he smiled so gentle and kind;
"Well, let's see if we can figure this out, let's just sit right here and talk,
And whenever you're good and ready Mister, then we can go for a walk;
I saw you coming up the road, so you must live down thata way,
The old man replied, well I don't know, but I guess it's whatever you say;
Well, is it OK if I call you Franklin, 'cause that was my Grandpappy's name,
You mean old Franklin who was President? Yes, Sir, they're one and the same;
Well, I'll be darned, the old man chuckled, The grandson of old Franklin D.,
And here we are on an old country road, Old Franklin's grandson and me;
They walked for hours, only stopping to rest, and now it was getting dark,
When the old man cupped his hand to his ear, saying, that's my old hound's bark;
About that time they saw the lane that led to the run-down shack,
The gate was hanging on one hinge, with tall weeds in the front and back;
The front door was standing open, cobwebs were everywhere,
There was only an old wood-burning stove, a bed and a rocking chair;
I reckon this must be your place, the little boy said with a grin,
Well I reckon you're right Mr. Roosevelt, won't you please come in;
I don't have much to offer you, but I'll share whatever I've got,
Inside the little boy saw the old stove, and a rusty coffee pot;
Now Franklin you just sit down here, and I'll go get some wood,
And you and me are gonna cook us up something really good;
The old man smiled and nearly stumbled into the old rocking chair,
Removing his old crumpled hat, exposing his silver hair;
The little boy ran all the way to his home, and got his Mom and Dad,
He said let's hurry Daddy, 'cause the old man's really bad;
I think he's sick from something, and he doesn't even know his name,
We can't just leave him all alone, 'cause it would be such a shame;

Arriving at the old man's home, the hound dog lay at the gate,
The little boy said, Hurry Daddy, I hope we're not too late;
Stepping inside, they saw the old man, but he made not a sound,
And thinking he was fast asleep, they started to look around;
In one corner of the one-room shack, a portrait hung on the wall,
A beautiful lady standing beside a soldier handsome and tall;
The identities of the couple wasn't very hard to guess,
The gorgeous young lady was wearing a snow-white wedding dress;
The little boy turned the portrait over, and read the names and the date,
Georgia and Franklin Brewster, Married , June 5th, 1938;
He couldn't help but notice all the medals on the soldier's chest,
And another little note saying, 1960, my Sweetheart was laid to rest;
Then the old man stirred just a little, and they all rushed to his side,
And the little boy was so relieved that the old man hadn't died;
 But the old man reached for the little boy's hand, struggling so hard for breath,
He whispered, Thank you Mr. Roosevelt, and closed his eyes in death;
Still holding to the old man's hand, he couldn't help but cry,
Then finally letting go he turned his face toward the sky;
He whispered, You're welcome Franklin, I'm gonna miss you so,
But I know you've gone to Heaven, and that's all I need to know.
2013 Arvil Jones

## Am I a Christian?

How easy it is to go online and claim to be a Christian,
To tell everyone how good and decent we are;
The places we've been, the deeds we've done, the testimonies we've given,
But can we show a single battle scar?

Are we well known for our eloquent speeches, our vast store of knowledge,
And how the public perceives us to be?
Is our life an open book, with nothing to keep hidden,
Are there things we do not want the people to see?

Do we have to advertise to gain some recognition,
Do we crave to be applauded and praised?
Does the life we live on a daily basis say all that needs to be said,
Can folks look at us and tell how we were raised?

How easy it is to go online and easily deceive,
And make folks think we're more than what we are;
Do we have the tendency to try to raise our stature,
And do we know where God has set the bar?

How many of our neighbors know that we can always be trusted,
To do what's right in every circumstance?
Or do they see us as hypocrites, playing out a role,
Always trying our own lot to enhance?
Am I a Christian every day, and how am I at night,
When none but the eyes of Jesus Christ can see?
And does it really matter if others know my name,
Can I say that I know Him, and He knows me?

And if I have to advertise in order to convince others,
That, my friend, in itself, is a pretty good sign;
That there is something missing, and I need to examine,
And know for sure I'm His, and He is mine!

## America loves...

I guess everybody loves something or someone,
At least to some degree;
Some love dolphins, some love owls,
And some love to hug a tree;
Some love all the animals, some love all the plants,
Some love having tattoos,
And some love holes in their pants;
Some love a Chevy, some love a Ford,
Some love a Studebaker;
Some love the fifties, some love the sixties,
And some love a mover and shaker;
Most young men love many sports,
And girls with pretty good looks;
Some love their hi-tech toys,
And some love to read books;
Some love fast food restaurants,
While others love their cooks;
But if there's one thing I've learned here lately,
From the upcoming heated election;
Neither political party has much of a selection,
And as much as America loves apple pie,
And looks and cooks and books;
There's one thing America loves even more,
America loves her CROOKS.

## I feel so much like an Orphan

I feel like a little orphan girl,
With no Mom or Dad in this cruel world;
Though brothers and sisters, I once had fifteen,
But now two are gone, leaving thirteen;

I've been blessed with a very large family,
We were taught about Jesus at our Mother's knee;
My Dad was a big and powerful man,
But as gentle as a man could be;
He was in the mountains the day when Jesus whispered,
Come to Me;

I would love to have been there that blessed day,
When my Daddy fell on his knees;
Asking the Lord's forgiveness,
In the hills, among the trees;
As he came running down the mountain side,
My Mother gasped with alarm;
But she knew what had happened when my Daddy,
Ran straight into her arms;

He said woman we're going to church Sunday morning,
The children, and you and me;
For I just called upon Jesus' Name,
And He heard my pitiful plea;

Our family and home were changed that day,
There was joy like we'd never known;
For Daddy was changed, saved and forgiven,

For all the wild seeds he had sown;

There was also a change in our dear Mother,
She seemed so much happier now;
We were never rich in material things,
But the Lord made a way somehow;

We had all the things that really mattered,
We had peace, and joy and love;
And now we had the Lord Jesus Christ,
Smiling down from above;

One day the health department came,
To have a talk with my Mother;
"Mrs. Jordan, they said, you have enough children,
And surely you don't want another";

Now don't be offended Mrs. Jordan,
We only want what's best;
If you abstain from having more children,
You can better care for the rest;

So we recommend you start birth control,
It's all in this little pill;
It prevents any further pregnancies,
And it won't even make you ill;

My Mother listened respectfully,
Being quiet all the while;
And when the nurse finished speaking,
My Mother gave her a smile;

She said, You know dear ladies,
I am extremely blessed;
My husband and I have a large family,
And we've withstood many a test;

We gather our children around us,
And we bow our heads to pray;
And we've never gone without warmth and shelter,
We've never seen a hungry day;

Birth control, from where I stand,
Is in the hands of my Lord;
He's been my Savior for many a year,
And I still trust in His Word;

And if He sees fit to honor me,
With another child to hold;
That child will never go hungry,
Nor shudder from the cold;

And speaking of children, it's now supper time,
And time for us to pray;
You're welcome to join us, but if not,
You may all be on your way.
© 2014 Carolyn Jordan-Jones

## And now...?

The number of our future days lies hidden from our view,
We know not if they will be many, or just a very few;
And would we really want to know how many lie ahead?
Which ones are filled with happiness, which ones are full of dread?
I count it good that God withholds the future from our eyes,
For surely we might tremble if we heard the mournful cries;
The cries that may lie dormant now within our peaceful soul,
Yet only waiting till the pain of time shall take its toll;
Nay, let us not be anxious about tomorrow's things,
But take sweet comfort in today, and all the good it brings;
And if today we've watched and prayed, and done our very best,
Then our pillow in the evening will surely give us rest;
And if we do indeed awake to the light of tomorrow's sun,
Today will then be a memory, and another day begun;
Ahh! The memories! Are they sweet? And did we make them so?
Did anyone say we were a friend that they were glad to know?
How many memories can we recall? How many would we repeat?
How many left a blessing? How many were bittersweet?
Do we not see the truth of it all, the memories we create?
These only may we carry with us to the Wicket Gate;
Soon this day will be a memory, and I shall go to rest,
And shall my pillow welcome me, and shall my sleep be blest?
Did I honor my Creator, and serve my fellow man?
Can I say to my Redeemer – I've done the best I can?
In the moments as the sun of today is sinking low,
Lord tell me, is there anything I can do before I go?
Lord is there not another soul to whom I yet may speak?
Any courage I might give to one who is growing weak?
Or is there not one wandering sheep that somehow lost its way,

To whom You might now send me while it is still today?
And if there is another one, then Lord don't let me sleep,
Till I have gone and searched and found that precious wandering sheep.
2016 Arvil Jones

## *Another Path, Another Road*

*Sometimes we're made to ponder the paths and roads we take*
*One road brought us to a place of suffering*
*And another to a quiet lake*
*The path we took not so long ago*
*May have led us to doubt and despair*
*But just around the next bend up ahead*
*Were some Friends who showed us they care*
*There were some very dark and treacherous paths*
*With some sights we'd rather not see*
*And we could think of many places*
*That we would much rather be*
*But then that dark valley opened up wide*
*With wondrous sights to behold*
*And as far as our grateful eyes could see*
*Were fields of glistening gold*
*There may have been times at the end of a road*
*We felt we just could not go on*
*Perhaps because of some failure*
*Or for something we had left undone*
*But just when we thought we had reached the end*
*A sweet Voice whispered...Go on*
*For I am walking beside you*
*And we took the Hand of God's Son.*
*© Arvil Jones*

## ....Before I Wake

"And if I die before I wake"...such innocent words to say
They've been repeated by many a child
As they knelt each night to pray
But what if when we sleep tonight, we awake on Earth no more
Oh then where will our spirit be, what destiny lies in store
If I should die before I wake, where will my spirit be
When I have traded all of time for that Eternity
When the Reaper Grim with his morbid scythe
Cuts the body and soul in twain
When a cold and lifeless stiffening form
Is all that shall remain
If I should die before I wake and lie quite still in death
When that Dread Angel hovers near to steal my final breath
Will the Angels bear my soul aloft in Heaven's fields to roam
Or will the burning flames of Hell be my Eternal home
To all my friends who loved me here I give my answer now
If I should die before I wake, before My King I'll bow
If I should die before I wake, I know where I shall go
The Blood of Jesus has prevailed, and washed me white a snow
To you I put the question now, my dear beloved friend
If you should die before you wake
Where will your soul be then?
© Arvil Jones

## Before Sin Entered

The morning stars sang together, the sons of God shouted for joy,
The Cherubim and Seraphim their voices did employ;
In highest praise and honor to the great King of glory,
The farthest reaches of the Universe resounded with the story;

Mighty angels hid their faces from the glory of His face,
They saw Him create every star, and set them in their place;
The angels bowed in silent wonder and reverence at His feet,
And watched in awe as Creation of the worlds was complete;

The hosts of Heaven watched Him spread the cosmos like a span,
They saw Him stoop down to the dust, and from it make a man;
With God's breath in his nostrils, he became a living soul,
Made to live eternally as ceaseless ages roll;

Made to live in peace and in communion with his God,
Made to have dominion o'er the earth on which he trod;
Before sin entered there was nothing to bring him any harm,
So long as he did lean upon the Everlasting arm;

But one day in the heavens, a secret was made known,
The glorious angel Lucifer was coveting God's Throne;
He said I will be greater than He who created me,
I will ascend above His Throne, and the universe will see;

That I am the most powerful and glorious one of all,
And all the angels of heaven will answer to my call;
But God in wrath did cast the angel from his lofty height,
As Lucifer became the devil, doomed to an awful plight;

Before sin entered the garden, there was peace and happiness,
As man and wife gazed upon the beauty that God had blessed;
There was no such thing as pollution, the air was crisp and clean,
Nothing decayed, nothing died, not a thistle could be seen;
Man could drink the waters from the river or the stream,
No storm cloud ever rose to hide the beautiful sunbeam;
Their perfect bodies never felt the splash of a drop of rain,
They were happy, healthy, holy and humble, and never had a pain;

Before sin entered Adam and Eve never had a reason to cry,
They never had a quarrel, they never uttered a sigh;
They walked together naked, without a blush of shame,
God brought the creatures to Adam, and he gave them each a name;

How long this state of bliss continued, no one can really say,
But many to this day contend that it lasted less than a day;
How long they enjoyed Paradise? It matters not at all,
Because one day sin entered, and brought man's horrible fall;

Thousands of years later, God looked down from above,
He never forgot His covenant that He made with them in love;
And although sin has entered and defiled man's body and soul,
God gave His only begotten Son on a cross to make men whole.
 2014 Arvil Jones

## Beneath The Hickory Nut Tree

For those who have never lived in the country,
And enjoyed all those simple things;
Like the soothing sound of a babbling brook,
Or the song that the robin sings;
There are so many wonders to behold,
And so much beauty to see;
Like watching a little squirrel playing,
While standing under a hickory nut tree;
We could learn a lot by just standing still,
And watching God's creatures at play;
And taking in all the sights and sounds,
Just letting the time slip away;
No, I'll never forget the simple joys,
My Father taught to me;
As we stood still and watched and laughed,
Underneath that old hickory nut tree.
© 2013 Arvil Jones

## Big Brother Jack - 2010 by Arvil Jones

Now when Jack was born
His Mom called him Lois
'Cause he had a twin sister
Whose name was Joyce
He was raised down in the Kentucky hills
With the snakes and the possums and the whip-poor-wills
And with Mom's country cooking, it didn't take long
He grew up handsome, tall and strong.

Well Jack soon learned to live off the land
And with the guidance of his Daddy's strong hand
He learned to live by the golden rule
How to shoot a gun, and plow with a mule
Jack never cared much about book learnin
It was out in the woods his heart kept yearnin
Sometimes he'd stay in the woods for days
Just watching the creatures, and learning their ways.

While the other boys sweated over thick school books
Jack fished the streams, and waded the brooks
Whenever he could get away from home
It was over the hills that he loved to roam
And whenever you met him, he was always the same
And folks in the country respected his name
He never cared much for fashion and style
But he always wore a friendly smile.

Now Jack was tough, but he wasn't mean
His nerves were steel and his eyes were keen
His Daddy had taught him how to hunt and track
Not an animal living could hide from Jack.
Now I once heard that Jack shot a squirrel
From a hickory tree so high
When it hit the ground, he had the skillet hot
And the squirrel was ready to fry.
In loving memory of my brother-in-law,
Jack Jordan.

## Blessed Are The Children

You work and save and you worry and pray
For their health and for all that they need
And when one of them is sick or hurt your heart just seems to bleed
Whey they're so small and helpless, you pray to see them grown
Then suddenly you're wondering where all the years have gone
And for the three that God gave me, I simply must confess
I can't imagine how one man could be so richly blessed
It's so easy to take their love for granted when all is going well
But when unexpected tragedy will strike, none of us can tell
And one such tragedy came to me in the form of a heart attack
Then my wife suddenly suffered a pulled muscle in her back
So there wasn't much that either of us could really do for the other
But guess who came running to the side of dear old Father and Mother
In the blink of an eye it seemed they were here, doing all that had to be done
They cut the grass and cooked and cleaned, and made it all look like fun
They did the laundry and washed the dished and dusted everything in sight
And everything they did for us, they did with all their might
And neither of them would leave until they knew our needs were met
Just thinking of how they showed us their love, my eyes get kind of wet
The did all this for us while tending to families of their own
No finer children in the world has any parent known
If any Father on Earth has been honored, that Father has been me
And I want them to know that a prouder Father, there could never be
We are grateful for every friend who came, and for all who said a prayer
But most of all we thank our children, who showed us that they care.
Dedicated to Travis Jones, Tracy Webb, and Erica Phelps
Blessed are our children
© 2012 Arvil and Carolyn Jones

## Blessed is the man...

Ungodly man, I will not partake of your bread, your beans, nor your rice,
I will not visit your ungodly house, nor take your ungodly advice;
I refuse to listen to your subtlety, though my patience you sorely test,
I spurn your very ungodly appearance, for you see, I am richly blessed;

I care not to spend even one hour within your house of scorn,
For my Father's house is of purest gold, and I have been twice born;
In the law of my Lord I meditate, you have nothing to offer me,
Morning and evening I seek His face, but with you I disagree;

I am as a tree whose roots run deep into a living stream,
Your fruit is rotten, and all your dainties are never what they seem;
My leaves never wither, my fruit is alive, and many may sit in my shade,
But you are weightless and worthless chaff, cut away by the reaper's blade;

And when at last the harvest is come, and the work of the sickle is done,
I shall stand before Him dressed in white, but you, the ungodly shall run;
You will pray for the mountains to fall on you, to hide you from His face,
While all the blessed of the Lord shall bathe in His matchless grace.
© 2013 Arvil Jones

## But I Ain't Complaining...

This morning my wife made the coffee too strong,
Left it in the microwave too long;
(but I ain't complaining)

Had a tiny spot on my new white shirt,
Right after I fell in the dirt;
(but I ain't complaining)

I thought the weather was a little hot,
Still a little worried about that spot;
(but I ain't complaining)

The weather man predicted a chance of rain,
I suddenly felt another pain;
(but I ain't complaining)

Another crazy driver cut in front of me,
Made me drive into a tree;
(but I ain't complaining)

Got some mud on my newly shined shoes,
Just one more reason to get the blues;
(but I ain't complaining)

Some more illegals crossed the border,
The lady at McDonald's messed up my order;
(but I ain't complaining)

When I got my breakfast it was way too hot,
Still a little worried about that spot;
(but I ain't complaining)

Well I finally made it late to work,
Saw a lot of folks who wanted to shirk;
(but I ain't complaining)

The weather is either too hot or too cold,
Women are either too young or too old;
(but I ain't complaining)

A man is either a man or a mouse,
A politician a liar or louse;
(I may start complaining)

They charge too much for the clothes I wear,
And no one cares about the burdens I bear;
(I may start complaining)

My wife says I should be thinner,
The preacher implied I might be a sinner;
(But am I complaining)

You can call me a loser, or call me a winner,
But just don't call me late for dinner;
(Or I may start complaining)

And if according to some polls projection,
If Hillary Clinton should win the election;
(........................)!
I ain't gonna say it!

## But Tomorrow Never Came

Billy and Susan grew up together, they were neighbors and close friends,
They walked to school together every day;
They liked each other quite a lot, their friendship just kept growing,
And life was simple, full of fun and play;
Then suddenly they were ten years old, their braces now all gone,
And life was just a game of childhood bliss;
Susan ran ahead of Billy, giggling as she ran,
Billy caught her, and gave her her first kiss;
They grew up quickly – all too quickly, Oh how the years did fly,
And before they knew it they were in their teens;
Billy got a motorcycle, and a black leather vest,
And Susan wore her tight-fitting jeans;
Both their parents had careers, at which they spent long hours,
It seemed that money mattered most of all;
Billy and Susan went to college, where soon they both discovered,
Illicit sex, with drugs and alcohol;
Neither they nor their parents had time for church, yet they claimed to believe in God,
Or at least in a supreme being up above;
They learned a lot about evolution, chemistry and quantum theory,
But they never learned about Jesus and His love;
There were a few Christians on the campus who witnessed to them both,
And told them that Jesus loved them very much;
But Billy and Susan wouldn't listen, they only longed for each other,
Just wanting to feel each other's tender touch;
And so they partied and drank a lot, and sneaked into each other's room,
And life was Oh so wonderful and wild;
High on alcohol and drugs, throwing caution to the wind,
Susan discovered she was pregnant with Billy's child;

"What are we going to do Billy?" I'm only nineteen and pregnant,
"Well you'll just have to get rid of it I guess!"
Oh God Billy, I don't know, do you mean an abortion?
I never thought our lives would be such a mess;
Now listen babe, I know this doctor who can take care of this today,
And no one else will ever have to know;
But Billy, I'm already three months, the baby has a heartbeat,
And as you can easily see, I'm starting to show;
Well I ain't ready to be a Daddy, so babe, you're on your own,
I've got bigger and better fish to fry;
He could tell her heart was broken, but Billy couldn't care less,
He walked away as Susan began to cry;
She could no longer concentrate upon her college studies,
On Wednesday morning she decided she would quit;
All she made was failing grades, her classmates all kept staring,
Noticing Susan's clothes no longer fit;
One day Amanda, a Christian girl, met Susan on the street,
Giving her a big hug and a beaming smile;
How are you doing, Amanda asked, are you still dating Billy?
Susan blushed, asking, Can we talk a while?
I'm pregnant Amanda, with Billy's baby, almost four months now,
Oh God, Amanda, I don't know what to do!
Well honey, you just sit right here, and let me be your friend,
Whatever you've done, Jesus still loves you;
Billy wants me to have an abortion, he says it's the only option,
He says if I don't he will never marry me;
Susan, that would be cold-blooded murder, and the baby deserves to live,
He's just covering his own butt, can't you see?
Susan, you and Billy need Jesus, He is your only hope,
If only you will call upon His name;
I know you're right Amanda, and I'll do it tomorrow,

Tomorrow in church – But tomorrow never came;
Billy pulled up on his motorcycle, flashing his sexy smile,
"Hey gorgeous, would you like to go for a ride?"
She quickly dismissed her friend Amanda, and the cycle sped away,
The evening News said – Today three more have died!
Two young college students – a boy and his pregnant girlfriend,
Speeding along with whiskey on their breath;
Billy ignored the speed limit signs, losing control of the cycle,
As a boy, a girl, and a baby met their death.
2015 Arvil Jones

## Calluses on My Knees - by Arvil Jones

So often since The Lord found me I've gone to Him in Prayer
And I've brought before Him many things, my wants, my needs, my cares
Sometimes I folded my humble hands, and bowed my humble head
And I found myself repeating lines that I had often said
I was always careful to tell Him how grateful I had been
And I always asked for cleansing from any secret sin
And I realized I was telling the Lord things that He already knew
Then one blessed day He said to me, I need to talk to You
It seemed that I could feel His Hand pressing me to the floor
And I felt a sweet humility I had never felt before
But that old floor was cold and hard, and my knees began to ache
And I felt that if I stayed there, my legs would surely break
But with a humble reverence I stayed there on my knees
And for the first time in my life, I knew He had heard my pleas
And though the pain was very real I knew what I must do
Down on my aching knees I cried, Lord let me talk to You
And the more I knelt the more I felt the pain had gone away
And I knew that He was listening to what I had to say
Down on my knees it seemed that I could see His blessed Face
And I felt His Holy Presence as my soul He did embrace
And I cried Oh Lord please hear my prayer
I humbly beg You Please
If You never give me anything else
Give me calluses on my knees.
© 2012 Arvil Jones

## Cindi and Sophie

Cindi and Sophie went for a stroll on a beautiful summer day,
Just running and jumping and having fun, just passing the time away;
Sophie is Cindi's little dog, a tiny greyhound pup,
And sometimes Sophie runs so fast, Cindi can hardly keep up;

They love to sit on the bench in the park, and watch the people pass by,
Then sometimes they run across the meadow, chasing a butterfly;
Cindi loves to watch little Sophie drinking from the stream,
As Cindi lifts her tiny hands, trying to catch a sunbeam;

Cindi and Sophie are the best of friends, and seldom are they apart,
For Cindi loves her tiny greyhound pup with all her heart;
But they never stray too far from home, For Mom and Dad are near,
To wash off the mud, to give them a hug, or brush away a tear;

And then it's time for supper near the end of another day,
As the family gathers around the table, and they bow their heads to pray;
Then Cindi is tucked into bed as Mama hums a tune so sweet,
And pats the head of little Sophie, curled at Cindi's feet.

So teach us to number our days, that we may apply our hearts unto wisdom
-Psalm 90:12

## Counting our days, or making our days count?

Yes, we spend our years as a tale that is told,
As is recorded by the Psalmist of old;
And if we have lived to be threescore and ten,
What have we done? And where have we been?
Do we value our days by just the amount?
Or do we try to make each day count?
Did yesterday count for anything?
What joy to some heart did we bring?
Did we dwell upon all that we thought to be wrong?
Or face the day with a smile and a song?
What is the value of a single day,
If by our neglect we waste it away?
Yesterday's page has now been torn,
And tomorrow's page is not yet born;
Today is the day that we must live,
For our God may not another day give;
Oh then let us value each tick of the clock,
Before the death angel comes to knock;
The rich man cannot another day buy,
When the day arrives that he must die;
But neither can the poor man stay,
When God has allotted his final day;
No, days are not measured by their amount,
But by how we made each day to count.
© 2013 Arvil Jones

## Country Proud, and Country Loud

Now this here's 'bout us country folk, who come from down in the hills,
We's raised on cornbread, pinto beans, and the song of the whip-poor-wills;
We don't care much for fancy talk like the politicians use,
An if ye's gonna talk to us, be careful of the words ye choose;
We don't aim ta put up with cussin, nor any of yer black gyardin talk,
And if ye cain't just tell the truth, we'll tell ye to take a walk;
Now ye may not cotton to the way we talk, and ye might even try to correct us,
But as long as ye understand what we say, we don't aim to let it affect us;
Ya see, it's like this where we come from, everybody knows each other,
An if one of us is in trouble, we treat him like a brother;
Ain't nobody goin hungry or cold, as long as we got the makins,
We learned the hard way about being a neighbor, and the givins and the takins;
Now if y'all want to call taters potatoes, we don't aim to argue with you,
An if ye want to call maters tomatoes, well, let me give ye a clue;
Y'all been wastin a lot of breath, till y'alls faces turn blue,
Why pronounce three syllables, when only two will do?
Now ye hafta admit, when we say maters, ye know what we's talkin about,
An when we say taters instead of potatoes, still there ain't no doubt;
An while we's on the subject of talkin, let me tell ye a little bit more,
If'n some of y'all would talk a bit less, ye jaws wouldn't be so sore;
We's jest about had it with ye polytishuns, a cussin and debatin,
A slingin ye mud at one another, a fussin and a hatin;
Y'all needs fer ye mama and papa to take ye to Sunday School,
Where's a good ol fashion preacher can tell ye all 'bout the Golden rule;
Well, I hope and pray ye all git ta Heaven when ye life on earth is through,
An if'n some of ye don't make, well, I did all I could do.

## Dear little one

I know you may not hear me child, or quite discern my voice,
But before this procedure is done, I have made my choice;
Something deep within me says it's as wrong as it can be,
But after all is said and done, the choice is up to me;

They tell me this is best for me, because my life in is danger,
And yes, little one, it was my fault that I slept with a stranger;
But he doesn't want to marry me now that I am with child,
He wants to have his freedom, a life carefree and wild;

Yes, little one, I thought things over, through many stressful nights,
They told me you are not a person, and that you have no rights;
They say that if I let you live you may even be deformed,
Yes, little one, I have the facts, I have been informed;

Many times I've pondered this thing called motherhood,
And at this time I've decided it is not for my good;
What a burden you would be, me being single and all,
So I guess I'll never get to see you smile, or laugh, or crawl;

Yes, little one, it's for the best that I dispose of you,
May God forgive and understand this thing that I now do;
"What's that Doctor? Yes, I'm ready, just thinking out loud,"
"Well, dear our staff wants you to know, you've made us very proud;"
Just think about it this way dear, after his procedure is done,
You won't have two mouths to feed, you'll have only one;
And you won't have to go on welfare, like so many others do,
Yes, my dear, all of us are very proud of you;

And after all dear lady, you aren't taking a life,
You're not the one with the needle, nor are you holding the knife;
The brilliant legal minds from many years ago,

Determined abortions are not murder, and I think they should know;

But Doctor, it's not the legal aspect that really worries me now,
It's like this little one inside me is calling out somehow;
No, I can't explain it, but it seems I can hear a voice,
A voice from within that says, this is an evil choice;

Somehow I know there is a life that I am about to take,
Dear God, if you are listening, am I making a huge mistake?
Dear child, the fact that you have doubts, is that not enough?
I understand you're thinking this choice is very tough;

Your heart and soul are troubled, for there is another life,
A life that will soon be ended by this butcher's knife;
You still have time to re-consider, and put your trust in Me,
I will provide for you and your child if you'll only let it be;

I am the God of all creation, all the world is mine,
And yes, dear child, I understand, you're waiting for a sign;
Your sign is already given, for it's Me who is talking to you,
That little one inside you is telling you what to do;

"Doctor, I have changed my mind, I want my child to live,
For life is not a thing that you or I can take or give;
To end this life is murder, I understand it now,
I simply trust that God above will provide for us somehow;

My little one, I love you, no matter what the cost,
I realize it's not my life, but yours that matters most;
I take responsibility for all that I have done,
Today I put my faith in Christ, God's only begotten Son.
2016 Arvil Jones

## Dear Mama

She was walking home from the Senior Prom, she had just turned eighteen,
The night had been so wonderful with all the friends she had seen;
She decided to take a shortcut to her home not far away,
When a total stranger blocked her path, there in the alleyway;
He quickly overpowered her, and threw her on the ground,
He gripped her tightly by her throat, so she could not make a sound;
She was brutally raped by the stranger, and she never knew his name,
And she walked the rest of the way to her home in horror and in shame;
Two months of terror slowly passed, and she desperately wanted to know,
Then her greatest fear was realized, she had now begun to show;
She never told her parents about that horrible night,
She simply didn't want them to know about her awful plight;
She found an abortion clinic, and was welcomed with open arms,
The doctor said "*I can fix your problem, and there will be no harm;*"
She asked no further questions, and the gruesome procedure began,
A child was taken from her womb, and tossed into a garbage can;
And now she began to wonder what course her life would take,
As terrible images plagued her mind, as each night she lay awake;
She tried to pretend that nothing was wrong, and everything was good,
But she cried each time she saw a child, playing in the neighborhood;
She returned to the clinic where her child was aborted, and asked the doctor for pills,
She complained of having panic attacks, and Oh, such horrible chills;
The doctor smiled and gave her the pills, saying, "*These will help you to sleep,*"
But the pills didn't stop the bitter tears, as she began to weep;
The horrors that swept her soul each night, no mortal tongue could tell,
As she wept and trembled each evening, as slowly the darkness fell;
She could find no peace or contentment, no matter how hard she tried,

And the pills no longer helped her, as she lay awake and cried;
As images of a little girl kept running through her head,
And then one night she woke up screaming, and knelt beside her bed;
She cried, *"Oh Lord, if you are there, please make these nightmares cease,"*
*If you are the God of love and mercy, can you give me any peace?"*
The tears that flowed from her swollen eyes now came in a steady stream,
Then finally she fell asleep, and there came the strangest dream;

The postman smiled as he gently placed a letter in her hand,
He said, *"This letter came today, from some exotic land,"*
As she opened the letter, her heart was touched, and suddenly she smiled,
For it was plain that every word had been written by a child;
"Dear Mama," she began to read, "I'm Lori, your little girl,
And I'm up here in Heaven now, and My, what a beautiful world!"
Jesus has answered all my questions, He's the King up here you know,
And I'm not hurting anymore Mama, like I did down there below;
When I arrived I saw so many children with a Mom and Dad,
And how my heart was longing for the Mama I never had;
And one day I asked Jesus if He had a Mama for me,
And He led me to Heaven's balcony, and He let me look down and see;
I've watched you Mama, from day to day, as you pretended everything was alright;
But then I saw the tears in your eyes, while you cried and screamed at night,
I asked the Lord why you and the doctor didn't want me to live;
But He asked me if I could find enough love in my heart to forgive,
Dear Mama, I love you with all my heart, and I pray someday we will meet;
And Jesus told me to tell you about that little church down the street,
Where Grandma and Grandpa go each Sunday, kneeling down to pray;
Across the street from the clinic where that doctor threw me away,
Yes, Dear Mama, I felt the pain, but I had no voice to scream;

And that's why Jesus is letting me appear to you in a dream,
Dear Mama, in a few more hours, when once again you awake;
To face the dawn of another day, you have a choice to make,
I know your heart is troubled Mama, over all the mistakes of the past;
But Jesus says that He can give you eternal joy that will last,
And now Dear Mama, I must go, and bow at my Master's feet;
And I pray someday by the grace of God, that you and I will meet,
Here in the bliss of Paradise where Jesus reigns Supreme;
Where there are no abortion clinics, and the children never scream,
Dear Mama, Jesus loves you, and He feels your horrible pain;
But if you want to see me Mama, you must be born again.
I love you Mama,
Lori
 2012 Arvil Jones

## Deep in thought...

The elderly gentleman was deep in thought, sitting on the old porch swing,
His body was there, but his mind was far away;
He quickly brushed away a tear, hoping no one had seen,
Reliving memories from a bygone day;
Slowly his mind drifted back again, and again his old heart pounded,
He thought he could almost reach and touch her hand;
Although he knew she wasn't there, and yet she seemed so near,
As once again he gazed at his wedding band;
His precious wife of sixty years, the only love he'd known,
Had passed away several years ago;
They used to sit on that old porch swing and watch the sun go down,
Or hear the chimes as the evening breeze would blow;
He could still recall the touch of her hand, the scent of her perfume,
And the little coral pin she wore in her hair;
And how he'd always hold the swing, for her to sit down first,
Now the loneliness was almost too much to bear;
Sometimes he'd catch himself talking to her, as if she were sitting there,
And sometimes he even thought she answered him;
He remembered the sweetness of her voice as she used to hum a tune,
Or help him read as his eyes were growing dim;
He could see her in her flower garden, singing as she worked,
And how her beauty took his breath away;
It had been so hard to give her up, but deep inside he knew,
That he would see his love again someday;
With his old heart aching he bowed his head and whispered a silent prayer,
Saying Lord I just can't make it all alone;
You know she meant the world to me, and Oh I love her so,
We did everything together, and now she's gone;
But Lord if it could be your will, I've lived long enough,

And surely there's not much more for me to do;
I'd surely love to see her, and hold her close again,
So Lord I have this one request of You;
The old man slowly closed his eyes and waited patiently,
Then leaning back he smiled the sweetest smile;
I'll be waiting for your answer Lord, so any time you're ready,
I'll just sit right here and rest a while;
The evening breeze blew softly across the old wind chimes,
But now he didn't even hear their sound;
What he heard was her sweet voice saying come on home sweetheart,
As a mighty choir of angels gathered round;
His old heart raced with gladness as again she touched his hand,
As together they gazed upon the jasper walls;
Hand in hand they strolled along the avenues of Heaven,
Rejoicing as they walked the golden halls.
2016 Arvil Jones

## Depending upon who you ask...

If you want to know who loves to walk along a path by a babbling brook,
Or the one who cherishes that narrow mountain trail that he once took;
Then visit a Veteran's Hospital, where you are sure to meet,
The brave young men from a battlefield where they lost both their feet;

If you want to know who loves to see the beauty of the starry skies,
Or the simple joy of watching the flight of a hundred fireflies;
Then visit a Veteran's Hospital, for there my friend, there lies,
A hundred men from the battlefield who lost both their eyes;

If you want to know who would love to touch the face of his loving wife,
Or the one who for your freedom has risked his very life;
Then visit a Veteran's Hospital, with very few comforts and charms,
Where you'll see the men from the battlefield, who lost both their arms;

If you want to know who it is who is most apt to pray,
Who has no knees to fall upon, yet prays for peace each day;
Then visit a Veteran's Hospital, and stop by every bed,
And meet the men who gave you the freedom to say what you just said;

If you want to know who are the most dedicated men alive,
Who risked their lives on a battlefield so that liberty could survive;
Then visit a Veteran's Hospital, and join at one bedside,
The mother of a son from the battlefield who just closed his eyes and died;
If you want to know, well, don't ask me, for my knowledge is so small,
Ask the ones who volunteered in answer to their country's call;

Ask the ones who bound themselves with an oath to fulfill their task,
The answers to your questions depend upon who you ask.
2016 Arvil Jones

## Echoes of Calvary - The Cries from The Cross

Hearing the Gospel story told, to the renewed heart, never grows old,
How one Man was willing to suffer such loss;
Dying for sinners, enduring the Cross,

We cannot measure the pain He endured for sinners like me and you,
Crying Father forgive them, for they know not what they do;
It was a cry from the lips of Grace, more than two thousand years ago,
But that cry still echoes around the world, that His mercy we may know;

The lips that spoke all things into being, creating the land and sea,
Cried from the Cross, My God, My God, Why hast Thou forsaken Me;
And although He was Man at his best, He was murdered by men at their worst,
And the voice that created the mighty oceans, through parched lips cried -
I thirst;

The eyes that wept for Israel and the world, beheld His Mother so dear,
As He said Woman, behold thy son, and John drew Mary near;
Then He said to John, Behold thy Mother, as His death drew closer now,
And He knew by only those few words, they both understood somehow;

And yet with all the pain and suffering, His heart still longed to save,
A dying thief whose wasted life had brought him near his grave;
While the other thief died in his sins, his heart as cold as ice,
Christ said to the other, This day you'll be with Me in paradise;

Hanging there in the blazing sun, scorned and mocked by all,
They trembled as the earth trembled, and watched the darkness fall;

My Lord cried It is finished! And He bowed His lovely head,
Into Thy hands I commend my spirit, and the Son of God was dead;

But death and the grave could not silence Him, for His voice still echoes today,
And the One who cried from the Cross is still the Truth, the Life, the Way;
Today He cries Come unto me, and I will give you rest,
And all who come in simple faith are then forever blessed.
© 2014 Arvil Jones

## Enough

I meet so many folks who say they have never had enough,
But we must always define our terms, of course;
Enough, if I have the right definition, simply means sufficient,
Sufficient to feed my family, or my horse;
But enough can have another meaning, used in another sense,
And I, for one, know exactly what it means;
I've about had enough of politicians, and the news media too,
Who don't seem to know their biscuits from their beans;
Enough, I say, of the rhetoric, and enough of the debates,
Enough of the media, trying to steal the show;
Enough of Cruz, enough of Clinton, enough of Kasich and Sanders,
And enough of Trump and Marco Rubio;
Give me another Ronald Reagan, a man of integrity,
Even if you must go and dig him up;
Better a dead Reagan than a lying Hillary,
That's my conviction, and I will not give it up;
Enough of lies and liars, enough of slinging mud,
Enough of using up our precious time;
Listening to men and women who fain would be our leaders,
One under investigation for crime;
Enough of crooked government, full of deceit and corruption,
Enough of neglect of our veterans, the sick and the old;
Enough if filthy rich Senators and lying presidents,
While homeless veterans shiver in the cold;
Enough is enough, and too much is nasty,
And I, for one, have simply had enough;
In fact, I've had more than enough, I've had it up to my gills,
And if you think my words are callous and rough;
I've worked hard since I was fifteen, always made my own way,

And I've seen a lot of leaders come and go;
Each one promising to make things better for all Americans,
Eager to tell all of us how much they know;
Enough of empty promises that you don't intend to keep,
For my future is in a Man much greater than you;
He has never broken a promise, He has never told a lie,
And whatever He says He will do, that He will do;
My future is not in the hands of men, and for that I am very grateful,
My future is in the hands of my risen Lord;
So enough of putting your trust in men who sprang from nothing but clay,
Put your trust in Jesus and His Word.
2016 Arvil Jones

## Face it now...

I suppose we all had some childhood fears that kept us awake at night,
Things like storms with horrible lightning, or tales that were filled with fright;
And then there were the monsters that crept into our dreams,
Or those creepy frightening sounds that woke us up with screams;
Then there were the bullies who pushed us around,
And the times we really needed a friend, but no friend could be found;
We learned the sooner we faced our fears, the sooner they would leave,
We somehow had to find the courage and the faith to believe;
And as we grew we slowly began to set aside those fears,
Only to learn there were other things that brought us many tears;
With many there comes the dreaded fear of simply growing old,
While others sit and worry about what the future might hold;
Some are afraid they will wind up in a nursing home somewhere,
Afraid their friends and family may no longer care;
Yes, there are a lot of fears, and things we dread to face,
But over the years I've learned to lean on God's amazing grace;
I've learned His perfect love is able to cast out all my fears,
And He even promised someday He would wipe away my tears;
I've traded all my fears for the joy His love can bring,
His blood has forever removed even death's fearful sting;
No, I can't in my own strength face my fears alone,
But when I look to Calvary, then all my fears are gone!
2016 Arvil Jones

## Facing the Dawn

The wicked man slowly opened his eyes, grumbling with every breath,
Giving no thought, no word of thanks, that God had spared him from death;
The sweet light of dawn held no promise for him, he faced the day with great dread,
Not thankful to be among the living, instead of among the dead;

Rising up slowly, he groaned with remorse, his soul felt nothing but gloom,
Then lying down, he covered his head, not wanting to leave his room;
He began to plot how to spend his day, should he go to work, or just sleep?
There was really nothing for him to gain, and what he had he would keep;

There is no profit at all for me to rise up early and toil,
I'll let those other foolish ones go out and till the soil;
Let them go and bend their backs, and bruise their hands and feet,
Perhaps at the end of the day someone will bring me something to eat;

It is only for myself I must care, and let others fare as they may,
I need no sentimental religion, no matter what they might say;
If there is a God, then it is His fault that I am what I am,
And if there is a Heaven or Hell, I give not a tinker's damn;

The wise man opened his eyes and smiled, being thankful for the light of day,
And with a heart of gratefulness, he knelt by his bedside to pray;

Then he picked up his Bible and read the words...it is good to behold the light,
Again he smiled and thanked the Lord for keeping him through the night;

Still gazing upward, he thanked the Lord for the roof above his head,
Then looking back to his Holy Bible, he turned each page and read;
Such great and precious promises, each one was his to claim,
Given from the lips of Him who is forever and ever the same;

With every beat of his thankful heart, God's mercies he embraced,
Knowing for certain that Christ was his keeper, no matter what he faced;
With deep humility he asked - Lord, let me be your witness today,
If only I may win one soul, or one sheep that has gone astray;

I know I must face and fight the devil, so I gird on your armor divine,
And by Your Spirit and Your Word, the victory shall be mine;
Dear God if You will prosper my way in all that I shall do,
I promise to bow my unworthy head, and give the glory to You.
 Arvil Jones

## Facing the Last Enemy

When David faced Goliath with a sling and five smooth stones
Goliath was Oh so confident and roared in fearful tones
All of those who watched believed that David could not win
But David was a man of God, and Goliath a man of sin
Yes, it was David who loaded the sling and gave the stone a throw
But the Spirit of the Living God delivered the deadly blow
It was God Who guided the stone toward Goliath's head
The battle was over in a moment, and the giant lay there dead
Then David severed Goliath's head and also took his sword
And David returned in victory giving Glory to his Lord
Goliath was only one of many giants in David's life
He faced temptation, cruelty, rejection, pain and strife
And so many others in God's Great Book
Had to fight against the odds
They faced the fiery furnace and defied the Heathen gods
And for us it is no different, there are giants we must face
They come in many different forms and lurk in every place
But like those who came before us we have no need to fear
We have a Mighty Warrior King who brings His Army near
And They encamp around us with their gleaming fiery swords
And then we hear the Victory shout...The Battle is The Lord's!
Then come Oh dreadful Enemy with foul and morbid breath
Oh yes, I know thee who thou art, the one whose name is Death
I know thou hast been tracking me even from my Mother's womb
But my Lord hath defeated thee when He rose up from the Tomb!
© Arvil Jones

## Faith

Faith can never be stronger than the object in which it is placed,
Faith is not measured by the size of the enemies we have faced;
Faith in mortal men is equal to faith in a pile of dust,
Faith in money is faith in something that will someday canker and rust;
Faith is strengthened day by day with much time spent in prayer,
For prayer is the Christian's vital breathe, it is his native air;
Faith reaches much higher than reason can ever go,
Faith believes in things unseen, which reason can never know;
Faith gives the one who has it rest and peace and hope,
Faith sees things that cannot be detected by a microscope;
Faith accepts eternal truth found in the Word of God,
Faith knows we are only pilgrims while here on earth we trod;
Faith claims every promise of the One who cannot lie,
Faith believes we shall live again in a mansion beyond the sky;
Faith that is real is a faith that is given by the Spirit of God above,
It's only object is Jesus Christ, and it only works by Love.
© 2014 Arvil Jones

## Godly or Godless, which am I? And how may I truly know?

Is there some sign, some evidence by which my life may show;
That I indeed do know the Lord and that I love Him too,
Do others think me godly by the things I say and do?
'Tis in my own immortal soul I must settle the question first,
Am I only godly at my best, and godless at my worst?
Am I a godly man at all, or godless through and through?
And let me answer for myself, before I look at you;
Search me O God, and try my heart, my will, my soul, my reins,
Draw out into the light of day my foul and ugly stains;
Lay me bare before Thy throne, expose each wicked way,
Whatever Thou dost find within, before Thee I will lay;
Oh, cut me deep with Thy gleaming sword, that not one sin may hide,
Let not one secret thing remain, ere I must cross the tide;
Let no ungodly counsel find its way into my heart,
Let godly men draw near me, let godless ones depart;
Draw near me Lord as I meditate in Thy Word each night and day,
And let my soul with joy attend to what You have to say;
If I be not a godly man, Oh Lord I wish to be,
For a godly man I must become if I am to dwell with Thee;
Oh count me not with godless men, let me not in their presence dwell,
Deliver me before I hear that lonely mournful knell;
That calls me from this realm of time into eternity,
Come Thou blessed Hope of glory, Come, abide with me.

## Grandpa and Mandy

The little girl of five years old sat holding her Grandpa's hand,
Her tiny fingers gently rubbing his well-worn wedding band;
Five days a week he was her only companion from nine till noon,
Her little heart fluttered with joy and gladness while Grandpa whistled a tune;

Now what's the name of that song Grandpa, I think I've heard it before,
I think it's the same one you whistled yesterday down at the candy store;
No, wait, don't tell me Grandpa, It's coming back to me now,
Yes, I remember, you told me Grandpa, God will make a way somehow;

But tell me Grandpa, How does God make a way for the birds to fly?
And how does He make a way for a rainbow to reach across the sky?
And Grandpa, How does He make a way for the sky to be so blue?
And Grandpa, Can God make a way for me to be as wise as you?

Well, Miss Mandy, I tell you what, I'll have to think on that a while,
But I suspect He did all that the same way He made your smile;
By the glow on her little face he knew she understood somehow,
That his short and simple answer was good enough for now;

Her tiny hand gripped his fingers, and she laid her head in his lap,
He quickly wiped away a tear, and watched as she took a nap;
His old heart pounded with a tender love, as he quietly whispered a prayer,
Watching his little granddaughter sleep, as he stroked her golden hair;

He was about to drift off to sleep when he felt a gentle tug,
Then both her arms were around his neck, with a big old kiss and a hug;
You know what Grandpa, When I grow up, I know what I'm gonna do,

I'm gonna ask God to make a way for me to be as smart as you;

Well, Miss Mandy, I'm really honored that you would feel that way,
And I'm gonna surely ask the Lord to grant your wish someday;
But I have a little secret Mandy, and now I'm gonna share,
You don't have to wait till you grow up darlin, 'Cause I think you're already there!
Arvil Jones

## Had He not risen...

Had Christ not risen from the dead,
Then our preaching would be in vain;
And each of us would yet be polluted,
With sin's dark ugly stain;
Had He not risen from the grave,
We'd have no message of hope;
And all who ever lived and died,
Would in the darkness grope;
Had He not risen to life again,
Up from the borrowed grave;
Then worthless was the blood He shed,
And vain the life He gave;
If only on the cross He suffered,
Never to rise again;
Then all our prayers are useless,
As well as all His pain;
And if our Christ is yet entombed,

## Hand-me-downs
by Carolyn Jordan-Jones

I remember a day when a dear man came,
And gave us a box of used clothes;
And I couldn't wait for him to leave,
So that we could go through those;
There were checked shirts, and of course, Blue Jeans,
Underwear, socks, and a ton of things;
And my childish heart just beat with joy,
Even though those jeans had belonged to a boy;
Yes, I knew the little boy who had worn them you see,
But it really didn't matter to me;
I only wanted to get them on, and Oh, how good it felt,
They fit my figure perfectly, I didn't even need a belt;
That little girl was suddenly changed into a little tomboy that day,
And as quickly as we could get permission, it was off to the woods to play;
Climbing trees, playing skin-the-cat, and riding on slick tree bark,
Choosing to be either cowboy or Indian, playing until it was dark;
The time and the fun seemed to never end as from hill to hill we'd roam,
And then we'd hear Mama's voice yelling,
And we knew it was time to go home;
But I'll never forget those tight-fitting Jeans,
And I'll never forget the boy;
It was Lonnie Merida's faded Jeans,
That brought me so much joy.
© 2013 Carolyn Jordan-Jones

## Harnessed

Back when I was very young, I learned to harness a horse,
And then my Daddy taught me how to plow;
Many acres had to be tilled, all to my great remorse,
But I knew I had to get it done somehow;
The days were long, the sun was hot, I had a farmer's tan,
But the hard work somehow made my back grow strong;
Following that horse and plow, I learned to be a man,
I also learned the difference between right and wrong;
A good horse doesn't mind being harnessed, if you will treat him right,
And give him some rest, and corn at the end of the day;
He'll pull a plow or a corn sled from morning until night,
Your ever gee and haw he will obey;
Gee means you want him to go to the right, Haw means to the left,
Giddyup means go, and Whoa means stop, of course;
Of the meaning of these simple commands, the horse is not bereft,
For God gave this much sense to even a horse;
Now I know what some of you are thinking – What's the lesson in all of this?
And I, of course, am about to give it to you;
If you haven't already guessed it, if something you have missed,
Perhaps the next few lines will furnish the clue;
We've learned to harness many things, we've learned to harness rivers,
We've harnessed electricity, horses and mules;
We've harnessed oxen, we've harnessed the wind, we've even harnessed donkeys,
But we've never learned to harness the mouths of fools.

## He Came To Me

When I was lost and helpless, without a ray of hope,
When in my sin and ignorance in vain I tried to cope;
He came to me.

When I searched for life's answers and no answer could be found,
When I searched for compassion with not a friend around;
He came to me.

When I was sorely tempted, about to go astray,
When from the heat of battle I wanted to run away;
He came to me.

When I was sorely tested, and asked to take a stand,
To face a deadly enemy, no weapon in my hand;
He came to me.

When all the powers of hell arose, compassing me around,
When I felt they would surely strike me to the ground;
He came to me.

When all my friends forsook me, and I was left alone,
When heartache, pain and sorrow touched my flesh and bone;
He came to me.

When all life's angry billows around my heart did roll,
When bitterness and anger crept into my soul;

**He came to me.**

He came to me in sadness, and brought to me a smile,
He came to me in weakness, and I went another mile;
He came to me in sickness, to comfort and to heal,
And when He came His presence was always Oh so real;
He comes when I am lonely, He comes when I am sad,
He comes when I am weary, and His coming makes me glad;
And yet again in glory on the clouds my Lord will come,
And I shall rise to meet Him as the angels take me home!
2016 Arvil Jones

## He knows...

Each time a little sparrow falls from its lofty nest,
Each time a weary pilgrim is put to the test;
He knows.

Each time a weeping mother holds her hungry child,
Each time the hungry lioness roars in the wild;
He knows.

Each time a homeless stranger is kindly taken in,
Each time a home is broken by some careless sin;
He knows.

## He Saw Me

Before I was fashioned in the womb,
And began my journey toward my tomb;
He saw me.

When my first deep breath I took,
When Mama gave me her loving look;
He saw me.

When with my first step I stumbled,
When with my first toy I fumbled;
He saw me.

When with my first word I mumbled,
When for the first time I grumbled;
He saw me.

When in infancy I cried,
When I whimpered, stole or lied;
He saw me.

When I scampered off to school,
When I learned the Golden Rule;
He saw me.

When betimes I broke the rules,
When I walked with friends or fools;
He saw me.

He saw me wrong, He saw me right,
He saw me run, He saw me fight;

He saw me stand, He saw me fall,
He saw my back against the wall;
He saw me lose, He saw me win,
He saw me weep, He saw me sin;
He saw me doing as I please,
And then He saw me on my knees;
He saw me bow my head in shame,
He heard me call upon His Name;
He saw my need, my broken heart,
He saw my life all torn apart;
He saw what needed to be done,
He saw, and sent His only Son!
2016 Arvil Jones

## He speaks...and the sound of His voice...

We hear so much about great speakers who can really hold a crowd,
Some have a soothing, melodious voice, while others are very loud;
Some speakers are quite interesting in a philosophical way,
While others do a lot of talking, but don't have much to say;
Some speak in a monotone, quite boring, to say the least,
Then there are those whose voice can soothe the savage beast;
There are those, who after hearing them, we want to hear no more,
But there are others whose gracious words we often come to adore;
'Tis said the wind has a voice, along with the raging sea,
And then there was Shakespeare's Hamlet...to be or not to be;
A wounded child longs to hear the voice of its Mother,
For it seems her voice can soothe the hurt more than any other;
And so the Mother loves to hear the laughter of her child,
Whether sitting in her lap, or playing, running wild;
Even the beasts of the forest have a voice all their own,
And by the sound of each one's voice, the other beast is known;
Each bird that flies into the skies has a clear and distinct call,
As when the eagle soars aloft, his voice is known by all;
And yet there is another Voice, distinct from all the rest,
The Voice by which both man and beast and fish a fowl are blest;
It is the Voice that has the power to command the wind and sea,
It is the Voice that shakes the earth and makes the demons flee;
The Voice that created the worlds and all therein,
The Voice that brings comfort unto the souls of men;
It is the Voice that creates, and the Voice that redeems,
The Voice that commands the stars, and made the bright sunbeams;
It is the Voice before whose power no army of earth can stand,
The Voice of One who spoke the Word, and made the sea and land;
Sometimes it comes with awesome strength like a rushing mighty wind,

Sometimes it is a still small Voice that calms the soul within;
That Voice is unmistakable whenever He chooses to speak,
It can break the mighty cedars, or comfort the poor and weak;
 The Voice that causes the strongest of men to bow before Him in fear,
And yet the Voice of One who stoops to wipe away a tear;
The Voice that whispers in the night, and says that all is well,
The Voice that leads men to Heaven, and saves the soul from hell;
It is the Voice of peace and hope, coming from above,
It is the Voice of Jesus, it is the Voice of Love.
2016 Arvil Jones

## He waits...

*At the Father's right hand, in glorious splendor,*
*Adorned with many crowns;*
*He waits,*

*He sees the good, He sees the bad,*
*He sees the smiles and frowns;*
*He waits,*

*He hears the cries, He hears the praise,*
*He hears the prayers of all;*
*He waits,*

*He knows each time a golden leaf,*
*Or a tiny sparrow falls;*
*He waits,*

*He intercedes for erring saints,*
*And watches as they sleep;*
*He waits,*

*He sends His Spirit in darkest night,*
*And finds the wandering sheep;*
*He waits,*

*He calls and sends his servants out,*
*To preach in every land;*
*He waits,*

*He blesses their every effort,*
*He covers them with His hand;*
*He waits,*

*He knows someday He will return,*
*And set all things aright;*
*He waits,*

*His coming will be sudden and swift,*
*Like a thief in the night;*
*He waits,*

*He waits until that last poor soul,*
*Has heard His precious Word;*
*He waits,*

*He waits as time and ages roll,*
*Till all the world has heard;*
*He waits,*

*So long now He has waited,*
*What patience, Oh what Love!*
*He waits,*

*But soon the waiting will be done,*
*As He comes from above;*
*He comes! He comes!*
*He comes with clouds of glory,*
*He comes with angel bands;*
*He comes with saints of ages,*
*With nail prints in His hands;*

*He comes with fire of vengeance,*
*To conquer all His foes;*
*His angels holding back the winds,*
*Pronouncing countless woes;*
*He comes with rod of iron to rule,*
*The nations of the world;*
*And kings before His feet shall bow,*
*As His banner is unfurled;*
*New heavens and new earth He makes,*
*Expelling all evil things;*
*He comes, We crown Him Lord of lords,*
*We crown Him King of kings!*
*2016 Arvil Jones*

## He Was There

When the morning stars together sang,
When the voices of the sons of God rang;
He was there.
Before there was an angel bright,
Before there was a day or night;
He was there.
Before the oceans came to be,
Before the sun, before the sea;
He was there.
When the waters heard His decree,
Here shall thy utmost borders be;
He was there.
Before the rivers, before the flood,
Before there was a drop of blood;
He was there.
Before the angel Lucifer fell,
And millions of angels did rebel;
He was there.
Before the rocks, before the trees,
Before the moving of the breeze;
He was there.
Before there was a hand to till,
Before there was a man to kill;
He was there.
He was there when man was made,
He walked and talked in the evening shade;
He knew each bird, He knew each blade,
And He blessed all that He had made;
When man first felt the gentle wind,

When the man and woman sinned,
He was there.
When they tried to cover their sins,
When they were clothed with coats of skins;
He was there.
When they first knew one another,
When the brother slew his brother;
He was there.
When Abram heard Him call his name,
When from his loins Isaac came;
He was there.
When on the altar Isaac lay,
When his father's hand was raised to slay;
He was there.
When Jacob wrestled in the night,
When Jacob saw the ladder's height;
He was there.
When Israel called upon His name,
When from his loins Joseph came;
He was there.
When Israel became a mighty band,
When they were slaves in Egypt's land;
He was there.
When the sacred law was given,
When Mount Sinai's slopes were riven;
He was there.
When Israel forgot His name,
When the fiery serpents came;
He was there.
When the Prophets prophesied,
When the last of them had died;

He was there.
When the shepherds watched by night,
Bathed in Heaven's glorious light;
He was there.
When wise men came from lands afar,
Guided by the shining star;
He was there.
When their honors they had paid,
When at His feet their gifts they laid;
He was there.
When in the fullness of the time,
When man committed his worst crime;
When the sun refused to shine,
When all sin, both yours and mine;
Were placed on Him upon the tree,
When He died for you and me;
He was there.
When in the grave three days He'd lain,
When He rose to life again;
He was there.
Into Heaven He has gone,
And yet my heart shall be His throne;
He is here!

## He was...

He was destined for greatness, though he never knew,
He just wanted a simple life;
A loving wife and family, maybe a little farm,
Free from the hustle and bustle and daily strife;
He became well known for his honesty, even in his younger days,
Dependable and trustworthy in every way;
A hard-working, God-fearing, law-abiding man,
Humble and quiet, with never too much to say;
A pillar of strength in adversity, never haughty or proud,
He seldom raised his voice to anyone;
He was a perfect gentleman, never caustic or loud,
With a great sense of humor, he loved a little fun;
He volunteered to go and serve on a foreign battlefield,
As a decorated hero, he returned;
Where again he resumed his life alongside his loving wife,
Enjoying all those things for which he'd yearned;
He played catch with his little boy, and often took him fishing,
And more than once repaired his bicycle chain;
He did everything a father should do to provide for his family,
Even if it meant he must suffer pain;
His neighbors always spoke highly of him, trusting him completely,
And he always proved himself to be their friend;
He was generous, thoughtful, reverent and kind,
And folks said his charity knew no end;
Yes, this man was quite a gentleman, but only in our minds,
For you see, he was murdered, and a garbage can was his tomb;
He could have been a lot of things if he'd been given the chance,
But he was aborted from his mother's womb!
2016 Arvil Jones

## He who watches o'er the sheep

In counting all my blessings which I have enjoyed today,
I simply cannot help but bow my grateful head and pray;
Today I had enough to eat, a roof above my head,
Tonight as I lie down to sleep, I have a nice warm bed;

But all of these are material things, and I thank God for them all,
But then I'm reminded that the greatest things are not really things at all;
The greatest blessings that I enjoy are the family and friends I know,
And yet there's another special blessing that God chose to bestow;

We call him Pastor, we call him counselor, minister and teacher,
But most often all of us simply call him Preacher;
This man of God wears many hats, and shepherds many souls,
On any given day of the week, he fills many roles;

He visits the sick, he comforts the grieving, he prays for all the lost,
He studies his Bible, he stands for the right, no matter what the cost;
He often receives criticism from those he loves so dear,
And even when he's being ridiculed, he lends a listening ear;

He preaches the Word, he raises a family, he cherishes his wife,
For any member of family or church, he'd gladly lay down his life;
Sometimes he's disrespected, often he's underpaid,
As day by day, so many problems at his feet are laid;
But with all of this, he yet goes on, wielding the mighty Sword,
And when he's gone, someone will say - This man loved the Lord.
In honor of my Pastor, Brother Tim Smith, East River Road Baptist Church

## Heart Search

Search me, O God, and know my heart: try me, and know
my thoughts: And see if there be any wicked way in me,
and lead me in the way everlasting (Psalm 139:23,24 KJV).

For Oh so long he neglected things, the important things in life,
Enamored with self, he even neglected his children and his wife;
He knew that he should think of others, but in his life they had no part,
He even neglected the spiritual condition of his heart;

Utterly consumed by his lust and greed, he lost his family and friends,
Knowing he had done them wrong, he never made amends;
Self was all that mattered to him, so he took whatever he could,
He took and he took, but never gave back, even though he knew that he
should;

He was often warned that sooner or later, he would surely lose everything,
He was warned by parents, and by his own conscience, but again, he
neglected the sting;
One day he heard a preacher preaching on a street corner in his town,
At the moment he had nothing better to do, so he slowly walked on down;

The preacher was saying something about a verse called 3:16,
And on his face was a radiant glow, like nothing he'd ever seen;
Something began to tug at his heart, and he didn't understand it at all,
But the longer he listened to the preacher, he began to feel very small;

Suddenly without any warning, tears began to flow,
He hid his trembling hands behind him, not wanting the preacher to know;
It was as if he was seeing himself for the first time in his life,

He thought about his hungry children, his abused and neglected wife;

He listened closer as the preacher told of an awful burning Hell,
And the horror that now gripped his heart no mortal tongue could tell;
It seemed the preacher was bringing his whole life into the light,
As he felt the gentle drawing of a Spirit he couldn't fight;
As the preacher kept on preaching, a crowd had gathered by then,
And the preacher told them every one, that Jesus was the cure for their sin;
The man had now been reduced to a beggar, homeless, lonely and cold,
But somehow he felt a certain warmth in the story the preacher told;

He could stand on his feet no longer, so he fell upon his knees,
Then others knelt there with him, crying, Lord forgive us please;
With broken heart and spirit, he believed the blessed Word,
And another hopeless sinner made Jesus Christ his Lord.
© 2014 Arvil Jones

## Here in Sodom, U.S. A. -by Arvil Jones, Ph.D.

We once called her the finest country, way back in her day;
When asked where we were from we replied - "The Good Old U.S.A.,
We admired her beauty, we respected her leaders, we loved and honored her name;
We proudly held our heads up high, without any cause for shame,
We built her with our blood and sweat, with Faith in our God above;
Who guarded us and guided us, and blessed us with His love,

We waved her flag with dignity from sea to shining sea,
Then slowly but surely we defiled the garments of Lady Liberty;
So come now stranger and let me show you a sick and sorrowful land,
A nation who despises the name of her Maker, yet takes the good of His hand;
A nation whose moral standards have long been swept away,
A nation whose name could rightly be called - Sodom, U.S.A.

Where there's liberty and justice -for all those who can pay,
Where women are proud to call themselves "Lezzies", and men are proud to be Gay;
Where the dogs return to their own vomit, and the sows wallow in their mire,
Where there should be a sign over Washington saying - "Crooked Politicians For Hire";
Where women have sex with other women, and men have sex with men,
And nothing their filthy minds can conceive is ever labeled as Sin;

Where perverted men in little white collars use Children as their sexual prey,
And cover it over with the sign of the Cross, here in Sodom, U.S.A.

Where little innocent babies are murdered with gross impunity,
And the high Court turns and closes its eyes, pretending not to see;
Where the gays and lesbians, Muslims and Aliens, and liberals get their way,
Where God has been expelled from our schools, and children can no longer pray;

The men of Sodom in the days of Lot demanded their rights I'm told,
The right to have sex with other men, so brazen and so bold;
With fire and brimstone they were burned alive, Oh can't you hear them yell,
As they heard the voice of demons crying, Gentlemen, welcome to Hell;
May I say to our leaders, The time will come, when you all will regret the day,
When you turned our Beloved America, into Sodom, U.S.A.
  Arvil Jones, Ph.D.

## Hey you, in the mirror!

I've never made a habit of passing in front of a mirror too much,
I've learned he has his own habit of revealing wrinkles and such;
I've tried to teach him better habits, like being more gentle and kind,
But that old stubborn mirror just won't change his mind;
He seldom pays me a compliment, and he wounds my ego a lot,
He never hesitates to tell me 'bout all the faults I've got;
He says he always tells the truth, and would never tell me a lie,
Pointing out I shouldn't have had that second slice of pie;
I ask him for a second opinion as I stand and turn and twist,
Surely, I inform him, there must be something you missed;
You know I can remove you any time I choose,
And yet he keeps reminding me of all the pounds I should lose;
Oh the audacity! Now he's trying to tell me how to dress,
The nerve of a piece of glass who says my hair is just a mess;
How dare he even insinuate that I look like a slob,
I'm beginning to wonder, who was the genius who ever gave him this job;
If I were not such a gentleman, I'd punch him in the face,
Ouch! That hurts! And now I have a mirror to replace!
I promise myself the next mirror will not be quite so large,
And perhaps he won't be so bold as to make me look like a barge;
All he will ever see of me is my glorious handsome face,
And he'd better always treat me with dignity and grace;
What's that? I ask, Did you just say what I thought you said?
How dare you say my teeth are dingy, and my eyes are bloodshot red?
Ouch! That hurts............! Arvil Jones

## How I Destroyed America – by Lucifer

Long ago her beauty shone from sea to shining sea
A beacon of faith, hope and charity for all the world to see
Like great peals of thunder, freedom rang from every mountainside
Her God adorned her with majesty, as if she were His bride
She quickly became the envy of all who cherished freedom's flame
And by whatever means they could attain, by the millions pilgrims came
Her soil was rich and fertile, her waters clean and clear
Her God had His hand upon her heart, and I began to fear
To what heights of grandeur will this lady come if I leave her thus alone
I must somehow corrupt her, I must touch her flesh and bone
Such righteousness and charity my soul cannot allow
And without her knowledge I devised my plan to destroy her somehow
I studied her massive foundations, searching for the tiniest flaw
And at her very spiritual roots, I slowly began to claw
I began to whisper in the ears of her leaders, and it didn't take too long
I had them convinced that light was darkness, I convinced them that right was wrong
By my subtlety I seduced her to abandon the truth of her God
My decadent plan was working quite well, while at her heart I did prod
I introduced her to evolution and I poisoned her mind
I convinced her that in herself alone the greatest joys she could find
I distracted her with entertainment, pornography and pride
And in her religious institutions, I found a place to hide
I crept into her government, Federal, State and City
I gave her children mind-bending drugs, and on them I showed no pity
I gave them new forms of sexual pleasures, but called it by a different name
Now her men marry men, and women marry women, without a blush of shame
I taught her to murder within her own laws through legalized abortion

I taught her financial experts to steal by deception and extortion
Ahh, Yes, I almost have her now, worshiping at my feet
I only had to promise her that her every need I could meet
Most of her beauty has now decayed, as I sit upon her throne
As I and my demons rejoice to see how far down she as gone
And the only things that stand in my way, as my evil plan I pursue
Are that old black Book – the Bible, and the prayers of a faithful few.

  Arvil Jones

## How I Saved America - by Emmanuel

I watched in the depths of sorrow, I wept at the sight of her shame,
I patiently withheld my wrath, as she slowly forgot my Name;
I saw her glory quickly fading, as Lucifer laid his plan,
I heard his cruel demons rejoice at the death of each fallen man;
I saw her children drugged and damned, revolting in the streets,
I watched as men of learning bowed, and worshiped at Satan's feet;
I let the wicked have their time, I allowed them to raise their voice,
I gave them time to do their worst, to boast and to rejoice;
I saw them steeped in drunkenness, and bloated in their pride,
I watched them pass their wicked laws, as millions of innocents died;
But all the while I watched them, I remembered My promise of old,
How I someday would redeem to Myself, a number yet untold;
I have raised up a mighty Army, whom I sent forth to the fight,
And each of them I have endowed with my Spirit and with might;
My Word is in their heart and mouth, and none of them shall fall,
Until that Gospel has been heard around the world by all;
And let the earth and heaven know, though all may seem to be lost,
I will yet redeem America, by the Blood of an Old Rugged Cross!
Arvil Jones

## How I Spell Mother

Do we not stand in awe and wonder at the mighty hand of God,
Who from the dust created Man upon the earth to trod;
But yet there was no helper for the man that God had made,
And so God put the man to sleep there in Eden's shade;
And from his rib God made a woman to walk close by his side,
To be his friend, his mate, his lover, his helper and his bride;
But more than this, the woman was given a calling like no other,
The highest honor of the fairer sex, the gift of being a Mother;
The "M" in Mother stands for the Mender of bruises and broken hearts,
The one who gave us encouragement in all our stops and starts;
The "O" in Mother stands for One, and only One can there be,
The One who took us to her breast, and bounced us on her knee;
The "t" in Mother stands for Teacher, but also for Tenderness,
She taught us the difference between right and wrong,
While embraced in her tender caress;
The "h" in Mother stands for Honor, and yes, she deserves so much,
For the many tears she wiped away with a single gentle touch;
The "e" in Mother stands for Everlasting, for such was her love for me,
Lifting up my name to God upon her bended knee;
The "r" in Mother stands for Reward, and great shall it be up there,
When my Mother stands in a robe of white amidst that beauty rare;
For while she lived here on the earth, she withstood every test,
And was carried by the holy Angels, to her eternal rest.
© 2013 Arvil Jones

### *How Much Was Spent For Him*

*As the years of my life slip quickly away*
*And I reflect upon all that I've done*
*The people I've met, the sights I have seen*
*And the many places I've gone*
*I find myself asking some serious questions*
*About how my life has been spent*
*Are there many things that need to be changed*
*Of which I need to repent*
*How much of my life was wasted on me*
*With no thought of God's Glory in mind*
*And I wonder what kind of Testimony*
*I'm going to leave behind*
*How much of my life did I give to my Lord*
*Did I make Him my All in All*
*Was all of my service acceptable*
*Did I listen to His every call*
*Did I feed the poor and the hungry*
*Did I lend a helping hand*
*Did I give shelter to the homeless*
*Did I help the feeble to stand*
*And when all my life has ended*
*And my race is finally run*
*And when I see Him face to face*
*Will I hear Him say...Well done*
*© Arvil Jones*

## How to become The President

Now I know what you're all thinking as you start to read these lines,
"Not everyone can be President in these fast and modern times"
And there are a few requirements, of course, that simply must be met,
And the first one is that you must enjoy riding in a fancy jet;
You must love to travel from East to West, and to fly from North to South,
But first be sure you have learned to talk out of both sides of your mouth;
Sometimes you'll have to whisper, and then get really loud,
Because all that really matters is that you speak to suit the crowd;
You should cover as much of your past as you can, not leaving many traces,
While being able to win the hearts of all religions and races;
You must convince the masses that you will be at their beck and call,
But be sure that when you mess things up, someone else takes the fall;
You must make a lot of promises, whether you can keep them or not,
Just keep thinking about all the power, and the wealth and fame you've got;
You must be able to make folks believe that you in fact do care,
And in all their pain and poverty, you'd even be willing to share;
You must look your best, stand straight and tall, while striking so many poses,
While you and all your Beltway Boys sit and look down your noses;
So what if a million more babies must die with every passing year,
You must convince yourself and others that they have nothing to fear;
You must simply believe that you are in fact the world's most powerful man,
And convince yourself that not even God could have a better plan;
And it helps to have a silver tongue, and to know a lot of lawyer tricks,
For these are basic necessities when you're practicing politics;
And when you make a bunch of foolish remarks, be sure they are undetected,

And once you have mastered all of the above, you're sure to be re-elected.
2012 Arvil Jones

## How Vonda Got Her Name: By Arvil Jones

Oh how the Crouchers did rejoice,
At the birth of this sweet child;
She brought so much of happiness,
To this family meek and mild.

But as it is with any child,
With this one it was the same;
First things must always come first,
And they had to find her a name.

At first it didn't seem much of a problem,
They had plenty of books at hand;
These books of course were full of names,
And some of them quite grand.

They wanted a special name of course,
Not just any old name would do;
And so between the two of them,
They began to try out a few.

Shall we name her after my relatives?
Asked Roy with a sly little grin;
He was hoping that Velma would quickly agree,
As he kissed the little girl's chin.

That's certainly an option she said,
But let's ponder this for a while;
She sure is a beautiful baby,
Then they saw her first little smile.

They decided to take their good easy time,
For this was a moment quite rare;
And the name that would follow her all of her life,
Must be chosen with caution and care.

So they put their little girl back in her crib,
And they bowed their heads in prayer;
Her name could wait just a day or two,
And it was something they both would share.

And the next day they got together again,
And searched for a name that was fitting;

But after long hours without a result,
Sometimes they both felt like quitting.

But then they hit upon a brilliant plan,
To just go through the alphabet;
But after going from A to Z,
They hadn't found a name yet.

They quickly discarded Amy and Alice,
And Laura and Lucy and Lola;
And neither of them cared for Carey or Cassie,
Or Victoria or Viola.

Perhaps we should name her after a flower,
Or a river, or maybe a tree;
 We could call her Pansy, Petunia, or Daisy,
Or Cindy or Sarah Lee.

We could call her Betsy, or Beulah or Brenda,
Or Rachel or Emmy Lou;
We could call her Ardilla, or maybe Priscilla,
Or Sally or Peggy Sue.

By now the child was three days old,
And still not a name was in sight;
And then their eyes began to shine,
As if someone had turned on the light.

We could name her after someone in the Bible,
Like Deborah or Delilah;
But if we have another girl,
We'll name her Dawna or Twila.

Then Roy exclaimed, I think love got it,
It's the best idea so far;
Well name our little bundle of joy,
The name of a great vintage car.

And so they began to think of some names,
And by process of elimination;
They couldn't call her a Ford or a Falcon,
Or Chevy or Citation.
From the front she looked like a Volvo,
But from the rear, like a Honda;
So finally the couple just compromised,
And called their little girl ....VONDA!

## I Am The One - by Arvil Jones

I was the Beggar with nothing to eat
I was the Cripple who was lame in his feet
I was the Blind man who could not see
And I was the Leper who stood hopelessly
I was the Thief who was hung by His side
And I watched in horror as He slowly died
I was the Mocker who spat in His face
Who spurned His Mercy and despised His Grace
I was the Soldier who platted the thorns
And sat down to gamble for the robe He had worn
Yes, I am the Sinner, the worst of them all
I am also the one whom He came to call
Yes, I am the man who was swollen with pride
But I'm also the one for whom Jesus died
And although I was blind, thank God I now see
For the Blood of Christ has availed for me.
© Arvil Jones

## I and My Conscience

I and my conscience went for a walk, though I asked him to stay behind,
But my conscience insisted that I, without him, would be walking totally blind;
I told my conscience I could survive without him, and do nothing wrong,
But in spite of all my objections, he still wanted to come along;

I kept insisting that he stay behind, and allow me to fend for myself,
But old conscience just would not allow me to put him on the shelf;
So, in spite of all my objections, my conscience came tagging along,
And before we had gotten very far, the temptations became very strong;

There in the road lay a very large purse, which both me and my conscience saw,
I opened it up and looked inside, and was immediately struck with awe;
Thousands of dollars were tucked inside, and my heart began to race,
And immediately old conscience stepped in and looked me in the face;

Those thousands of dollars were mine for the taking, and no one would know but me,
But that mean old conscience just had to butt in, saying, "look closer for an ID;
I tried hard to ignore him at first, but he spoke even louder then,
In fact, he literally screamed in my head, "You know this is a sin,"

As the voice of my conscience grew louder, I could no longer ignore,
I found the ID, it belonged to the owner of the local liquor store;
Aha! I quickly reminded my conscience, Do you see who owns this purse?
The old sinner woman who sells alcohol, now conscience, I ask, what is worse?

Should I return this money to her, so she can continue her trade?
Or give it to the Girl Scouts selling cookies and Lemonade?
I will argue with you no longer, my conscience quickly replied,
Then my conscience fell so quiet, I thought that he had died;

But my conscience had made his point, and I knew what I had to do,
I took the purse to its owner and said, I believe this belongs to you;
She quickly looked me up and down, then I saw a tear in her eye,
She said this money is for my daughter, who they say is going to die;

And aren't you a preacher Sir? I know I've seen you somewhere,
Yes, I replied, I am a preacher, at that Church right over there;
Her tears now flowed uncontrollably, and her knees sank to the floor,
Then I saw her precious daughter standing just inside the door;
As I knelt beside the woman, her daughter knelt there too,
And both of them were saying, "We thank God for sending you;"
The three of us prayed together, and I opened up God's Word,
And in a moment two precious souls claimed Jesus as their Lord;

I and my conscience went for a walk, both of us singing loud,
Praising the blessed Lamb of God, of whom we are so proud;
On Sunday, the lady stood in our church, and she had something to say,
Through tear-stained eyes she announced to us, her daughter had passed away;

But through her tears, she managed a smile, and took me by the hand,
Saying, "Thanks to God, and this man's conscience, my girl is in a better land;

I and my conscience are the best of friends, and I really like it that way,
And now, more than ever, I listen better to what old conscience has to say.

## ...I find no fault in this man (Matthew 23:4 KJV)

As He stood there before Pilate, the crowd all gathered 'round,
Many hateful slanderous accusations did abound;
The Lamb of God stood silent, uttering not a sound,
But with all the lies and accusations, no fault in Him was found;

And though they found no fault in Him, the multitude yet cried,
This man does not deserve to live, let him be crucified;
Three times in desperation Pilate tried to let Him go,
But the murderous hearts of His countrymen had now begun to show;

No earthly device can measure the lengths to which men have gone,
In all their futile attempts to find one fault with God's own Son;
Some attempted to find a fault concerning His Virgin birth,
Not knowing He was God in flesh, the Deity on Earth;

They could find no fault in His character, for He was the perfect man,
They could find no fault in His doctrine, for He taught salvation's plan;
They could find no fault in His teaching, wherever His voice was heard,
They could find no fault in the works He did, and no fault in His Word;

For never man spake like this Man, His every word was pure,
His every act was merciful, His every step was sure;
I challenge all to examine Him, then tell me if you can,
With all your searching can you find a single fault in this Man?

There was no fault in His earthly life, and yet He was made to be sin,
Condemned to die the death of the Cross in the place of sinful men;
There was no fault even in His death, as He writhed in unspeakable pain,
And to prove His death was faultless, He arose to live again;

I find no fault in this Man, by those words I will live and die,
And if you find no fault in Him, then may I ask you - Why?
Why do you not consider Him, and take Him at His Word?
And why do you not ask Him now to be your Savior and Lord?

## I Followed Him - by Arvil Jones

I followed Him from Heaven's Throne
To a stable in Bethlehem
Where quietly He lay in a manger
While men came to honor Him
Then I followed Him down into Egypt
Where He sojourned for a while
Then I followed Him back to Nazareth
Pondering each weary mile
I followed Him to the Jordan River
And watched Him baptized there
And I heard a voice from on High
As it mightily pierced the air
I followed Him to the Synagogues
Where He preached, and healed, and blessed
And yet He was scorned and ridiculed
And was put to many a test
I followed Him to a lovely Garden
Where in agony He prayed
And I followed Him to Pilate's hall
Since now He had been betrayed
I saw Him beaten, mocked and scorned
While all His friends had fled
And I watched as they placed a crown of thorns
Upon His bleeding Head
And the longer I followed the more it seemed
That my soul would surely be lost
Still I followed Him, and I followed Him
Then I found Him at the Cross.
© Arvil Jones

## I Remember

I remember a brother who wanted to serve,
They tested his mettle and tried his nerve;
In the swamps and jungles of Vietnam,
He valiantly honored his Uncle Sam;
I remember the thousands who left their wives,
To sail o'er the oceans and lay down their lives;
I remember the brave ones who stormed the beach,
For a target that some of them did not reach;
I remember the cold, the heat and disease,
They endured so that we could all rest at ease;
I remember the pilots who risked it all,
All the sailors and soldiers who answered the call;
I remember the fox holes in which they slept,
The all night marches, and the honor they kept;
I remember the charge, and I hear their cry,
Advancing forward, yelling Semper Fi;
I remember the rockets, the mortars and shells,
As before the onslaught, the enemy fell;
I remember Iwo Jima's sand,
And the flag that was raised by the little band;
I remember the joy and the jubilation,
As they came back home to a grateful nation;
And Oh yes- that Star - Spangled Banner does wave,
O'er the land of the free, and the home of the brave.
2012 Arvil Jones

### *I Think Of...*

*When the journey has been a little rough,*
*When I've driven too many miles;*
*When I've seen too many faces frowning,*
*And I'm running low on smiles;*
*When the task before me seems to tough,*
*And the troubles come in piles;*
*I stop and reflect, and think about,*
*My dear friend, Trisa Liles;*
*Who never lets anything keep her down,*
*A lady who'd rather smile than frown;*
*Who lives her life in her own way,*
*Trusting her God from day to day;*
*She never frets over fashions and styles,*
*She's just who she is, Trisa Liles;*
*What you see is what you get,*
*On any given day;*
*She'll speak her mind, and you'll always find,*
*She says what she has to say;*
*So if you've hit a rough place in the road,*
*If you've been carrying a heavy load;*
*If you think you've given more than your share,*
*Or when your patience begins to wear;*
*When you think you've traveled too many miles,*
*Think of my dear friend, Trisa Liles!*

## I Turn To Him

When the day has been so long and dreary,
When the body soul and spirit are weary;
I turn to Him.

When the road has been so rugged and rough,
When all my strength seemed not enough;
I turn to Him.

When not a friend came to my side,
When many nights I sat and cried;
I turn to Him.

When all the demons gather round,
And there's no courage to be found;
I turn to Him.

When the winds become a gale,
And all the sky is a darkened veil;
I turn to Him.

When my tears like a river flow,
When not a comfort I may know;
I turn to Him.

When temptation blocks my path,
When I hear the voice or wrath;
I turn to Him.

When the pain I cannot bear,
When I see death's cold dark stare;
I turn to Him.

When the tempests o'er me roll,
When the devils vex my soul;
I turn to Him.

I turn to Him in the morning light,
I turn to Him in the dark of night;
I turn to Him throughout the day,
I turn to Him to guard my way;

When loved ones go to their new home,
No more on earth again to roam;
I turn to Him

And when it comes my time to go,
There is one thing I surely know;
Whether the day be bright or dim,
I'll close my eyes, and go to Him.

## I was just passing by - By Arvil Jones
## The Parable of The Good Samaritan

'Twas just another day for me, and all my duties I had faithfully done,
And I took the same road home, as I had done many times before;
I expected nothing extraordinary, nothing to upset my routine,
I only wanted to get home to my family, and nothing more;

I had been in the sacred Temple of Jehovah, performing my priestly duties,
And I was quite satisfied that I had given God my very best;
All day long I had served God and man, ministering in the holy place,
And my tired old body only wanted some peace and rest;

As I slowly and cautiously made my way down the slope toward Jericho,
Upon my ear there resounded such a pitiful cry;
And suddenly, there in a ditch stained with blood, lay a wounded Jewish brother,
But I must hurry on, 'twas no business of mine, for you see, I am just passing by;

Surely the Levite who works with me in the Temple will stop and help,
After all, such menial duties as this are his to perform;
In spiritual matters I outrank him by far, and I dare not stain my garments,
Compared to me, he is as lowly as a worm;

And when he comes by and sees this wounded brother,
I'm confident that he will not just let him die;
As for me, I must get home and study the Law of Moses,
For you see, I am just passing by;

If I should take the time to stop, and help this fallen man,
Perhaps those who beat him are still lurking somewhere near;

My heart surely goes out to him, and I wish him all the best,
But for my own life and safety I greatly fear;

'Tis not the duty of a man of my stature, to do what the Levite can do,
And perhaps this all happened just to put him to the test;
And it won't be long till he passes this way, and sees this brother's plight,
While I get on home to my family, and enjoy my well-deserved rest;

I will say a prayer for this unfortunate one, and pronounce my blessing upon him,
For I must reach my home 'ere the darkness clothes the sky;
My dear friend the Levite is not far behind, and I'm sure he will see this fellow,
And I'm sure the Levite would never pass him by.
I am a lowly Levite, and I minister about holy things,
I serve with the priests in the Temple day by day;
And having faithfully done all my work, and keeping the candles burning,
I now long for home, and I must be on my way;

I haven't much time before darkness falls, and many dangers abound,
But I have great faith that my God will get me home;
I have gone from Jerusalem to Jericho so many times before,
And thus far, no real danger or harm has come;

But what is this, up ahead of me, lying in that ditch by the road,
A wounded man, and Oh, what a mournful sigh!
He looks as if he was badly beaten, Why he's nearly at death's door;
But I dare not go near him, for I'm only passing by;

I wonder why the Priest did not stop, and aid this dying brother,
For he says he's a much holier man than I;

But I suppose that he, like myself, feared for his own safety,
And he, like myself, was only passing by;

Surely no one in a right state of mind will blame us for going around,
It is likely too late to save this man anyway;
I'm sure the Priest said a prayer for him, and I will do the same;
What a pity, this poor man's luck was so awful today;

And who knows but that he deserved this fate, he was probably a horrible
sinner,
And not nearly as holy as the blessed Priest and I;
But enough of this senseless reckoning, and lingering till dark,
After all, like the Priest, I am just passing by.

There is just enough of daylight left for me to reach my home,
And perhaps some stranger will pass this way ere long;
And like the Priest has warned me so many times before,
My friend, you know, survival is for the strong.

And now I see the candle glowing in the window of my home,
No more am I able to hear the wounded man's cry;
I will shut the whole sordid scene from my mind, and rest in sweet repose;
For after all, I was only passing by.

I am a Samaritan, just a common stranger, to the Jews of Jerusalem,
And so often they have shunned me and cursed my name;
And though I have often offered my hand as a gesture of friendship to
them,
Yet they spit upon me, and look upon me with shame;

So many times my heart has been broken, as I've walked this road alone,
Just wanting to be a generous neighbor and friend;

But it seems that no one of their religion can even speak to me,
For to do so, they claim, would be to greatly offend;

But wait, it seems I hear a sound, up ahead just around the bend,
It sounds like the painful screams of a dying man;
Oh God, I must hurry, and get to his side, ere he breathes his final breath,
I must somehow give this fellow a helping hand;

His body is covered with his own dried blood, his face is ashen white,
And it seems his every breath will be his last;
Dear God, I beg You, show me what to do, help me to save this man,
For I must do something, and Lord I must do it fast;

This dear man cannot help himself, and I see that he is a Jew,
But it matters not, for I cannot let him die;
I will do what I can to save his life, I will give all that I have;
Even though today I was only passing by;

I can see by the tracks on the side of the road, that others have come this way,
But didn't they stop to help this man at all?
Did they not see his wounded body, and the blood upon his face?
And surely they could hear his pitiful call;

But I must pour in oil and wine, and bind his open wounds,
Now is that a spark of life I see in his eye?
Yes, I believe he is going to live, if I get him the proper care;
Thank God, I saw him, and couldn't just pass him by.
© 2013 by Arvil Jones

**I will come again (John 14:3).**

There were so many things for which to look forward,
Especially in our younger days;
A brand new bike, or a set of blocks to stack a thousand ways,

The girls looked forward to a Barbie doll, the boys just wanted a kiss,
And then it was on to high school;
And four years of careless bliss,

Then the hallowed halls of college loomed,
And  it was time to knuckle down,
Sitting under the watchful eye of old Professor Frown;

But love, of course, was in the air, and we knew it wouldn't be long,
Till we met the one and only;
Who would be our heart's sweet song,

The looking forward, in itself, made life somehow worthwhile;
And then one day - there she was,
That angelic, radiant smile;

The lump in your throat was hard to swallow, just to ask her for a date,
But ask you must, and you found the courage;
Before it was too late,

Nothing more noble than the heart of a man, captured by that first love;
He will make her his wife,
If he has to move the earth and Heaven above;

Nothing more sacred than the love of two, united together as one,

While friends and family, and angels watch;
And the ceremony is done,

Nothing more precious than the birth of a child, shall we name him
Lonnie, or Lee;
We will love him all the days of our life,
Looking forward to what he will be;

We will train him up in the ways of our God, and teach him the sacred
Word,
We will nurture and admonish him;
And show him the love of our Lord,

Looking forward, we count our blessings, and name them one by one,
Holding hands on the old porch swing;
Till another day is done,

Looking forward, our hearts turn upward, searching the Eastern sky;
Watching for the return of our Lord,
Who promised to come by and by;

Somehow His promise makes us forget about all the tears and pain,
Looking forward, ever forward;
For He said - I will come again.
© 2014 Arvil Jones

## I Will, Saith the Lord

From the dust let us create him, in our image let him be,
I will breathe in him the breath of life, that he may live like Me;
I will give him ears to hear Me, I will give him eyes to see,
I will give him soul and spirit that will live eternally;

In my garden I will place him so that he may dress and keep,
And to him I'll give dominion o'er the land and o'er the deep;
I will make the man the master o'er the earth that I have made,
Every beast shall be his servant, every tree shall be his shade;

But yet the man is lonely, so a helper I will give,
The two of them shall be as one, together they shall live;
I will give to them My blessing, and My voice they shall hear,
As in My garden they shall walk, and I will be quite near;

I will give him every herb to eat, the fruit of every tree,
But by one tree I'll test him, and by the test I'll see;
With all that I have given, will the man now stand or fall?
Will he hearken to his Maker, or heed the serpent's call?

In a moment he has fallen, in his shame he hides his face,
Among the trees the man and woman tremble in disgrace;
But yet I go to find him, calling out his name,
While each of them are gathering leaves with which to hide their shame;

And though the fig leaves sewn together may conceal their skin,
They have no covering that can hide the fearfulness of sin;
And he who once walked with his God, now walks behind a plow,
His back is bent, his body wet with sweat from off his brow;

The soft breeze that once cooled him now howls with gale and gust,
He knows that he is destined to return unto the dust;
As a hireling he fulfills his day, with trouble and with tears,
The night winds that once whispered peace now fill his heart with fears;

Yet I will look upon him with an eye of tenderness,
And though he disobey Me, My creature I will bless;
If he stumble I will catch him, if he cry I'll hear his call,
For in mercy I have promised I will save him from the fall;

In his sorrow I will comfort, in his pain I will console,
In weakness I will give him strength, though time shall take its toll;
It matters not how great his sin, how measureless his loss,
For now I only see him through the blood of Calvary's Cross;

With the Bread of life I'll feed him, in green pastures he shall lie,
He shall drink from living Waters, and his soul shall never die;
And when his days on Earth are spent, and the grave becomes his bed,
I will call and he will answer, I will raise him from the dead;

I have a place prepared for him, with Me he shall abide,
Around My Father's table, in a body glorified;

There in the bliss of Heaven, never more again to roam,
I will say to all My blessed children - Welcome Home.
© 2014 Arvil Jones

## *I Wonder...*

I wonder how God feels each time someone tells a lie,
And how He feels each time a little unborn child must die;
And how does the mother feel when the child is taken from her womb,
Not even given the smallest respect of even a decent tomb;
I wonder how the father feels, or if he knows or cares,
About the life in which he and the mother shares;
I wonder how the doctor feels who takes that precious life,
I wonder how the nurses feel who handed him the knife;
And none will ever know how much that little one could give,
If only he or she had been given the chance to live;
I wonder how God feels each time a soldier has to die,
Somewhere on a battlefield beneath a foreign sky;
To protect our foreign interests, so the politicians say,
How many lives are our interests worth, can anyone really say?
I wonder how we all will feel when comes that judgment day,
When each of us must give account for each idle word we say;
What will I say, how will I feel, when my record I must face?
I claim nothing else but Jesus' blood, and God's amazing grace!
2016 Arvil Jones

## If ever you have wondered...

If ever you have wondered how some folks made it through life,
Enduring hardship, poverty, sickness, war and strife;
Sometimes not even knowing from where the next meal would come,
Sometimes enduring the bitter cold till their fingers and toes were numb;
Or sweating in the prickly heat, no air conditioning or fan,
Without a steady income, without a viable plan;
Without a visible means of support, and a family of fourteen,
When many times the cupboard was bare and all the children were lean;
When there seemed to be no hope of rising above the circumstance,
And even on the far horizon there seemed to be little chance;
When the greatest struggle everyone faced was the struggle to survive,
When it seemed you were the only ones who knew you were alive;
When the only means of living was living off the land,
And we were thankful for anyone who would lend a helping hand;
When all the children walked to school with patches and hanging threads,
And all of us were thankful for the roof above our heads;
They were both willing to sacrifice to see that the family was fed,
And sometimes as many as six of us would sleep on a single bed;
How did we survive? You ask, well let me tell you how,
We gathered around an old oak table, and all our heads would bow;
While Mama thanked the Lord above for the little that we had,
Believing someday God would make things better for her and Dad;
It took a while, but the good Lord answered the prayers my Mama
prayed,
Not once did she ever doubt Him, as upon her knees she stayed;
She was faithful in the smallest of things, and taught us to do the same,
To cast our cares all upon Him, and to trust His Holy Name;
I've never gone to bed hungry, and I've always had a place,
To lay my weary head at night by trusting in His grace;

His grace has never failed me, though I'm put to many a test,
But through it all I awake each day and know that I am blessed.
But more than this I am certain when my record is laid bare,
I'm not afraid to look in the Book, for I know my name is there.
2016 Arvil Jones

## If He Came This Very Day

The scriptures and the Prophets all declared that He would come,
a promise some did not believe, but held so dear by some;
The centuries passed slowly, and the faithful watched the sky,
Believing their Messiah would come to them by-and-by;
When the fullness of the time was come, God sent forth His Son,
And so many just could not perceive the way that it was done;
There was no pomp and circumstance, no trumpets loud and long,
Just a few lowly shepherds listening to the angels' song;
In a manger in a stable, the Great I Am did lay,
As wise men came to offer gifts, and bowed their heads to pray;
He grew in grace and stature, was baptized in Jordan's stream,
Then far and wide He spread the news about Salvation's theme;
And many who had waited knew He was God's beloved Son,
And wondered at the power of the miracles He'd done;
They followed Him from place to place to hear His wondrous Word,
Such grace and power and mercy none of them had ever heard;
But why, they asked, must He now die upon a wooden cross?
And why should such a man as He endure such pain and loss?
It seemed they'd all forgotten His words, that He must rise again,
Up from the cold dark tomb where His wounded body had lain;
And He left them with the precious words that in their hearts did burn,
That each of them should watch and pray, and wait for His return;
Yes, His return is just as certain as His death upon the tree,
And before Him every knee shall bow, and every eye shall see;
And so the question must be asked - Who over our hearts holds sway?
And would He find us watching, if He came this very day?
© 2012 Arvil Jones

## If He'd Just Walked Away

No one could have blamed Him if He had just walked away,
From a world that hated Him so;
A world that had long been held captive by sin,
Whose religion was but a vain show;
No one could have blamed Him if He had just left us,
To perish in our own sin and shame;
For after all, the world despised Him, and cursed His very name,
The world spat in the face of God, and beat Him with a whip;
Not knowing He had come to deliver them,
From sin and its horrible grip;
He could have simply walked away, and left the world alone,
But if He had just walked away, who then could atone;
For there was no priest or prophet, nor any earthly king,
Who could deliver His lost sheep from sin and its deadly sting;
If Jesus had only walked away, the world would surely be lost,
For there was no earthly sacrifice that could pay the awful cost;
He could have called ten thousand angels from Heaven's throne above,
But then the world would never have known the depths of redeeming
love,
But no man took His life from Him, He freely laid it down;
That He might take it up again, and receive the golden crown,
Let us rejoice, and be exceeding glad, and honor Him this day;
Let us be forever thankful that He didn't just walk away.
© 2013 Arvil Jon

**If I had a nickel...**

If I had a nickel for every time I've heard a politician lie,
My stack of nickels would probably reach beyond the starry sky;
If I had a nickel for every promise a politician breaks,
I'd have enough nickels to buy the world ten pounds of porterhouse
steaks;
If I had a nickel for every time Hillary Clinton has lied,
I could buy the leaning tower of Pisa and the Taj Mahal beside.

## If My People.....II Chronicles 7:14

Why did God have to add an "if" to what He was about to say?
Because there was the likelihood that His people would not pray;
And this alone should cause each child of God to blush with shame,
For after all He loves us enough to call us by His name;
And I guess what God had to say next really applies to me,
Because I know my strongest suit is not humility;
And yet at times I humble myself, and fervently ask for grace,
Upon my bended knees in prayer, seeking the Master's face;
He asks me, Son, where have you been, I've not heard from you in days,
But I'm glad to see that you are here, turning from your wicked ways;
And as He promised, He hears our pleas from Heaven up above,
Ever willing to forgive, and bless us with His love;
And if our land ever needed healing, Dear God, the time is now,
If only all God's people were willing to humbly bow.
2013 Arvil Jones

## If Not For The Cross

If not for the Cross there could be no Peace
We would have no reason to smile
For it was by the Blood of His Cross
That He came to Reconcile
If not for the Cross there could be no Pardon
For all the crimes we have done
For it was by the Blood of His Cross
That He came to Atone
If not for the Cross there could be no Promise
No Covenant to Embrace
For it was by the Blood of His Cross
That he opened the Fountain of Grace
If not for the Cross no one could be Pure
From our foul corruption within
For it is by the Blood of His Cross
That He washes away All Sin
© Arvil Jones

## If Only I Could...

If only I could turn back the sweeping hands of time,
And could still know all the things that I know now;
I've often asked myself, Are there many things I'd change,
If only I could change the past somehow;
I know it is impossible, merely wishful thinking,
But I guess we all have entertained the thought;
How much of our lives would we change, how much would we keep the
same,
How much was spent for good, how much for nought;
There were certainly some childish things we could have done without,
Some fleeting fantasies, some unreachable stars;
So many foolhardy whims and mistakes, so many plans and dreams,
So many sorrows that left invisible scars;
What relationships would we cherish, how many would we let go,
How many words would we choose not to speak;
How different would our outlook be concerning things to come,
Would the portrait of our life be bright or bleak;
How much of our time would we use more wisely, for more important
things,
How many trivial vanities would we lay aside;
How much more honest would we be, how much more transparent,
How many secrets would we still try to hide;
How early would we seek our God, and search until we found Him,
Instead of putting Him off till near the last;
How much better would we prepare for our eternity,
Instead of holding grudges from the past;
Ahh, 'tis all but wishful thinking, to hope to change what's done,
For the past is written, and lies in the tomb of time;
And though it were played in the minor key, as a sad and solemn refrain,

The future yet holds hope for a sweeter chime;
Bury it, bury the solemn past, beneath the blood of Christ,
Who on the Cross in agony suffered and bled;
So deep His blood has covered our past, so far He has cast our sins,
That never again can they raise their ugly head.
2015 Arvil Jones

## If only, if only!

How many young men in the skid row gutter now have a lot of time to think,
If only, If only, I had never taken that first drink!

How many dying with cancer, heart attack or stroke,
Are saying, If only I had never lit up that first smoke!

How many with venereal disease, their bodies ravaged with pain,
Are saying, If only with the prostitutes, I had never lain!

And how many from the flames of Hell, now scream with a tortured tongue,
If only I had called upon Jesus, way back when I was young!

Now is the accepted time,
Today is the day of salvation;
Tomorrow is a misty illusion,
And it may spell your damnation!
© 2014 Arvil Jones

### *If you want my...*

*If you want my attention, then please be discreet, and keep your*
*sentences short,*
*If you want my attention, say something of value, and I don't need a*
*lengthy report;*
*If you want my attention, please be honest, and never tell me a lie,*
*If you want my attention, be specific, and look me in the eye;*
*If you want my attention, be transparent, having nothing to hide,*
*If you want my attention, be consistent, and don't let your words collide;*
*If you want my attention, please speak clearly, so I understand each word,*
*Do you want my attention, or just my opinion, about what I've just heard?*
*If you want my opinion, be ready to listen, as I have listened to you,*
*Give me the same courtesy, and listen to my view;*
*Please do not interrupt me, please do not be rude,*
*For I have listened to your words, however clever or crude;*
*If I give my attention, if I give my opinion,*
*If as friends you and I may part;*
*I have really given you nothing,*
*Unless I gave you my heart.*

## If You Want To...

If you want to argue politics, I am not available,
But if you want to discuss it, I'll be there;
There is no political view that is totally unassailable,
And I won't argue, but it's not that I don't care;
It's just that neither you nor I know all there is to know,
And if we argue, neither will be convinced;
But if we sit down and discuss it like two gentlemen should,
Then neither of us will wind up being incensed;
I've never studied political science, though I guess I probably should,
It's just that I have a real issue with lying;
And as far as my limited knowledge goes, forgive me if I'm wrong,
It seems politicians can lie without even trying;
And if you want to argue religion, I am not available,
But I'll gladly sit down and discuss your point of view;
For there is a certain religious conviction, totally unassailable,
The fact that Jesus died for me and you;
If you want to argue morality, I am not available,
But surely we may discuss it without a fight;
For in the realm of morals, some things are unassailable,
Quite simply my friend, it's either wrong or right!
2016 Arvil Jones

## If

If you knew there was a raging fire burning at your front door,
Would you simply ignore it, or pretend it wasn't there?
If a venomous snake was about to strike at the heart of your only child,
Would you do nothing but stand there and stare?
If your child was about to drink deadly poison, and had it to his lips,
Would you not take the bottle from his hand?
If a murderous gang of thugs tried to force him to join them,
Would you let him go, or firmly take a stand?
If you knew your child was taking drugs that would eventually end his life,
Would you turn your head, or try to intervene?
Would you rather see your child in church, learning about the Lord,
Or find him dead at a bloody murder scene?
You might say to me these are foolish questions that don't deserve and
answer,
And none of these things will ever happen to you;
But they happen somewhere every day, to someone's precious child,
And it seems that those who care are very few;
But something even worse than these must now be considered,
Do you know the condition of your child's eternal soul?
Are you willing to let him choose for himself, without any guidance from
you,
As a godless liberal society takes its toll?
Are you willing to let a crooked politician, or a liberal professor,
Decide your children's destiny and fate?
Will you let them teach him evolution, and a homosexual lifestyle,
Without so much as a conscientious debate?
Are you so caught up with success, and making more and more money,
As to bury your head, and pretend that all is well?
Have you taken the time to love your child enough to chasten him,

Or would you rather let him go to hell?
If we have given our children everything money can buy,
And yet have failed to tell them of the Lord;
We haven't really loved them at all, and we have given them nothing,
Except an empty life, and our empty word;
A child left to himself will bring his mother to shame,
The words of a very wise king from long ago;
If we do not teach our children the faithful Word of God,
The we, and they, will reap just what we sow.

## I'm glad you're not...

I'm glad not everyone is just like me,
And I know you want me to explain;
Because if you were just like me,
You'd have a lot of pain;

And if you are not just like me,
Another reason to be glad;
Believe it or not, this kind old man,
Sometimes gets pretty mad;

I'm glad you aren't just like me,
For you'd have little time to spare;
You'd have a lot of wrinkles,
And not a lot of hair;

Dear friend if you were just like me,
Your eyes would be getting dim;
You'd have a bulging waistband,
Instead of being slim and trim;

And the biggest reasons I am glad,
My life is not your life;
You'd be as handsome as I am,
And you'd be in love with my wife!

## In 2015 I....

Well, now the year has come and gone, and as I sit here all alone,
Reflecting on the highs and lows, and on how quickly the time goes;
I thought about all the things I've done in this past year that now has gone,
I grumbled, I stumbled, I mumbled, I fumbled, and once or twice I was greatly humbled;
I published a book, I tried to cook, I refused to hate, and I gained some weight,
I drove a hundred thousand miles, I saw some frowns, I saw some smiles;
I laughed a lot at the politics, with all its fancy words and tricks,
I often bowed my head and cried for all my fellow men who died;
I saw so many in so much pain, I prayed that none had died in vain,
I saw the tragedies that swept our land, and many who offered a helping hand;
I counted my blessings day by day each night as I bowed my head to pray,
And in spite of all I saw and heard, my faith is unshaken in God and His Word;
What the New Year holds, I have no clue, but I already know what I'm going to do,
I will thank Him each time I open my eyes, and look toward the eastern skies;
Each passing moment my heart will yearn, as I watch and wait for His return.

## In a World Gone Mad, by Arvil Jones, Ph.D.

In my more than sixty years of living, I like to think that I have learned a little,
About life and love, and right and wrong, and a thing called The Golden rule;
I am absolutely certain about some things, but not so much about some others,
But at the end of the day, I'm still nobody's fool,

I know the difference between night and day, and how some folks don't mean what they say;
And how most folks simply look out for old number one,
I've seen folks cheat and I've heard folks lie, and talk about Heaven and the by and by;
And excuse themselves for it all when the day is done,

Living in a land where the leaders are elected, supposedly to serve their fellow man,
I've seen my country sink to levels that break my heart;
I was taught to have faith and confidence in our great government,
And that as a taxpaying voter I shared a part;

But the longer I live and try to do the right thing, and pay the bills and all that,
It seems to me that only a few can have their say;
I'm told that us Bible believing Christians are just too narrow-minded,
And that we should just shut up and get out of the way,

We're being told that our brilliant leaders, some of whom are gay and lesbian,

Know more about what we need than we could possibly know;
That we should accept men kissing men, and women kissing women,
And that there's nothing wrong with a pornographic show;

And when we object to such practices, based upon the Holy Bible,
We're told that we should be quiet, and make no remark;
But some of us still call sin by its name, and we recognize filth when we see it,
And it's a shame to even speak of what these folks do in the dark;

While hurricanes, tornadoes, wildfires, floods, and all sorts of catastrophes,
Keep sweeping this land with unnatural intensity;
While the whole world braces itself for war, and famines and droughts and such;
And some still say - "whatever will be will be",

Well, I for one, speaking strictly for myself, believe that judgement is imminent,
And that what we are seeing will only intensify;
For as long as out nation keeps killing little babies, and catering to the Devil's crowd,
And convince themselves it's alright to cheat and lie;

This nation is headed for a rendezvous with a horrible destiny,
If she doesn't repent and return to faith in her God;
Our children and grandchildren are going to Hell with every passing day,
While we train Muslims to kill us on our own sod;

The politicians have no answers, scientists and teachers are baffled,
How such a great nation could come to such a sorry state;

But unless and until we return to Christ, and ask for His forgiveness,
We are doomed, that is, if it isn't already too late;

I know the evening of my life is now swiftly approaching,
And I may have waited too long to say these things;
But what I have written, I have written, and I make no apology,
I am ready to face whatever tomorrow brings;

I know that I am ready to go, and to stand before my Maker,
And I wish that all the world could say the same;
But if some of you who read this cannot make that same statement,
I beg of you, please call upon Jesus' Name.
Arvil Jones, Ph.D.

## In The Creek

Now some folks may not understand us country girls and boys,
And probably because they've never known those simple country joys;
Like waking up to the sound of a Mother singing while she cooks,
Who was more concerned about her children than about her looks;
Or maybe you've never known the joy of the song of a whip-poor-will,
Or sat in a swing on the old front porch in the evening quiet and still;
Perhaps there are those who have never held a plow in his callused hand,
Or walked barefoot down an old dirt road, leaving footprints in the sand;
How sad that some have never heard the sound of a babbling brook,
Or dug a worm and watched it squirm while baiting an old fish hook;
And there are some who never wore a pair of patched overalls,
Or milked a cow, or slopped a hog, or shoveled out the stalls;
Some ain't never ate fried chicken straight from an old chop block,
Or kissed his childhood sweetheart, carving hearts upon a rock;
God help the ones who never fished in the creek till the light grew dim,
Or when the fish quit biting, just jumped in the creek for a swim;
Some never saw an old baptizing down at the swimming hole,
And pity the boy who never had a pipe-cane fishing pole;
Ahh! The simple joys of life on that small Kentucky farm,
Where everyone was your neighbor, and no one meant any harm;
When the days were long, and filled with wonder, and the greatest thing
was love,
When children were taught to work and play, and trust in God above.
2016 Arvil Jones

## In The Fork of The Road

So often my heart goes drifting back to a beautiful sacred Place
To a little Church in the fork of the road where I found God's Saving Grace
God only knows how many lost souls have laid down their heavy load
At the Altar of that little Church that sits in the fork of the road
It was there that many a poor lost sinner found Eternal Life
And there that many a country boy met his future Wife
I can still hear the Old Country Preacher as his voice rang loud and clear
Like the bell on Sunday morning saying Worship time was near
I can still hear the Church Choir singing and the glow on every face
And the Spirit always touched my soul when they sang Amazing Grace
So many precious memories and joys still abound
As I recall those all day meetings and Dinner on the ground
I can hear the children's laughter as they went to Sunday School
Where we learned the Ten Commandments and the precious Golden Rule
I recall the testimonies of the ones who have gone before
How they longed to leave this vale of tears for Heaven's peaceful Shore
They left behind a Legacy of Truth and Hope and Love
To join the ranks of Heaven's Choir in Mansions up above
But here on Earth the work goes on and the bell still loudly rings
And the country folks still worship
At the Church called Dripping Springs.
© Arvil Jones

## Independence Day!

Two-hundred and forty years ago the Declaration was signed
Sometimes hailed, sometimes Hallowed, and other times maligned
And those who signed it thought it right that they should separate
From tyranny and oppression, and to form a better state
They all knew that Liberty for all would not be cheap
Yet they planted the seeds of Freedom for the rest of us to reap
Thousands paid the highest cost - their blood that soaked the sod
Giving all that they possessed for Country and for God
The Flag that flew above us then was honored by one and all
And not one proud American would dare to let it fall
America, America! There are those who love you still
As we hear the shout of Freedom ring from every blessed hill
And there are yet a few of us who trust in God above
As the one and only Source of strength, Who guards us with His love
But let us not forsake Him, lest we surely then shall fall
And may we never drift so far we cannot hear His call
For the amber waves of grain that grow spring from His loving hand
Who created the soil from which it grows, and waters our thirsty land
And to all of those who would do us harm, and spurn our righteous law
Our Captain wields a might Sword, He whets the Eagle's claw
No weapon formed against us can prosper in the end
For Christ is our Protector, our Redeemer and our Friend
So as you fly your Flag today, and shoot rockets to the skies
Please say a prayer for this Nation that the Flag does symbolize
© Arvil Jones

## Is it AMERICA? Or is it just - me?

I could almost swear the spirit of Hussien Obama was dictating this! lol

The A is now gone from America, for our Ancestors no longer matter,
The Almighty has long been expelled, so we listen to political chatter;
The R is now missing, for there is no Respect, and no Responsibility,
And no Remembrance of the glory that shined from sea to shining sea;
And the only meaning left in the I, is that I get my way,
And that I, and those who agree with I, are the ones who have our say;
The C that once stood for unflinching Courage now bows before Muslim kings,
And Courage has turned into Cowardice, and the shame that Cowardice brings;
The last A once meant that All could be what they wanted to be,
But without the Almighty, Respect and Courage; I guess that just leaves...*me*!
© 2013 Arvil Jones

## *Is There Anything...?*

*Is there anything as lovely as the face of a little child?*
*Is there anything as touching, as gentle, meek and mild?*
*Is there anything as innocent as a little baby's heart?*
*And to whom on earth more sweetness did the Lord impart?*
*Is there anything that can touch the heart more than an infant's smile?*
*Is there anything more precious than holding him for a while?*
*Is there anything more fragile than that precious little life?*
*Whose little cry can cut your heart deeper than a knife?*
*Is there anything as gentle as his tiny finger's grip?*
*Or as funny as his first small step, or the time you saw him trip?*
*Can anyone describe the joy of that first spoken word?*
*To a Mom or Dad it's the sweetest sound they have ever heard!*
*The answer is No, there is nothing as precious or as sweet,*
*As hearing the pitter-patter of his tiny little feet!*
*2016 Arvil Jones*

## Is This The Hour?

The storm clouds have long been gathering o'er the land of Israel,
The long awaited prophesies that the Prophets had to tell;
The nations are all now poised, prepared to do their worst,
And now it is only a matter of which one will strike first;
Is this the hour in which the Word of God will be fulfilled?
When by the many millions, men of Earth will be killed?
All the nations around God's favored land are ready to advance,
While all the puny politicians maneuver and take their stance;
Little do they know that none of them are in control,
Is this the hour the thunder of God's mighty wrath shall roll?
I see the armies gathering, and the thousands in their ships,
But wait, is that an Angel with a trumpet to his lips?
Do men believe that they can rid the world of tyrants at last?
Do they not know that God can destroy them all with a single blast?
But the Scriptures of the prophets, they all must come to pass,
And then when all is said and done, our God will reign at last;
He shall come in power and glory, and sit upon Zion's hill,
And all the nations of the Earth shall bow before His will;
No idle word shall go un-punished, every sin shall be made known,
And every knee shall bow before the One upon the Throne;
And every man shall give account of how he has behaved,
And so the question must be asked, my friend, do you know you're
saved?
© Arvil Jones

## Joseph, I Thank You

There was never a great deal written of you,
My dear and faithful friend;
Things I believe the world ought to know,

How you and your friend Nicodemus came,
The day I was crucified;
With tears in your eyes, and both your heads bowed low;

And though my body hung dead on the Cross,
I saw your broken hearts;
As from My hands you pulled the driven nails,

I felt your care and gentleness, as you carried my Body away;
And off in the distance,
I heard all the mournful wails;

I saw you remove the crown of thorns,
From off My bleeding head;
I felt your humble kindness and gentle grace,

I saw you wipe the blood from my Body,
And I saw the clean linen clothes;
And the napkin that you placed upon my face,

I saw you and Nicodemus, preparing the sweet spices,
And wrapping my wounded Body;
With the greatest of care,

And though you may not have known it,
I was smiling at both of you;
As the fragrance of the spices filled the air,

I watched as you carried Me to your own tomb;
And laid my Body to rest,
I saw you roll the stone into its place;

But I also saw you looking upward,
Knowing I would rise again;
Ever trusting in My mercy and My grace,

I thank you Joseph, for the loan of your tomb;
And for all you did for Me,
And now my friend, before I go away;

I just wanted to tell the world some of the things you did,
And that you and I;
Will meet in Heaven someday,
Jesus of Nazareth.
2013 Arvil Jones

## Just Thinking of You

In our many years of walking with Him,
Sometimes the way looked hopeless and dim;
There were times when it seemed that the sun would not rise,
And nothing but dark clouds covered the skies;
But He always sent us a new ray of hope,
And a blessing or two that helped us to cope.

Those blessings He sent us were not earthly things,
Not silver or gold, or big diamond rings;
He always supplied our heart's greatest yearning,
With undying love, and lessons worth learning;
He gave us those things that make the heart glad,
The kind word of a friend, when our souls were so sad.

Oh yes, we are blessed, more than can be counted,
And as the years pass, our blessings have mounted;
He gives us mercy, and grace beyond measure,
And fills our hearts with Heavenly pleasure;
And whenever we need a blessing or two,
We can just close our eyes, and think of you.

Our words cannot say what a blessing you've been,
Our dear Savior knew that we needed a friend;
So He sent you to us, with your warm loving smile,
To help us enjoy each moment and mile;
And so before our earth's sojourn ends,
Thank you so much for just being our friends.
To Mike and Phyllis from Arvil and Carolyn

## Just Wondering

The longer I live, the older I get, the more the lines crease my face,
As each step seems a little harder, and I struggle to finish my race;
So many memories come flooding in, as I close my eyes and wonder,
What will it be like when Heaven I see, what awaits me over yonder;
Now don't take me wrong, my life has been good, and I don't wish to
leave today,
But if it be His will to call me, I'll be happy either way;
And I guess I can say with so many others – I only wish I'd done more,
For the glory of my Master, and laying up in store;
More of those heavenly treasures of which He speaks in His Word,
For I feel I've done so little for by blessed Savior and Lord;
I've lived to see four generations in my family here below,
Oh what great mercy, what great blessings He chooses to bestow;
And I so undeserving of even the smallest grace,
He lets me look by faith and see the glory of His face;
To me, who failed Him so many times, He yet says – I forgive,
As daily I'm reminded – He died that I might live;
Oh the wonder of it all, rejoice my soul rejoice,
That God Almighty would allow a worm to know his voice;
That a heart that once was hard as stone, He softened with a touch,
To one who was wretched, blind and poor, He chooses to give so much;
And more than this, He has prepared a mansion up above,
Where at last I will forever know the wonder of His love.
My last poem of 2015

## Learning from the children...
## An Ice-skating lesson:

I watched intently as two small children played outside one day,
My heart and mind were deeply touched by what they had to say;
A little boy and a little girl – they appeared to be about eight,
And it was obvious the little girl was teaching him how to skate;
She held his hand securely as she showed him how to stride,
Being careful not to criticize or wound his youthful pride;
Each time he stumbled she steadied him, slowing down their pace,
Saying – "Jimmy, don't look at your feet, look me in the face;"
Each time he fell, she picked him up, making him try again,
Saying, "Jimmy if you're gonna skate, expect a little pain;"
"I just can't seem to get it right," Jimmy said with a grin,
"But Jimmy, if you're gonna skate, it has to come from within;"
"Now watch me closely Jimmy, and never mind my feet,
Just visualize yourself gliding across this icy sheet;"
She skated away from Jimmy, a hundred feet or so,
Then glided back toward him, gracefully and slow;
He watched her skate around him with such ease and grace,
Remembering her gentle words – "Look into my face;"
As she twirled around him, she watched him slowly turn,
And as he turned his feet grew steady, now he was starting to learn;
She skated in a wider circle, then he heard her yell,
He didn't know, but she was only pretending that she fell;
All he could see was his closest friend lying on the ice,
As she motioned for him to come, he remembered her advice;
Jimmy forgot all about his feet, nothing else mattered now,
He simply had to cross that ice and get to his friend somehow;
She smiled as Jimmy bent his knees, his eyes looking straight ahead,

Never looking at his feet, but looking at her instead;
He suddenly found his balance, he conquered all his fear,
Then he saw her rising up just as he drew near;
Their little hands clasped each other, their little hearts were bound,
As Jennifer and Jimmy skated around, and around, and around.
2016 Arvil Jones

## Let Us Pray

Let us pray for a Nation that has lost its way,
Let us pray for the homeless with no place to stay;
Let us pray for the lost, the sick and the dying,
Let us pray for the ones who want to quit trying;

Let us pray for our leaders who seem to have strayed,
From the righteous path our forefathers laid;
Let us pray for the baby in its mother's womb,
That the abortion clinic won't be his tomb;

Let us pray for the misguided women and men,
Whose lives have been tortured and ravaged by sin;
Let us pray for the greedy who spend all their time,
Just trying to make that extra dime;

Let us pray for our Pastors, their children and wives,
For the teachers and counselors who have touched our lives;
Let us pray for those who travel afar,
For the missionaries wherever they are;

Let us pray for the youth and the very old,
Let us pray for the soldier who sleeps in the cold;
Let us pray for Israel and her protection,
That God will give her leaders direction;

Let us pray for the orphans in every State,
As they hope for a parent, and patiently wait;
Let us pray for the families torn apart,

For the child who cries from a broken heart;

Let us pray for our friends and our enemies too,
Let us honor our Lord in whatever we do;
If you run out of folks for whom to pray,
Then pray for me at the end of the day;

For my needs are many, but my God is great,
And I know that many blessings await;
And as your daily life you pursue,
Just know that I am praying for you.

© 2014 Arvil Jones

## Life! With God- or Without God?

Understanding life is not all that complicated, if you have the right
information,
It takes an idiot to believe in evolution, a wise man to embrace Creation;
But what about all the crime and hate, all the murder and disease,
Has God abandoned the human race, to do just as they please?

No, God has not abandoned us, He gave us all a will and a choice,
He endowed the human race with intelligence, a brain, a mind and a
voice;
If men turn out to be killers or thieves, it's because they choose to be,
And so they can murder an innocent baby, but spend millions to save a
tree;

We see folks pleading for all of us to save a dog or a cat,
Now God knows I love animals, and I have no problem with that;
I am all for saving the planet, and things that live in the wild,
But how many folks do we hear pleading for the life of an unborn child?

Life was so simple and beautiful when God first created man,
There was absolutely nothing hurtful or harmful as long as man followed
God's plan;
The man and his wife lived in Paradise, with everything holy and pure,
Their lives were blessed by God Himself, their steps were steady and sure;

But then one day in the Garden, a stranger's voice was heard,
The devil softly whispering to Eve that she should question God's Word;
At first God's Word was questioned, and then His Word was denied,
And then God's Word was disobeyed, and they knew the devil had lied;

And though their bodies were still alive, they were dead in spirit and soul,
As the dreaded fear death and judgement began to take their toll;
At the end of each day of labor and sweat, men knew their lives were
vain,
And Oh how the souls of men did groan, for sin had left its stain;

Generation after generation, they watched each other die,
Knowing this was all because man had listened to Satan's lie;
And yet within the human breast a ray of hope did burn,
The hope of a blessed Redeemer for which they all did yearn;

And according to the promise of God, one day the Redeemer came,
Born of a Virgin in Bethlehem, and Jesus is His name;
And again men have a choice to make while here on Earth they trod,
They can choose to live, or live without the blessed Lamb of God;

To choose to live without the Lord is a desperate mistake,
For it means you'll spend eternity in that awful burning Lake;
Receive Him as your Lord and Savior, and then all shall be well,
And you can live in Heaven, instead of a burning Hell.
© 2013 Arvil Jones

## Looking Forward With Hope and Faith

When I look around and see the way the world is going,
I brush a tear of sadness from my eye;
And yet there is a ray of hope, though I have no way of knowing,
Just when my Lord will come in the eastern sky;

I'm often tempted to complain when I see the hate and greed,
And watch as thousands of families fall apart;
It seems our hearts are focused upon our wants instead of our needs,
And it seems our elected leaders have no heart;

Yes, the future of America does look very grim,
If we continue to forsake the Lord;
He is the only hope for America and the world,
If only we would heed His blessed Word;

The path our leaders have chosen to follow can only end in disaster,
Unless we repent and turn to Him again;

## Lord, I'm Sorry

Dear Lord, I'm sorry for every time I failed to kneel and pray,
And for each time I neglected You at the start of a new day;
I'm sorry for each and every time I rushed to finish a prayer,
And for each time I saw a need, but didn't show that I care;

Dear Lord, I'm sorry for every time I failed to read your Word,
And for listening to another's voice, when Your voice I should have heard;
I'm sorry for often being so weak, for failing to take a stand,
For giving back so little, and yet taking from Your hand;

Dear Lord, I'm sorry for being silent when it was time to speak,
And for the times I often failed to help the poor and weak;
I'm sorry for sometimes speaking when I shouldn't speak at all,
And for the many times I didn't listen to Your call;

Dear Lord, I'm sorry for each time my words were harsh or mean,
And each time I failed to give my brother an arm on which to lean;
I'm sorry for every time that I was Oh so quick to judge,
And for the many days I wasted, holding onto a grudge;

Dear Lord, I'm sorry for tearing down when I should have lifted up,
For each time I failed to drop a few coins in a lonely beggar's cup;
I'm sorry for the wrong I've done, and the good that I didn't do,
For only going a single mile, when I knew I could go two;

And while I'm here on my knees dear Lord, repenting of my sin,
I guess my heart breaks most of all for the souls I failed to win;
And yet dear Lord, I know You love me, in spite of all I've done,

And for no other reason than the fact that I have accepted Your Son;

Lord, if You give me another day, I'll begin it on my knees,
And early will I seek your face, and You will hear my pleas;
I love you Lord, even though I fail to show it every day,
But if tonight You should decide to take my soul away;
If somewhere in my slumbering I hear that lonely knell,
I know that I can sing that song;
It is well, It is well.
Arvil Jones

## Lord, Let Me See England
## By Arvil Jones

Each night I lay dreaming of a land far away,
'Tis a vision so sweet, I care not for the day;
But then the day breaks, and I waken once more,
Still dreaming and longing for England's fair shore!

My forefathers sailed from her shores long ago,
For whatever reason, I yet do not know;
In my own yearning bosom there is but one care,
To walk on the shores of great England so fair!

In the eye of my soul, her great ramparts I see,
And the white cliffs of Dover are beckoning me;
And I see a great Tower that reaches up high,
Lord, let me see England before I die!

I dream of her castles, her Ladies and Lords,
Her Poets, Her Princes, Her shields and Her swords;
And I dreamed that I stood at great Westminster's door,
Oh how my heart longs to see England's bright shore!

And my thoughts go a drifting, as if by a call,
To the shining courts of Balmoral's hall;
But no knave poor as I has a right to be seen,
In the very presence of Earth's Fairest Queen!

And yet I am dreaming, perhaps by God's Grace,
Someday I may look on Her Majesty's face;
Would He grant such an honor to one such as I?
Lord, let me see England before I die!

## Meet Me At The Cross

The years that I have lived have taught me many things,
Time has a way of making us more wise;
Some things I was taught to believe, I no longer believe,
Slowly, with time, I began to realize;
That most other folks around the world, with very few exceptions,
Are really not all that different from me;
We eat, we drink, we work, we sleep, we dream, we play, we worship,
And we all sprang from the same family tree;
I will not be so foolish as to judge another man,
By nothing more than the pigment of his skin;
But let me get to know him, put myself in his place,
And try to understand what lies within;
What is it then that separates us, making us so different?
What is it that makes men hate each other so?
Is it tradition? Is it color? Is it our place of origin?
Is it the air we breathe, or the places we go?
Nay my friend, it is none of these that ultimately divides us,
But something far beyond our mortal ken;
There is but one object, in the shape of a cross,
Which ultimately divides men from men;
If you can meet me at the Cross, then you and I can worship,
Whatever stripe, or color, or creed, or name;
If you can meet me at the Cross, then you and I are brothers,
For the Cross alone makes us different, or the same;
For the Cross is undeniable, whatever men may say,
It's the Cross, and that alone that stands between;
It's the Cross that separates time from eternity,
And it matters not who you are or where you've been;
The One who died upon that Cross is none other than God Himself,

Come in flesh to redeem the souls of men;
If you can meet me at the Cross, there the ground is level,
It was at the Cross God dealt with human sin;
If you, like me, were once confused, not knowing where to turn,
Your heart and soul by sin's dark tempest tossed;
Peace awaits for every soul ruined by the Fall,
If only you will meet Him at the Cross.
2016 Arvil Jones

## Precious memories – Precious hope!

How far back do your memories go? For each it is different I guess,
Different memories, different times, yet so much alike, more or less;
Childhood memories, some bitter, some sweet, all about family and
home,
The cuts, the bruises, the spankings and hugs, the hills where we used to
roam;
The brothers and sisters, the blessings and blisters, and dear old Mom
and Dad,
The little white lies we often told, and all the fun we had;
The old dirt road, the swimming hole, the little two-room school,
Reading, writing and arithmetic and the good old Golden Rule;
So many friends that came and went, so many gone before,
Walking down the railroad track to the little country store;
Homemade toys, homemade clothes, homemade bedtime stories,
Mama with her Bible telling of Heaven and all its glories;
The sadness of watching a brother or sister move so far away,
Wondering if we would ever get to see them again someday;
The harsh realities of everyday life often quenched many a dream,
As we worked the fields and watered the crops from the gently flowing
stream;
We often wondered where that stream began, and where it went,
Sometimes I followed its winding course till most of the day was spent;
Observing the life that stream sustained, the minnows, the crawdads and
snakes,
Watching my sister's sit by its banks, making little mud cakes;
Sometimes I dreamed of following that stream in order to find its source,
But Oh the joys I found instead just following its course;
It taught me just to pause and look, and take my good sweet time,

To see what was in front of me in nature so sublime;
To see the many wonders in a simple narrow stream,
Which, as it flowed, it seemed time slowed, and I was taught to dream;
To see the many miracles right before my eyes,
While learning that everything that's born eventually dies;

## "Mommy – Mommy!"

It happens about every thirty seconds, another baby dies,
No funeral, no flowers, no one stands and cries;
No minister is present to offer a comforting word,
No tears of sorrow, no broken hearts, no dying voice is heard;
Just a doctor and some nurses, in a clinic somewhere,
No Daddy is present, and Mommy dearest sheds not a single tear;
Another life is ended, for the law says it's OK,
With no concern for right or wrong, just another working day;
But somewhere in that distant realm, somewhere beyond the sky,
Another little voice was heard, asking, Mommy, Mommy, Why?
Why do you not want me Mommy? Did I do something bad?
Am I so undesirable, or did I make you sad?
Is it because I'm a horrible child that you want me to die?
Please give me an answer Mommy, please tell me why!
You say you can't afford me? That I would cost too much,
Mommy, I just want your love, to feel my Mommy's touch;
Mommy, I'm not asking for money, wealth or fame,
All I'm asking is my life, I don't even need a name;
If you don't want me Mommy, there are others who do,
Why do you want to kill me Mommy, I've done nothing to you?
Mommy! Mommy! I'm begging you, don't let them take my life!
Mommy! Mommy! Mommy! That doctor has a knife...!
2016 Arvil Jones

## Mother

Many songs and many poems have been written of a Mother's love,
Her care has even been compared to that of God above;
And I suppose in each of us there is a special place,
Which we hold dear all through the years, remembering Mother's face;

Men have fought their wars for freedom,
With pride and flags unfurled;
But...the hand that rocks the cradle,
Is the hand that rules the world;

While others sleep she stays awake, and cares for those she loves,
Rising early each morning as gently as a dove;
To clean the house or cook a meal, or wipe a fevered brow;
To give a smile and carry on, with grace we knew not how;

With no complaints, and no words of praise, she labored day by day,
And when it seemed all hope was gone, she'd always find a way;
To keep the children happy all through the good and bad,
Teaching us to be thankful for all the blessings we had;

Fourteen children she has borne, and now we realize,
The value of that deep and caring love in Mother's eyes;
Oh yes, we love her dearly, and we'll miss her when she's gone,
But with Mother we will live again, up there around God's throne.

## Moving Toward...?

In my own humble opinion, but with many years of experience upon which to rely, some things have advanced far beyond the apparent to the painfully evident to me. There will always be some who will adamantly disagree with my opinions, and, as has been so vehemently demonstrated lately, will also lash out, and even become belligerent or even violent toward anyone who disagrees with their own opinions. Opinions are opinions, and all of them are based upon one or more assumptions, with a few – a very few, being based upon indubitable, undisputable, historically proven facts.

Fact: Every nation that ever existed on planet earth which has either neglected, rejected, or abandoned the teachings of the Holy Bible has, at one time or another, experienced moral decay, cultural decadence, spiritual debauchery, internal corruption, some degree of starvation, civil unrest and disobedience, with many of them ultimately facing decimation and/or destruction to a point of virtual or actual ruin.

Fact: The hungriest and/or poorest nations of the world are those who either reject the teachings of Christianity outright, or, to some degree, refuse to allow the teachings of Christianity to spread within their borders.

Fact: The more liberal a society becomes, throwing off all restraints, allowing anyone and everyone to do as he or she pleases, with no regard or acknowledgement for the clear teachings of the Holy Bible, and the more that society distances itself from the spiritual realities taught in the Holy Bible, the higher the crime rate becomes. And if the documented statistics of both modern and ancient societies hold any lessons for us today, it should be the fact that hardly any society seems to learn much of anything from the rise and fall of those societies, following blindly and irreverently in the same footsteps of those that fell!

Fact: In every case, with no exceptions, every nation that has ever neglected, rejected, or abandoned the teachings of the Holy Bible, has, eventually, been judged – either through financial ruin, internal strife, civil war, desolation and destruction by natural (and supernatural) disasters, diseases, tornadoes, earthquakes, wildfires, plagues of different kinds and degrees, and, in many cases, slowly destroyed from within by the actions of its own leaders and citizens, or by all of these.

We are being told by our leaders and would-be leaders that America is moving toward a brighter and more prosperous future than ever before in her history – perhaps I should say – her brief history. Yes, America has, to some degree, become the envy of the world! She has prospered financially; she has probably outdistanced every other nation in the world in the areas of technology, science and medicine, space research, and cultural "advancement", to name a few. And, yes, America boasts of being the most tolerant, the most diverse, and the most lenient of all the nations of the earth.

As any reader can probably discern from what I have written so far, I am moving toward a conclusion here – a conclusion which, I feel, is based upon solid historical facts. But, at the same time, I also feel that as a Bible-believing Christian, I must also reinforce what I have written, not only upon the statistical and historical facts as recorded in the archives, libraries and history books of the nations of the world, but upon the inspired writings of the Holy Bible itself. And a single statement, written by the inspired pen of single writer - the great and wise King Solomon, will suffice to sum up and demonstrate the truth of what I have written. It is found in the Book of Proverbs, chapter 14, verse 34, which reads:

Righteousness exalteth a nation: but sin is a reproach to any people.

America, my America, the nation once applauded and respected for her ethical, moral and spiritual rectitude, has fallen into reproach, and, in my opinion, is moving toward a horrible destiny unless she changes course immediately, and turns back to the God of Abraham, Isaac and Jacob, the God of Christianity, the Christ of Calvary. Time and time again I have posted a poem entitled – In a world gone mad...depicting the decadent and immoral standard and state into which our nation has fallen, and speaking of the certain judgments that would, and are, now falling upon us in rapid succession. But it seems no one listens; no one believes; no one gives any heed, in spite of all the tragedies and horrific disasters that are now striking at the heart and soul of this country. We keep murdering the unborn; we keep giving more and more rights to the debauched and depraved appetites of the wicked sodomites, as disaster after disaster devastates cities and towns, leaving death and destruction in their wake, and we attribute it all to natural phenomena. When will someone – anyone, like the magicians in the court of the ancient Pharaoh of Egypt, acknowledge...this is the hand of God?

## My Evening Thoughts

Again the evening shadows come, and I must lie down to rest,
But first I bow and count the many times that I was blessed;
Oh yes, my faith was sorely tested, and my patience sorely tried,
But through it all God humbled me, and crushed my foolish pride;

My grateful heart looks upward now, and seeks Your smiling face,
Just to say dear Lord I thank You for each mercy and each grace;
For I know at any moment You might call my soul away,
And yet You chose to grant to me another blessed day;

And how the days are flying now, and so quickly go the years,
And so many of the months are filled with so much pain and tears;
And yet in the very midst of sorrow, my soul doth yet rejoice,
For through the raging thunder I still hear my Master's voice;

He tells me I must wait a while, and tarry till He calls,
And Oh how sweet the heavenly tone upon my ear that falls;
For somewhere deep inside my heart, I know it won't be long,
Until I write my final line, and sing my final song;

And through my little window now, the light is growing dim,
As the evening shadows deepen, I commend my soul to Him;
Lord hide me in thy bosom as the lonely shadows come,
And if on Earth I wake no more, Lord lead me safely Home.
Amen.
© 2013 Arvil Jones

## My Favorite Season?

After a life of six decades, and two more years beside,
It seems the seasons pass so quickly, they almost collide;
I ask myself, Is the time really flying, or am I just getting slow?
Or are the answers to those questions something I don't want to know?

My favorite season? Now let me see, which one is the dearest to me?
Well it certainly isn't the Winter, so that narrows it down to three;
For the best that I remember there have always been just four,
That is unless the politicians have gone and added more;

I really do enjoy the Fall, for it's neither too hot nor cold,
But then again the Fall reminds me that I am growing old;
And I surely remember my childhood Summers, so full of joy and bliss,
It was Summer time inside an old barn where I got my first kiss;
I can never forget my little heart was thumping out a tune,
I remember it well, for name of the girl, and the name of the month was June;

But I guess if I had to narrow it down, my favorite season is Spring,
For that's when the flowers begin to bloom, and birds begin to sing;
Yes, I've decided that Spring is indeed my favorite season of life,
For it was the Spring of '66 when I met my beautiful wife.
© 2013 Arvil Jones

## My Friend

The "F" in Friend is Forever, in your heart, let come what may
The one who stands beside you, no matter what others might say

The "r" in Friend means Refreshing, whenever your spirit is low
The one who makes you smile again, and goes wherever you go

The "i" in Friend says I love you, just because you are you
And my love will never forsake you, though your days be many or few

The "e" in Friend means Endearing, growing closer with each passing day
And the bond that has formed between us, will never go away
The "n" in Friend means that Never, will our friendship be torn apart

For from the first day that I met you, you have been so dear to my hear

The "d" in Friend means Dependable, in the sunshine or stormy gale
And that we can count on each other that our love will never fail
© Arvil Jones

## My Life's Sweetest Memories

The great God of heaven has granted to me sixty years, plus one,
And I know I don't have as many years left as the years that have already gone;
Ahh! How gracious the Lord has been, with new mercies for me each day,
And bountiful blessings beyond measure, far more than mere words can say;
May I take a few moments of time to tell you how kind my Savior has been,
In showing me mercy and giving me grace, and forgiving all of my sin;
He has taught me some of His righteous ways, His truth has instructed me,
Through His Word and Holy Spirit He has caused my eyes to see;
I began to learn of His plan and purpose while I was but yet a child,
And yet I neglected Him so long, and began to be quite wild;
But still His angel followed me, no matter where I went,
And so many times He sent His Word, telling me to repent;
Although I tried to escape Him, He would not let me go,
For prayers were lifted up for me, how many I do not know;
I remember a weeping Mother falling on her bended knees,
With trembling voice and broken heart, sending up her pleas;
I recall the neighbors who loved my soul, who prayed for me so long,
Encouraging me to cherish the right, and always shun the wrong;
I remember the old country preacher who took my hand one day,
And lifted his eyes toward Heaven, as he began to pray;
He asked the Lord to watch over me wherever I might roam,
And if I should ever wander, to bring me safely home;
And I now know without a doubt, that old preacher's prayer was heard,
For the good Lord saved my wretched soul, and called me to preach His Word;

And it has been the purest joy, to tell of His saving grace,
As I've traveled half-way around the world, and gone from place to place;
And someday yonder in that land of peace, when Heaven's gates I see,
I want to meet all those dear old folks who said a prayer for me;
Then all of us can rejoice and sing together forever more,
In the presence of our Savior, there on Heaven's peaceful shore.

## My Old Friend Joe

Today I met an old friend of mine from many years ago,
And we had a lot of catching up to do;
Of course there was some small talk about how we'd missed each other,
And how we'd both gained a pound or two;
How many years has it been old friend? I reckon thirty or so!
Yeah, I guess you're right 'ol buddy, but I don't rightly know;
But as we both can easily see, time sure has taken its toll,
Then I noticed my friend was trying to hide a dirty cereal bowl;
What's that? I asked without thinking, as he turned his eyes away,
Oh it's just an old bowl I happened to find while fishing yesterday;
I meant to throw it in the trash, I guess I just forgot,
You know 'ol buddy at our age we tend to do that a lot;
For a moment I was at a loss for words to say to my friend,
But I somehow knew I couldn't let this meeting come to an end;
My friend was in some kind of trouble, and I didn't quite understand,
But then I couldn't help but notice the trembling in his hand;
Are you alright Joe? I quickly asked, trying hard not to stare,
No matter what's happened, I'm still your friend, and I hope you know I
care;
With his eyes still turned away from me, Joe let out a desperate sigh,
Then as he looked at me again, I saw a tear in his eye;
'Ol buddy, he moaned, I guess you can tell, I'm not who I used to be,
I've lost it all my dear old friend, I guess that's plain to see;
I lost my wife and children over twenty years ago,
And please don't ask me where they are, for I honestly don't know;
And as for this dirty little bowl, well that's my beggar's cup,
I sit right here from day to day, hoping someone will fill it up;
And beneath this bench is where I sleep, no pillow for my head,

And yes, my friend, there are those times I wish that I was dead;
I traded a loving wife and family and a lucrative career,
For this park bench, a dirty bowl, and a craving for whiskey and beer;
You wouldn't happen to have a drink for an old friend would you Sam?
Yes, I'm a little ashamed to ask, but that's how desperate I am;
If I only had a drink of two these shakes would go away,
And no, there's not much hope for me, or so the doctors say;
I've often been physically abused by several thieves and thugs,
And I just traded my wedding ring for a small handful of drugs;
My heart was broken for my friend, so much I could barely speak,
He looked so pale and hungry, his voice was low and weak;
I silently whispered a prayer to God to give me words to say,
Knowing it wasn't by accident that I found Joe that day;
Suddenly the words came easily, as I took the hand of my friend,
Joe, I don't think this is the way you want your life to end;
And yes, my friend, I can help you, but not the way you might hope,
I have something far better for you than beer or whiskey or dope;
I have a home not far from here, and a bedroom just for you,
But you must make the choice Joe, just tell me what you want to do;
Oh Sam, If only I could sleep in a nice warm bed for a night,
But I'm so dirty and grimy Sam, and I know I'm an awful sight;
And what would your wife and family say if I came home with you?
I'm kinda at a loss here Sam, but I'll go if you want me to;
As Joe and I walked slowly to my home not far away,
I quietly listened to every word my old friend had to say;
Now, how about you 'ol buddy? How's life been treating you?
If I may say so Sam 'ol buddy, you seem quite well to do;
Well, I'll tell you something Joe, my life's been pretty good,
But I've done some things I shouldn't, and neglected some things I
should;

You see my friend there was a time when I was just like you,
I was headed down that same old road, not knowing what to do;
But someone had other plans for me, and showed me a better way,
They gave me hope and comfort, and a nice warm place to stay;
Well, how about that, I'd have never guessed, looking at you now,
Well, Joe, it can happen for you too, and I can tell you how;
You see my friend, what I am today is not because of me,
It's because someone else loved me enough to set me free;
Oh come now Sam, are you telling me there's hope for my ornery soul?
A man who left his wife and kids and begged with a cereal bowl?
Don't get me wrong Sam 'ol buddy, I'm glad you're doing well,
But as for me, I've accepted my fate, I'm going straight to hell;
Well, Joe, I once felt the same, and had no hope at all,
I thought life was all about me, and drinking and having a ball;
But then I met this Christian lady, and when she entered my life,
She led me to the Savior, and then she became my wife;
My life has never been the same, as you can plainly see,
And Joe, the Lord can do for you just what He did for me;
Joe had a strange look on his face as we stepped inside my door,
He seemed almost afraid to step on the beautiful hardwood floor;
But his countenance changed when my lovely wife greeted him with a
smile,
I said honey, this is Joe, and he's gonna stay a while;
She shook Joe's hand and gave him a hug, and welcomed him inside,
His voice stammered a bit as he asked, Sam, is this your bride?
Why she's an angel 'ol buddy, you lucky son of a gun,
No wonder you asked her to marry you, that's just what I would have
done;
Carolyn blushed a little as she set the table with care,
And we could hear Joe sobbing as we bowed our heads in prayer;

No words were needed, because Joe's eyes said all that needed said,
Trembling, he reached for both our hands, and slowly bowed his head;
Dear Lord, he sobbed, I'm just an old sinner, as lost as I can be,
But my 'ol buddy Sam seems to think there's still some hope for me;
And Lord I know I'm not worth saving, but if you can find the grace,
Then here I am, the lowest man in all the human race;
I'm asking you Lord Jesus to come into my heart,
Forgive my sins, for they are many, and give me a brand new start;
I thank you Lord for saving me, and I'll never forget this day,
I praise you Lord for what you've done, and for sending Sam my way;
Joe slept like a baby that night, in a big four-poster bed,
He said it sure is nice to have a pillow under my head;
My wife and I had prayer with Joe, and talked a little while,
Then for the first time in many years, Joe drifted off with a smile;
Several months have now passed by, and Joe is a better man,
He found a job in marketing, and now he has a plan;
He bought himself a brand new suit, and new shoes for his feet,
And when I knew the time was right, I took Joe across the street;
When I asked him to ring the doorbell, he was hesitant at first,
He seemed to be a bit confused, expecting the very worst;
But when the door was opened, Joe got the shock of his life,
There before his very eyes stood his beautiful loving wife;
Joe was so happy he couldn't speak, not knowing what to do,
Then she threw her arms around him, crying Joseph, I love you;
For a moment I just stood there in the warmth of the summer sun,
As my old friend Joe embraced his wife, his daughter, and his son!
2016 Arvil Jones

## My Time Has Come

Seems I can hear a choir sing
And the gentle sound of rustling wings
There's someone standing on the shore
To guide my spirit safely o'er
I hear my Father calling me
My time has come to cross the Sea
I'd like to say before I go
That I have no fear, for I surely know
That the One who died on Calvary
Removed the sting of death for me
Oh yes I hate to leave you here
For you have been a friend so dear
But surely you will follow me
When it comes your time to cross the Sea
To all my friends that I leave behind
If you should search your heart and find
That I have caused one tear or pain
Forgive me 'til we meet again
Farewell my friends, don't cry for me
My time has come to cross the Sea.
© Arvil Jones

## My Voice – Is It Really Mine?

'Tis more than just a mechanism with which to form a word,
The human voice is an intricate thing, created by the Lord;
With my voice I may bless, or curse my fellow man,
'Twas given me that I might pray, or praise as best I can;
I may use my God-given voice to edify or abuse,
Of my voice I am but a steward, what then shall I choose?
Shall I speak words of kindness, shall I slander or degrade?
Shall I lift my voice in thankfulness for all that God has made?
As the finger leaves a fingerprint, the voice leaves its mark,
It may bless God in the daytime, or curse Him in the dark;
Yes, my voice is mine to use, however I may employ,
With it I may mourn and weep, or sing glad songs of joy;
But God will hold me accountable for how I used my voice,
'Twas He who gave me a heart and mind, and the will to make a choice;
And surely I am richly blessed in my earthly sojourn here,
To have met some very gifted folk I've learned to love so dear;
Whose voices are anointed to sing sweet harmony,
Who when they sing they always bring such great joy to me;
Their voices bless the hearers, and give praise to God above,
Their songs are filled with passion, and tell of Jesus' love;
Some of their songs tell of His suffering, His agony and loss,
And when they sing we can almost see Him hanging on the cross;
They sing of how He bled and died, of all His shame and pain,
But then their voices rise in praise of how He rose again;
Yes, my voice is mine to use, and I must make the choice,
So when I speak, do folks hear me, or do they hear His voice?
Dedicated to my friend – Bro. Ed Reid,
Whose anointed voice has blessed so many for so many years!
By Arvil Jones

## My Wish For You

I know it would be impossible to sum up one whole year,
With only a few simple poetic lines;
Each of us have our own reflections, and some which we've all shared,
We've shared some laughs, and some of the most horrible of times;
And there were times when our faith was tested, and our patience sorely
tried,
And sometimes we felt that we just couldn't take any more;
But then we heard of some poor soul who was far worse off than we,
And we realized there were some things worth waiting for;
There were all those things that made the headlines, all the politics and
such,
And the multi-million dollar movies from Hollywood;
There were scandals and wars, catastrophes and storms, debates and
reality shows,
And we heard all the bad news, but seldom heard any good;
But may I just take a little time at the close of another year,
To say a few things that have long been on my mind?
I realize there are so many who are so much smarter than me,
And I surely don't want to say anything unkind;
It is not my aim to hurt or offend, or to push my opinion on others,
But I've realized that time is not on my side;
There is something that burns inside my soul that I cannot help but share,
A testimony that I simply cannot hide;
My wish for you, and for all the world, in the year that is now upon us,
Is that you may come to know my Savior and Lord;
I wish for you a blessed home, and a godly family,
That each day gathers around His eternal Word;
I wish for you a life of prayer, and faithfulness and truth,

A life filled with peace and joy and happiness;
I wish for you the certainty that your soul is saved and safe,
And every blessing with which the Lord can bless;
And if you and I do not meet again in this unfriendly world,
If these few lines are indeed my last goodbye;
I wish for you that we shall meet in that land of eternal love,
In those mansions far beyond the starry sky.

Arvil Jones

## *No Longer A Stranger*

*Most of the friendships that we form in life*
*Are by meeting face to face*
*With some of those friends we remember the day*
*And may even remember the place*
*There is always that special something about them*
*That endears them to our heart*
*And we knew that we would become friends*
*Right from the very start*
*But then there are other dear friends we know*
*Whose faces we have never seen*
*Who are just as dear as the ones we have met*
*On whose shoulder we often lean*
*Some folks have a way of becoming a friend*
*Simply by the words that they speak*
*Who know how to give a word in due season*
*Who help you when you are weak*
*And though I haven't met you face to face*
*You're no longer a Stranger to me*
*And I know that someday God will grant*
*That your lovely face I will see.*
© 2012 Arvil Jones

## No Longer Indebted

I cannot remember what age I was, just that it was way back when,
I began to learn about right and wrong, of sorrow, sickness and sin;
At first I didn't think too much about what might lie ahead,
I lived a loose and carefree life, without any fear or dread;
Back then life was all about me, and all that I could get,
Once in a while I'd give a little, then curse myself with regret;
I always wanted more and more, but no matter how hard I tried,
No amount of material things ever kept me satisfied;
And so like Solomon of old, I tried many other things,
I tried the wine, the women and song, and gold and diamond rings;
I turned to all types of entertainment, movies and rock-n-roll,
And yet there was always an emptiness deep inside my soul;
But still I kept on searching, but with each mistake I made,
I never knew each sin I committed had become a debt unpain;
Those who knew me couldn't believe I had become so wild,
As to forsake a loving wife and a little hungry child;
Driven to desperation, I begged for something to eat,
I found myself sick and alone, a drunkard on the street;
Plunging ever deeper to the point of despair,
My life of selfishness and pride was more than I could bear;
One day on a dirty sidewalk my tears began to flow,
As I heard someone softly singing – "Where Could I Go";
A song I heard my Mother sing when I was just a lad,
I could see her in her rocking chair beside my dear old Dad;
The song was coming from a storefront church a couple blocks away,
And I asked myself the question – Should I go? Or should I stay?
Again my mind went running back to the place where I was born,
I could see our family in the fields a hoeing corn;

I remembered a little blonde-haired boy sitting on the floor each night,
Listening to Mama read the Bible by a coal-oil light;
I could see the smile on Mama's face as she slowly raised her head,
Saying – "Listen closely children to these words written in red";
Somehow I found the strength to rise from off that dirty street,
Making my way to that little church, and stumbling into a seat;
I was trembling with hunger, but more so from despair,
Then I saw a little old lady with silver in her hair;
She reminded me so much of Mama, her voice so soft and kind,
But when she stopped beside me, I could see that she was blind;
With all my strength I struggled as the preacher said – "Let us stand",
As the little lady with the silver hair took me by the hand;
"Come now Sir, she softly whispered, someone is waiting for you",
But Ma'am you don't know all I've done, and I don't know what to do;
I've lived a life of drunkenness, a life of sin and shame,
I've hurt so many others, and disgraced my family's name;
The little woman stopped, and lifted her hands to my face,
"Son, she whispered, all of us here are sinners saved by grace;
It matters not how far you've gone, or how big a mess you've made,
For long ago, on and old rugged Cross, your debt was fully paid;
If you will call on Jesus now, He has promised to set you free,
Just like He did your Mom and Dad, and like He did for me;
I could feel her hand still gripping mine, as we knelt there on the floor,
And I knew the load that I'd been carrying – I would carry it no more;
In a single moment of time, I knew the debt was paid,
As at the feet of Jesus Christ all my sins were laid;
And now I bless that happy day when the Savior heard my call,
No longer am I indebted, for Jesus paid it all.

## No more will I...

No more will I appoint myself to be the judge of my brother,
For if I understand my God, we are to love one another;
No more will I perceive that I am any better than he,
For the same God who created him also created me;
Although he may have committed wrongs, as much or more have I,
And wrong is wrong whether it be a murder or a lie;
No more will I justify myself, and condemn my fellow man,
For what judgment I may render will be rendered to me again;
No more will I esteem my works greater than another,
Nay, but I will condescend to lift up my dear brother;
No more will I consider the color of his skin,
But I will look into his eyes, and see what lies within;
No more will I determine that I alone will succeed,
Nay, but I will strive to help my brother in his need;
No more will I neglect the sister whose life is in despair,
No more will I lift up my head with a proud and arrogant air;
No more will I arrive at conclusions because of the clothes she wears,
For how do I know but that underneath the many scars she bears;
No more will I be bitter when my brother goes ahead,
For if I will be a leader, I must first be lead;
No more will I aspire to make for my own self a name,
But for the prize of humility let my heart lay claim;
No more will I lay down my head in anger, doubt or fear,
And when I close my eyes in death, then let my Lord be near.
2016 Arvil Jones

## Not your average kids!

Now I guess you all got a bit of schooling,
Some a little more than others;
Some of us went to a two-room school,
With all our sisters and brothers;
We had a chalk board, hard oak desks,
A few short pencils and paper;
And once in a while us naughty boys,
Would pull off a pretty good caper;
Like putting tacks in the teacher's chair,
Or cutting off a piece of a little girl's hair;
Pushing a friend down the slippery slide,
Or overturn the outhouse with someone inside;
Or slipping a frog in a girlfriend's lunch,
That really made her like me a bunch;
We played games like "Fox-n-Hound",
Never cared much for the merry-go-round;
We drank our milk from Mason jars,
Our swing were tires – (we called 'em tars);
We learned how to fish, and hunt and fight,
And some of us learned to read and write;
We know the difference 'tween a friend and a fool,
And we still believe in the Golden Rule;
We learned a bit about life and love,
And we learned to trust in God above;
Some say it's all about taking and giving,
But life without God just ain't worth living.

## Now - about the Church

A place where sinners, saved by grace,
Attend each Sunday, and take their place;
Of course we look at each other's clothing,
And talk about the ones we find to our loathing;

Some folks give a little more than others,
And some look better than their sisters and brothers;
Some of us simply can't carry a tune,
And some hope the sermon will end real soon;

But a few sweet ladies can sing quite well,
While some sound like they just came from Hell;
But the preacher, he's faithfully sowing the Seed,
And trying to minister to every need;

No, we're not perfect, not by a long shot,
But we do our best with what we've got;
None of us claim divine perfection,
And I, for one, could use some correction;

But whenever all is said and done,
And our earthly race is finally run;
There's one blessed thing we certainly know,
We have a better place to go;

We've trusted Jesus as Savior and Lord,
And we all still believe in His Holy Word;
We know He reigns in Heaven above,

## 192

And we know a little 'bout brotherly love;

We know how to lend a helping hand,
And to help a fallen brother to stand;
We know the difference between right and wrong,
And we know that life doesn't last very long;

So if you are somewhat imperfect like us,
And sometimes prone to argue and fuss;
And to confess that we all sin,
Well, brother we reckon you'd fit right in;

Sometimes we are many, sometimes we are few,
Sometimes we're happy, sometimes we're blue;
But we'd surely like to welcome you,
And we guarantee there's and empty pew.

## 'Ol Doc Sherman

The kindly old doctor from years ago whose days were growing few,
Still loved to make his house calls – so few doctors do;
He'd walk for miles to see a neighbor, and sit and chat for a while,
Sometimes even staying for dinner, that was just his style;
And while he was there he'd examine the family, each child in its turn,
Even looking in Grandma's ears as she sat at her old churn;
He'd listen to Papa's heart and lungs, telling him what he should quit,
As Mama, dipping her powdered snuff, turned to the fireplace to spit;
Sometimes he'd let the children listen through his stethoscope,
While another played with his pocket watch, dangling from a braided rope;
And if after each examination he didn't find anything wrong,
He'd join the family in front of the fireplace in a good old gospel song;
With Mama singing alto, Doc would sing the bass,
While sister's beautiful tenor brought a smile to every face;
Many times he stayed until the evening shadows fell,
But the doctor never left until he knew everyone was well;
He'd sit on the porch with Papa, listening to the crickets chirp,
He'd rock the baby in the rocking chair, listening for him to burp;
The family hated to see him leave but they knew he had to go,
He had another family to visit up the road a mile or so;
When folks saw his kerosene lantern swinging at his side,
Most would stop their wagon and offer him a ride;
But Doc would graciously refuse, saying he'd rather walk,
And as he walked he and Jesus always had a little talk;
He'd ask the Lord to forgive him if he'd offended anyone,
Asking God to show him if he'd left anything undone;
He prayed for every family God had given him to treat,

As he braved the chilly winter snows and the summer's prickly heat;
The weather never got too rough for him to make his rounds,
He'd been bitten by copperheads and chased by old coonhounds;
"Well, how much do we owe ye Doc?" The man of the house would say,
You don't owe me nothing Sir, Doc said as he walked away;
After a supper like your missus made, that's pay enough for me,
But could I take an apple or two from this old apple tree?
Doc was in his eighties now, and ninety was drawing near,
And all the folks on the old dirt road had now begun to fear;
What would they do without ol Doc if he should pass away?
He'd always been there for them all no matter, night or day;
Sixty years had come and gone since Doc made his first house call,
And the hundreds of families he had treated, he loved them one and all;
He lived in a little four-room house about half way up the trail,
He remembered the circuit-riding postman bringing him his mail;
Folks would sit on their front porches, watching for his lantern's light,
And then in late November, one cold and rainy night;
Doc stepped off his creaking porch to make his rounds once more,
All his joints were aching, and his tired old feet were sore;
The neighbors saw his lantern swinging at his side,
And just like always someone stopped and offered him a ride;
This time Doc accepted, climbing slowly onto the seat,
Asking John if he had any ailments he needed him to treat;
John just grinned, shaking his head, as the horses plodded along,
Then suddenly without any warning, ol Doc started singing a song;
"Well, I'm lookin over Jordan, and what do I see?
A comin for to carry me home?
I see a band of angels comin after me,
A comin for to carry me home!
Swing low, sweet chariot, comin for to carry me home,

Swing way down low sweet chariot, a comin for to carry me home.
John couldn't help but join in, singing the old melody,
Now the rain had stopped and the horses rested beneath a big oak tree;
Then suddenly Doc stopped singing, taking John by the hand,
Saying, John, my work is over, and I'm going to the Promised Land;
The folks all waited till Sunday night to carry Doc up the hill,
The preacher said before Doc died he wrote it in his will;
They wept for hours as Doc was laid beneath the big oak tree,
His old lantern still hangs where they left it, for all his friends to see;
Each November, rain or shine, all the families gather round,
To celebrate the life of the dearest friend they ever found;
The oldest man is given the honor of lighting Doc's lantern once more,
As ol Doc Sherman sings the bass on Heaven's golden shore.
By Arvil Jones

## Once Upon A Country Road

The handsome young man had dated quite a few ladies before,

If he were to count them, probably fifty or more;

He was dashing and daring, with money and a car,

He loved to frequent the night clubs and the local bar;

He was known for his silver tongue, with just the right words to say,

And far more often than not the young man got his way;

His motto was "love 'em and leave 'em, take what you can get,"

And over the years he'd taken a lot from every girl he met;

He never cared how many young lives he had shattered,

To him, his own pleasure was all that ever mattered;

Careless, reckless, boastful, arrogant and wild,

A few times he even left behind and unwanted child;

But his little game of pleasure was bound to meet its end,

For little did he know what waited just around the bend;

One bright Sunday morning he decided to go for a drive,

Feeling Oh so confident, feeling so alive;

And like so many days before, there was one thing on his mind,

He'd take whatever he wanted from the first girl he could find;

He was driving on a country road he'd never seen before,

Totally oblivious to what might lie in store;

He slowly passed a country church, when he heard a beautiful sound,

Some folks were singing and some were having dinner on the ground;

Something deep inside him said that he should stop a while,

And the very first thing that greeted him was a pretty young lady's smile;

"Come join us, she welcomed him, there's plenty here to eat,"

Why, looky here, she laughed, I think they've saved you a seat;"

She led him to a wooden chair beneath an old oak tree,

"Now what's your pleasure mister, a coke or sweet iced tea?"

Oh, by the way, I'm Nancy, and what do they call you?"

Without even thinking, he said – "they call me Hugh,"

He felt his heart begin to pound in a way he'd never known,

Such kindness and sincerity no one had ever shown;

There was something different about these folks, something he'd never

seen,

There was something different about this place than any place he'd been;

There was something different in their singing that touched his very soul,

Quite unlike what he was used to – rap and rock-n-roll;

There was something different about this girl, he couldn't figure it out,

He thought to himself – "I'll stick around and see what's she's about;"

She brought him a plate of fried chicken, with biscuits and mashed

potatoes,

Corn on the cob, fresh green beans, lettuce and sliced tomatoes;

"Now you just sit and enjoy yourself, and if you need anything,

I'll be happy to get it for you right after I sing;"

He couldn't help but admire her as she quickly walked away,

And for the first time in his life, he found he had nothing to say;

He finally managed a "thank you" as she re-joined the choir,

As the lovely hymn that rang from her voice set his soul on fire;

He almost choked on a biscuit as someone started to shout,

But a fire was burning in his heart, and he couldn't put it out;

Her voice was soft and melodious, gentle as a dove,

Then suddenly it hit him – he knew he was in love;

Nothing quite as powerful had ever gripped his mind,

As he slowly sat and reflected on the girls he'd left behind;

Nancy quickly noticed the strange look on his face,

As she and the other ladies softly sang Amazing Grace;

She saw him slowly bow his head and set his plate aside,

As the old country preacher sat down by his side;

The preacher said "Hello young man, everybody calls me Sam,"

As Nancy asked the choir to sing – Just As I Am;

She smiled as the sweet Holy Spirit moved among the trees,

She watched with grateful heart as Hugh fell upon his knees;

Another soul had come to Christ, and the church folk shouted Amen!

Hugh Hudson was delivered from a life of flagrant sin;

Three years he and Nancy courted, and then one early Spring,

He placed upon her lovely hand a golden wedding ring;

Later in the Summer time when life and love abound,

They had an all-day singing, with dinner on the ground;

He brought her a plate of fried chicken, with biscuits and mashed
potatoes,
"Now you just sit and enjoy yourself, and if you need anything,
I'll be happy to get it for you, right after I sing."
She smiled as she recollected that day three years ago,
How she had been so courteous to a man she didn't know;
As she watched him quickly walk away, she felt that Holy Fire,
As her handsome husband, Hugh Hudson, led the big church choir.

2016 Arvil Jones

### Our Grandson – Matt.

We often sit on the old porch swing,
In the evening when the day is done;
And we often talk about how we're blessed,
To have such a fine grandson;
Our minds and hearts drift back again,
To that day you came to us;
How everyone wanted to hold you,
And we all made a big fuss;
About how you and your twin sister,
Were so beautiful and small;
And when the day was over,
And you had been held by all;
We looked up to Heaven, and thanked the Lord,
For two more blessings we had;
As we prayed that you would grow up to be,
A strong and handsome young lad;
And surely our prayers have been answered,
And we are so proud of you Matt;
You have the love of both our hearts,
And we hope you'll remember that;
You have the greatest Mom and Dad,
And they love you as much as we;
And all of us will love and support you,
Whatever you decide to be.
With all our love,
Grandma and Grandpa Jones.
You've grown up tall and handsome,

***Our Little Granddaughter's Prayer***

# 201

*My Mama took the kids all to church on Sunday morning,*
*We learned to live by the Golden Rule, and walk the narrow way;*
*I can still recall sittin 'round an old oak table,*
*When all the family bowed our heads, and we heard our Mama pray.*

*She'd say, ALord, we want to thank you for the food that's on our table,*
*For the shoes on everybody's feet, and the roof above our head;*
*We know it's nothing fancy Lord, but teach us to be grateful,*
*You never said that we'd be feasted, You just promised we'd be fed.*

*Now a lot of years have gone, and there's been a lot of changes,*
*All the children scattered off since Mama passed away;*
*We seldom bow our heads, or even gather at the table,*
*And that Golden Rule got broken, somewhere along the way.*

*But we got another ray of hope, late last Sunday evening,*
*When our little granddaughter Brenna came home from Sunday School;*
*She was all bright-eyed and happy to tell us what she'd been doing,*
*She said her teacher taught her something 'bout a Golden Rule.*

*She gave us each a hug and kiss, and sat down at the table,*
*And none of us had a single clue, what she was about to say;*
*But it brought a tear to every eye, when without any warning,*
*Our little granddaughter folded her hands, and bowed her head to pray.*

*And she said*
*Now I way me downa sheep,*
*I pway da woid my soda keep,*
*Amen*
*© 2012 Arvil Jones*

## Perplexed

Not too many things in this old world surprise me anymore,
But I am perplexed about some things I see;
And most folks tell me that I should just let it ride,
And be content to simple let it be;
I'm told I shouldn't rock the boat, I'm told to not make waves,
I'm told I should let others run the show;
Some folks say the President, and all those who surround him,
Have forgotten more than I will ever know;
And while that may just be the truth, I certainly am no genius,
Yet I sit and wonder how these people sleep;
How men and women in high positions can lie with impunity,
Making promises they know they'll never keep;
But my perplexity runs deep, I just can't figure it out,
Just how gullible Americans can be;
Many who can be convinced that a lie is still the truth,
"There are none so blind as those who refuse to see."
Our politicians could sell ice cubes to an Eskimo,
Or hot sauce to a man in a burning hell;
And stand in the middle of a burning fire which they started themselves,
And yet convince the masses that all is well;
Now I may not be the sharpest knife in the kitchen drawer,
Nor the brightest bulb in the chandelier;
But until someone can prove to me that my vote really counts,
I say to you, my friends, I greatly fear;
The upcoming election has already been decided,
By the money, the media, and the moguls of this land;
I sincerely hope you can prove me wrong, and I really hope I am,
But until then, this is where I take my stand;

I further contend, hoping not to offend, there are also other things,
Which have been decided before the coin is tossed;
Like sports on the professional level – football, baseball, basketball,
Someone already knows who won – who lost;
But again this is only my opinion, I reserve the right to be wrong,
But if past experience teaches anything;
Politicians lie, money talks, and many a boxing match,
Was decided before the fighters entered the ring;
There is a lot more I could say, but now I need a nap,
I'm pretty tired from all this writing I've done;
So let me borrow a word or two from some of our politicians,
Would you believe it was all just for the fun?
2016 Arvil Jones

## Settling Accounts? Or, All Accounts Settled?

"I'll get you back," the young boy shouted as his classmate ran away,
"This fight ain't been settled yet, and there'll be another day";
His classmate stood at a good safe distance, sticking out his tongue,
And the fight became a war of words between two boys eight years
young;

"Your Mama is ugly as a monkey", Johnny shouted at Tim,
"Well, your's looks like a gorilla," Timmy shouted back at him;
"Well, your Daddy has the face of a donkey, and your sister has the face
of a frog",
"Well, your Daddy looks like Frankenstein, and your sister smells like a
hog";

The boys exchanged their insults for thirty minutes or so,
Till each of them ran out of words, and it was time to go;
Johnny stomped and fumed and muttered all the way to his house,
While Timmy laughed quietly under his breath, quiet as a mouse;

Johnny went home cursing that day, vowing he'd get revenge,
He found his Dad passed out on the sofa, from another drunken binge;
Johnny's stomach growled with hunger, but his Mom was nowhere
around,
He quickly searched the pantry and oven, and ate the crumbs he found;

The bottle of whiskey was almost empty, and Johnny drank the rest,
Then stole the last ten dollars from his Daddy's wrinkled vest;
He tucked the money under his mattress, he had fifty dollars now,
He drifted off to sleep while vowing, "I'll get that Timmy somehow;"

Ten years later, two young men met on a city street,
As Johnny yelled to Timmy, "I knew someday we'd meet";
"Why, Hello Johnny, How ya doing, let's go have some fun,"
But Johnny stood about five yards off, and quickly pulled the gun;

"It's time I settled things with you, like I told you I would,"
Timmy's face turned ghastly pale, and he ran as fast as he could;
"Go ahead and run you coward", Johnny began to yell,
He quickly fired six bullets, and Timmy's body fell;

Johnny stood over his classmate grinning, vengeance was his at last,
He'd finally settled an old account from way back in the past;
But just before he walked away, he thought he heard a sound,
Timmy was still breathing as he lay there on the ground;

But how could a man with six bullets in his back still live,
Leaning closer he heard Timmy moaning, "Johnny, I forgive";
Forgiveness was a term that Johnny never understood,
He only remembered being beaten by his Dad with a piece of wood;

The judge imposed Johnny's sentence - Life without parole,
Every day, Timmy's last words haunted Johnny's soul;
He tried so hard to forget about Timmy, but the memory wouldn't fade,
As night after night he laid and cried for all the mistakes he'd made;

Then one day, when Johnny turned fifty, an old country preacher came,
He stood and smiled at Johnny, asking, "Mister, what's your name?"
"What's it to you bible thumper?" Johnny quickly replied,
The preacher ignored the insult, and sat by Johnny's side;

"Do you know what forgiveness means?" the kindly old preacher said,
Johnny's heart leaped into his throat as he quickly turned his head;
That awful memory from long ago now suddenly returned,
As Timmy's last words - "I forgive" like a raging fire burned;

"Preacher can I be forgiven for the awful things I've done?"
"Yes, Johnny, you surely can, if you call upon God's Son";
"You see Johnny, there's a wonderful truth a lot of folks don't know,
That the old accounts were settled on a Cross so long ago;

It matters not how far you've gone, and neither how great your sin,
For the blood that flowed from Calvary's Cross is sufficient for all men;"
Johnny's eyes filled up with tears, and he slowly bowed his head,
And somehow found the will to believe the words the preacher said;

Jesus came into Johnny's heart, and washed him white as snow,
He knew he was forgiven for his sins from long ago;
His face now shined with happiness, and without any shame,
He shook the preacher's hand and asked - "Now preacher, what's your name?"

The old country preacher hugged Johnny's neck and looked him in the eye,
He said, "I'm Timmy's father, and before I say goodbye",
Just remember that wonderful truth that now I'm sure you know,
On an old rugged cross the old account was settled long ago."
© 2014 Arvil Jones

## Shall I Speak of Love?

'Tis a term so full of meaning and mystery, I dare not try to define it,
And for good reason, because you see, I never could design it;
How shall I define what I could not design, and lay all its meaning bare,
And yet possess enough of its truth that I cannot help but share;

Some poor deluded souls define love in the passion of a single kiss,
But with the passing of a single day, discover that something is amiss;
Still others would sum up all their love in a time of courtship and wooing,
Only to find love is not defined in the wooing, but in the doing;

And yet many others strongly insist that love is something we make,
While many more will loudly proclaim that love is something we take;
Shall I clothe my brother, my sister, my neighbor, with loving words alone,
Or shall I give him warmth and comfort with garments to put on?

Shall I say to the hungry, be ye filled, but give him no bread to eat,
And shall I welcome him to my home, but offer him not a seat?
Shall the groaning of his stomach be calmed by all the fine words that I say,
Shall his heart be impressed after I have blessed and sent him on his way?

If love be only of the flesh, then it is not love at all,
And if it stands in word alone, then surely it must fall;
It is not love, but carnal lust within the flesh that burns,
And lust is never satisfied by all for which it yearns;

No, love has never been a thing into which a man may fall,
Forever love must be a conscious choice to one and all;

## 208

And though a man may search for love across the widest sea,
A love that's true can only be found, as he looks to Calvary.

'Twas there upon the rugged Cross that Love was so displayed,
As in the lovely Son of God, the Way to Heaven was made;
And all His pain was not because that I had loved Him first,
But only because I knew no love, yet He loved me at my worst;

For many years I had been chased by Hell's most vicious hound,
But where my sin abounded, Love and grace did more abound;
So look, my friend, to Calvary, where Jesus bled and died,
For it was there the One whose Name is Love was crucified.
© 2013 Arvil Jones, Ph.D.

## She Lifter Her Voice

She was born in the hills of Clay County Kentucky
Along the banks of old Otter Creek
And she was the eighth of nine children
Of a family humble and meek
And of course every parent wonders
What their little ones will grow up to be
But for this little girl, it didn't take long for everyone to see
Her Mom and Dad were somewhat surprised
It was such a beautiful thing
For not long after she was able to talk
She lifted her voice to sing
Her voice had a quality all it's own, so clear, melodious and strong
And when she and her Mom and sisters were gathered
They would sing the whole day long
It was clear that God had blessed this young lady
And He had a plan for her life
And many a heart-smitten country boy wanted her to be his wife
When she and her family sang together it made the Heavens ring
And people traveled from miles around when she lifted her voice to sing
She's had her share of heartaches, and trials, she's known a few
But she still lifts her voice to honor her Lord
For she knows what her God can do
And no one could number the thousands of souls
That her voice has blessed through the years
When she lifted her voice the saints began shouting
And the sinner's eyes filled with tears
And when her journey down here is over
And her burdens are all laid down

Before her Lord and Savior she'll stand
And receive her Golden Crown
But until then she'll go on singing, til her race is finally run
And she can bow before the King, and hear Him say, Well Done.

## To my Special Friend Sherry, from Arvil Jones

She Looks Good In...
She looks good in red,
She looks good in blue;
She looks good in purple,
And lavender too;
She's lovely in green,
She's gorgeous in white;
She's pretty in pink,
Whether dark or light;
She can laugh, she can cry,
She can dance, she can sing;
This lady can do about anything;
She can report the weather or news,
She's our friend and neighbor;
Sherry Hughes

## She Played the Church Piano - A tribute to Ethel Smith-Jordan

So many poetic lines have been written about famous people we know,
Many who were great orators, and others who starred in a show;
Some were called heroes, some celebrities, and others super stars,
Some whose lives were measured by wealth, and fame and fancy cars;
But how do we really measure the life of a person whom we know well,
Or should we measure their life at all, for after all, who can tell;
There are so many little things that go unnoticed in life,
Like the tears that were shed on a lonely night, or the pain of inner strife;
There are some whose lives are never honored by the millions here on Earth,
Many of whom are not well known, nor come from noble birth;
But the little things they do mean a lot to those who have known them long,
Like playing the Church piano, or singing a sacred song;
I have known such a lady for many years, and a lovely lady indeed,
A lady of sweet and humble spirit, a rare and special breed;
She never sought for fortune or fame, no great status did she seek,
The daughter of a beloved country Preacher, from a family mild and meek;
She played the old upright piano faithfully, year after year,
She had her share of trials and troubles, and wiped away many a tear;
But the light of love that shone in her eyes always came from a grateful heart,
And it could always be said of her, she always did her part;
Her life has been a great influence on many a girl and boy,
Just playing the old Church piano, she brought us so much joy;
And when the roll is called in Heaven, and the crowns are given that day,
I want to be there and see her face, when Ethel sits down to play.
We love you Ethel,
Arvil and Carolyn Jones

## *Sherry Knows...*

*Before the morning sun rises to kiss the morning dew,*
*Before the sunbeams paint the clouds in a many-splendored hue;*
*Sherry knows.*
*And as the sunbeams travel westward, as the morning dew dissipates,*
*As the heat of the sun touches the rivers, and the water evaporates;*
*Sherry knows.*
*As all of us in the tri-state area wait with anticipation,*
*Wondering if there's going to be any precipitation;*
*Sherry knows.*
*As the winds from any given direction begin to pick up speed,*
*And if their direction and speed of travel no one else can read;*
*Sherry knows.*
*And be it a breeze, a gale or a zephyr, a tornado or hurricane,*
*And whether it brings a single drop, or rushing torrents of rain;*
*Sherry knows.*
*While the rest of us sit and watch the screen, catching our favorite shows,*
*Whether the weather is bright and clear, or threatening winter snows;*
*Sherry knows.*
*We know exactly how to prepare for whichever way the wind blows,*
*And we rest secure, safe in our homes, simply because...*
*Sherry knows!*
*To Sherry Hughes,*

## Standing at the Crossroad

Well I was born a country boy
Where the summer breezes whisper through the pines
Where the bluegrass grows and a river flows
And we wakened to the Sunday church bells chime
Yeah we listened to the whip-poor-will
Had apple pies on a window sill
And we left a lot of footprints in the sand
In the evening when the work was done,
Just before the setting sun
I remember Daddy took me by the hand

And we'd go down to the crossroad, where another road went winding far away,
In my young and foolish mind I swore that I would take that road someday,
I looked up into his eyes, said Daddy, tell me where that road will end,
He said, Son I took that road before, and you don't know what lies around the bend.
Chorus:
Don't ya let nobody tell you that it don't matter which way you go,
'Cause one road leas across the mountain high – and the other down below,
Well a lot of road might look the same, but once you choose you can't turn back the time,
When you're standing at the crossroad, Boy you've got to make up your mind
Repeat Chorus.

## Summer time in the mountains

When we were only little girls, down in the Kentucky hills,
We never had to wander far to find life's greatest thrills;
The simple wonders of Creation often warmed our heart and soul,
As we sat in the shade of a tall pine tree, or skipped across a grassy knoll,

We drank pure water from a flowing brook, and breathed the clean
mountain air;
We gazed for hours at the simple beauty of a field of flowers so fair;
We had no picnic basket to carry at our side,
For we knew that if we got hungry, that God Himself would provide;

We munched on leaves of Mountain Tea, and huckleberries sweet,
Whatever our hungry soul desired, was right there at our feet;
And no matter how long we romped and played,

And no matter how far we'd roam;
We always knew there was a loving Family,
Just waiting for us to come Home.
© 2012 Carolyn Jordan-Jones

## Tell me 'bout love...

The little boy, about seven now, went to his teacher one day,
The teacher waited patiently for what he had to say;
"Teacher, can you tell me 'bout love? I really need to know,
The teacher stared out the window, gazing at the new-fallen snow;
She was searching for an answer to give the little lad,
The little boy stood silently, his eyes looked so sad;
Not knowing quite how to answer him, she pulled him to her side,
When his Mother drove in the teacher smiled, saying Jimmy, there's your ride;
I'm sure you'll find the answer Jimmy, she cried as they drove away,
Jimmy sat in silence, with not a word to say;
What's wrong Jimmy? His Mama asked, are you not feeling well?
She knew Jimmy was thinking 'bout something, but what? She couldn't tell;
The snow was falling hard and fast, and she could barely see,
Suddenly she left the road, smashing into a tree;
Jimmy was thrown from the car, and into an icy stream,
Floundering in the water, he heard his Mama scream;
Jimmy didn't know how to swim, he was nearly frozen now,
Stumbling through the blinding snow, she had to reach him somehow;
Falling down the embankment, she heard her right arm crack,
And now she couldn't move her legs, the fall had broken her back;
With all her strength she drug her body to the water's edge,
Jimmy was sitting rigid on a narrow ledge;
With her left hand she pulled him close, as hot tears filled her eyes,
Knowing he was still alive, she heard his pitiful cries;
Tearing her clothes from her body, she wrapped him as best she could,
Praying Jesus would hear her cry, believing that He would;

The life of her son was all that mattered, she cared not for her own,
And now she felt the sweetest warmth she had ever known;
They found her frozen, nearly naked, her blood had stained the snow,
The officer noticed the temperature had dropped to five below;
Inside his little notebook, he quickly scribbled a note,
"We found the little boy alive, wrapped in his Mother's coat;
"Did you find the answer Jimmy? The teacher asked aloud,
Jimmy rose up from his seat, walking tall and proud;
Yes Ma'am, he smiled, as together they gazed upon the new-fallen snow,
"My Mama taught me all about love I'll ever need to know.
Arvil Jones

**Tell me Little Lamb - from Psalm 23...By Arvil Jones**

Tell me little lamb why you romp and play, and graze in the lush green fields all the day,

Are there not many dangers for which you should look, each time you drink from the cool gentle brook;

There are so many lions and wolves all around, and so many other great dangers abound,

And yet you seem quite content to feed, and to all my warnings you've given no heed;

But do you not fear for your safety at all, and continue to graze in the grasses tall,

Upon what defense do you hope to rely, or who will be present to hear your small cry;

And how will you fare in the shadows of night, when you wander in darkness without any light,

And if perchance you should stray from the flock, or injure yourself on the craggy rock;

And how will you feed when the winter winds blow, and the grass is deadened beneath the snow,

Then where will you shelter and keep yourself warm, and who will protect your family from harm;

And when your life's journey has come to it's end, then who, may I ask, will be your close friend,

To whom will you go when the cold hand of death encamps 'round your soul to take your last breath;

Little lamb, will there be any safety at all, when that final enemy comes to call,

Do you really believe that all will be well, even when you shall hear the death knell;

Tell me little lamb, is there a Secret place, where a lamb may hide from death's horrid face,

Is there really a place of sweet peace and rest, where all of our kind may be richly blessed;

Tell me little lamb, may I follow you there, to that Heavenly place with no fear or care,

Oh please little lamb, please tell me now, for that dreaded cold hand is now on my brow;

And I fear that this may be my last day, Little lamb won't you please show me the Way?

The Little Lamb Answers

Dear friend, I never have reason to fear, though thousands of enemies are crouching near,

Both I and my family are safe from all harm, we're well-fed and watered, and happy and warm;

And while we feed safely in these pastures below, there is a great Secret we've all come to know,

We dread not to drink from these waters so still, for just over yonder standing high on that Hill;

Is the One whom we've trusted for many a year, and rejoice each time His voice we hear,

In both darkness of night, or in brightest day, our Shepherd is never too far away;

In the chill of the night, or in winter's dread cold, He always leads us safe back to His fold,

In the warmth of His love we all lie down and sleep, knowing that each of our souls He will keep;

And yes, there were times when I slipped away, and in my foolishness I did stray,

And I found myself in a strange weary land, and thought I might perish at the enemy's hand;

But while in that fearful place I did roam, my Shepherd He found me, and brought me safe home,

And as through that vale of dark shadows we walked, I humbly listened as the Shepherd talked;

And He spoke only words of sweet comfort and cheer, words that I desperately needed to hear,

My bruises were many, my wounds were so deep, but the Shepherd whispered..."you're still my Sheep";

In the presence of all my foes I am fed, with His oil of gladness He anoints my head,

And He promised someday by His infinite love, we shall dwell forever in green pastures above;

And so my dear friend, if the Way you would know, it is through the Shepherd that we all must go,

And if this is indeed your final, day, just follow the Shepherd, for He is the Way.

 2012 Arvil Jones

## Thanksgiving Day

There is something about the Holidays that cause me to reflect,
And yes, I greatly fear there are some things we often neglect;
Thanksgiving has always preceded Christmas, but nowadays you wouldn't know,
It seems that Christmas now begins long before the first flake of snow;

But I like to keep the Holidays in their rightful order and place,
It seems we're living our lives too fast, running at a breakneck pace;
Christmas will be here soon enough, and if I am still living,
I don't want to celebrate Christmas first, before I enjoy Thanksgiving;

You see, I have so very much that I am thankful for,
In fact, when I count my daily blessings, I just couldn't ask for more;
I dare not neglect to be thankful for all that my Lord has done,
Why even this morning He opened my eyes to see the rising sun;

I was reminded of the thousands who recently lost their lives,
Who won't be at the family table when Thanksgiving Day arrives;
Thousands who won't even have a table at which to sit and eat,
And millions who will never have a pair of shoes for their feet;

I'm sure that many who read these lines are thankful for many things,
For the love of a family and the many joys the love of a family brings;
So let us keep the Holidays Holy, and in their proper place,
And let us be thankful to God above for His mercy and for grace;

May the Holidays bring out our best, and may God forgive our worst,
Let's celebrate Christmas in December, but enjoy Thanksgiving first;
Let the heathen fight and bicker about what to name their tree,

But for this old simple country boy, it's a Christmas tree to me;

So from one grateful American to all my family and friends,
I just wanted to share a few lines before another season ends;
And if when Christmas does arrive I am not among the living,
To all of you I wanted to wish a very Happy Thanksgiving!
Arvil Jones

## That First Christmas Night

So many words, hymns and stories have been written about that night,
As the world lay in spiritual darkness, in desperate need of Light;
And yet a burning ray of hope burned in the hearts of men,
A promise that God would someday save His people from sin;

The time of that promise had now drawn nigh, and a Virgin was
espoused,
To marry a man named Joseph, a descendant of David's house;
And though he was of David's seed, and a man so meek and mild,
Yet Joseph himself could never be the father of this Child;

The One who was to be the King, and sit upon David's throne,
Must be forever sinless, in order that He might atone;
And so it was that Mary herself, was of the Royal Seed,
And in her womb did bear the One who met man's greatest need;

The little town was overcrowded, every room was filled,
As somewhere on the outskirts, a stable was quiet and stilled;
But yonder in the heavens all the angels sang with joy,
Announcing the coming birth of a little baby boy;

Conceived by the Holy Spirit, He was Christ, both God and man,
The miracle of the Virgin Birth, wrought by God's own hand;
Gently wrapped in swaddling clothes, and laid in a lowly manger,
Wise men came from far away to see this little stranger;

Each one showed to Mary and Joseph the gift that he did bring,
Gold and frankincense and myrrh to lay before the King;

Then back to their own country each of them did trod,
Rejoicing, knowing they had looked into the face of God.

## *That Hateful word...Sin - by Arvil Jones*

All the years that God has allowed me to live
To enjoy all the Blessings that His Son did give
I could never measure all He's done for me
I 've a mouth to speak and two eyes that see
My two hands work well, I have ears to hear
And a loving Family that I hold so dear
The list of my Blessings could go on and on
All the things I possess because of God's Son
Then my spirit goes drifting to a lonely Hill
Where one Man hung dying, God's Plan to fulfill
There were many who gathered just to watch Him die
But only a few knew the Reason Why
Some say He died for the crimes He had done
But the Record proves He committed none
Then Why, you may ask, did He suffer so
To endure such agony, pain and woe
There is only one Reason, and Sin is its name
My Sin that put him to all of the Shame
It is Sin that has caused so much suffering and loss
My Sin that nailed Him to The Old Rugged Cross.

## That Little Town in Kentucky...

Some folks are still proud of our Nation, and many are proud of their
town,
Some are better known than others, cities of great renown;
Some great towns and cities are known for the murders committed there,
While others are famous for their smog that permeates the air;
Some major cities have gained headlines because of the rampant crime,
They are the cities that "never sleep", so busy all the time;
Some towns are known for the hustle and bustle, and the names of movie
stars,
With their names engraved in the sidewalks, and their fancy homes and
cars;
Some cities are known for their tolerance, a place where "anything goes",
Cities where no one can walk without stepping on someone's toes;
There are cities and towns where I wouldn't live if you gave me the whole
place,
And now I hear they're even planning for cities in outer space;
But there's this little town in Kentucky, a town that I love so well,
A place where you can still wake up to the sound of an old church bell;
You don't hear much about famous folks, but neither is there any smog,
But you can still walk in the morning dew, and watch the lifting fog;
You can view majestic hills and valleys, or drink from a mountain brook,
Where there's still lots of elbow room, in any direction you look;
No, it's not famous for anything, as the world defines fame,
But it's a place where everyone knows his neighbor's name;
It's a place where God is honored, and children are taught respect,
A place where you will seldom hear of child abuse or neglect;
A place where families can sleep at night without a deadbolt lock,
Where no one jumps and grabs a gun each time they hear a knock;

Where the days are filled with work and play, and nights are quiet and
still,
I'm proud to call it my hometown, the town of Barbourville.
2016 Arvil Jones

## The Anointing

Since the Mighty God of Heaven
First gave His Word to men
He gave that Word because mankind
Had fallen into Sin
And the God of Heaven always knew
That if men were to be reached
Then He must give to men His Word
And that Word then must be Preached
And in order for men to Preach that Word
They must first receive His Call
And Preach by His Holy Spirit
Or never Preach at all
For to Preach without the Spirit
Is a mockery at best
The Word must be Divinely Sent
And by His Sprit Blessed
When the Spirit and the Word combine
They are like a Two-edged Sword
They pierce the hardened sinner's heart
And lead him to The Lord.
© Arvil Jones

## The Attributes of God

In mercy He withholds the judgment that I do so deserve,
In grace He gives me every gift that I could never earn;
With pity He forgives me each time on Him I call,
In truth He teaches me what I need to learn;

But the greatest attribute of our great God,
Who dwells in Heaven above;
Was shown upon an old rugged Cross;
Where He demonstrated His Love;

In the Person of His beloved Son,
Dying for the fallen race;
No greater love was ever shown,
As He opened the fountain of Grace;

From the veins of God incarnate,
The blessed Immanuel;
There flowed the cleansing precious blood,
That saves us all from hell.
© 2014 Arvil Jones

## The Trial of the Cat that ate the Canary!

Now what do you have to say for yourself, you wicked little feline?
Did you not know that all in this house, including the birds are mine?
Honestly! I really don't know what I'm going to do with you,
That bird was a very costly bird, so I guess I'll have to sue;

I want a lawyer said the cat, and I demand a fair trial,
But you have a feather in your mouth, and are you still in denial?
I have my rights, and I am innocent, as my trial will certainly prove,
So until I see my lawyer sir, I refuse to make a move;

Then a trial you shall have my pet, if that will ease your mind,
Here's the phone, now call the greatest lawyer you can find;
But if it's all the same to you, I'll take that feather now,
And don't think you can bribe me with your purring and your meow;

Order in the courtroom, said the judge with a gruesome frown,
The crowded room grew silent as he laid his gavel down;
He quickly scanned the jury box with fiery piercing eyes,
Where sat twelve furry canines of every shape and size;

The cat looked at the jury, and let out an awful scream,
He ran up to the rafters, leaping fast from beam to beam;
The judge ordered the bailiff to climb up and bring him down,
With order restored once again, he brushed his flowing gown;

The cat's attorney took some notes of everything in sight,
I may not win this case, he sighed, but I'll sure put up a fight;
He whispered to his client, "I think that judge is a hound",

If that's the case the cat replied, my tail is jailhouse bound;

Now, now, my pretty feline, relax and do not fear,
I've never lost a case in my illustrious career;
The judge looked sternly at the cat and asked - How do you plead?
Not guilty, answered the attorney, and the judge began to read,

I see that you are charged with many crimes my furry friend,
But rest assured that justice will be served by this day's end;
The indictment says that, first of all, you ate a little bird,
Objection cried the lawyer, the charge is most absurd;

My client has no taste at all for any kind of fowl,
He's never had a robin, nor a finch or screeching owl;
Ere since he was a kitten he has eaten naught but fish,
I'll prove it if you let the jury smell my client's dish;

The stone-faced jury smelled the dish, slowly one by one,
As the trembling cat watched silently till all the sniffing was done;
The judge himself then sniffed the bowl, then set the dish aside,
I grant the dish does smell like fish, but methinks the cat has lied;

Then down the aisle came the prosecutor, with a proud and noble strut,
Don't worry whispered the cat's attorney, he's nothing but a mutt;
But then the prosecutor stepped up to the judge's stand,
Holding a yellow feather in his furry little hand;

Now see my fellow canines, the evidence is clear,
This feline felon has broken all the laws that we hold dear;
But do not base your verdict upon prejudice or hate,

Simply observe the evidence as you deliberate;

'Tis only justice that we seek, and justice shall be served,
And now both the cat and his attorney had become quite unnerved;
My friend, I do not think today that justice will be done,
So tell me Mr. Calico, how fast can you run?

Well Sir, the mutts and terriers, I can outrun them all,
None of them have claws like mine, so they can't climb the wall,
But the judge is a Doberman, the bailiff a Greyhound, and the Sheriff is a
fox,
But I think I'll be safe once I pass the jury box;
But if we can't outrun them Sir, then what else can we do?
Well, I don't have to outrun them, I just have to outrun you.

2014 Arvil Jones

## The Christmas Spirit

Ahh! The blessed Spirit of Christmas, how pleasant it is to see,
As we watch the shoppers come and go, and parents buying a tree;
It seems there are a lot more smiles around this time of year,
And many folks seem to forget about all of the trouble and fear;

It seems that so much joy abounds all other cares are forgotten,
And some who seemed so mean before, are now not quite so rotten;
It's a time when even sworn enemies are able to live and let live,
And some who once held horrible grudges are willing to forgive;

It's a time when many forget themselves, and just reach out to others,
A season in which all races and creeds can call themselves friends and brothers;
A time when neighbors come closer again, and lend a helping hand,
And a sound of hope and cheer and laughter is heard across the land;

A time when even the politicians give their differences a rest,
A time that seems to conceal our worst, and bring out our very best;
A time when the little child in us is seen in a smiling face,
A season when the hardest of men can show a bit of grace;

And what is this Spirit that causes folks to be a bit more loving,
If only for a week or so, instead of pushing and shoving;
Could it be the Spirit of Christ Himself, Who brings such goodness to mind,
And makes the meanest Scrooge in the world, so generous, gracious and kind.

© 2013 Arvil Jones

234

## The Conversation

A young man growing up on the farm came to his Dad one day,
And Daddy knew from his expression he had something to say;
He sat down on an old oak stump and waited for his son to speak,
He noticed the boy was a little timid, his voice a little weak;
What's on your mind today my son, the father asked with a smile,
The young boy stopped and cleared his throat, just staring for a while;
Well, you know Dad, I've always had a deep respect for you,
I've always admired your wisdom, and the little things you do;
How you've always loved your family, and worked hard all your life,
How you've always told all us boys what to look for in a wife;
Well Dad, I think the time has come for me to let you know,
I've met a beautiful woman, and Dad I love her so;
And I'm quite sure she loves me too, I can feel it in my heart,
Well, Son, as well you know, that's the most important part;
How long have you known this girl, and how did you meet her Son?
Well, Dad I've known little Carol since we were only one;
We went to school together, I've known her all my life,
And just the other day I asked her to be my wife;
Well, tell me a little more about her, that is, if you don't mind,
Well, Dad, she's pretty as an angel, and so well-mannered and kind;
Well, Son, I'm very happy for you, and for the fact she's pretty,
But tell me boy, is this here gal from the country or the city?
Oh, she's a southern country gal, with long black shiny hair,
And the very first time I kissed her, love was in the air;
She can milk a cow, and ride a horse, and she loves my hunting dogs,
I've seen her lift a bale of hay, and even slop the hogs;
I've seen her pull a crosscut saw, and then go split the wood,
Well, that's all fine and dandy, but is her cooking any good?
Yes Sir, that girl can skin a rabbit, and cut it up to fry,

And she can shoot a rifle, and knock out a cricket's eye;
Well, boy, it sounds to me like that all the courtin's done,
And afore the week is over, you better marry that woman Son!
2016 Arvil Jones

## The Country Girl

Well she came from a lowly backwoods family,
Somewhere in the hills of Tennessee;
And when she started growin, folks said, child where are ya goin?
She said I'm gonna be a big star on TV,
I'm gonna make you country folks remember me.
Now when she thought that she was grown, she just up and left her home,
With thoughts of fame and fortune in her head,
But when she got to California, she found it like they warned her,
'Cause there was no place to lay her pretty head,
Then one night she wound up in a stranger's bed;
Well, it was easy to seduce her, He said I'm a big producer,
Honey I can make your every dream come true;
You gonna be the biggest thing that ever played the silver screen,
Just stick with me and darlin, when I'm through,
We gonna make them country folks remember you.
Now with the city lights all glowin, and that whiskey river flowin,
He soon found it wasn't hard to lead her on,
But next morning she awakened, and her body started shakin,
When she looked around and saw that he was gone,
Well then she started weepin, she had nothing left worth keepin,
He had taken all her innocence and pride,
All he left was an open door, and twenty dollars on the floor,
And that country girl just bowed her head and cried;
As she reacalled her Sunday learnin, in her soul a fire was burnin,
As she realized that what she'd done was wrong,
She cried, Lord I'm so ashamed, but I promise You I'll change,
If you'll only let me live to get back home.
Repeat first stanza...Yeah, she came from a lowly backwoods family...
The next lines fade out

## The Cross - by Arvil Jones

The "C" in the Cross stands for Christ the Lord
The One Who hung upon it

The "r" stands for redemption from sin
He died to save us from it

The "o" stands for Omnipotence
The Power above all others

The first "s" means Salvation
That makes all of us Brothers

The last "s" stands for Savior
The One Who sets men free
The One who hung and bled and died
Upon a cruel Tree.

## The Day We Met - by Carolyn Jordan-Jones

It was early one Easter morning, and the sun was shining bright;
And everything in my little world seemed to be just right;
I was wearing a beautiful dress of yellow,
When suddenly I met this handsome fellow;
I was just a sweet young thing, I had barely turned fifteen;
But to make the longer story short, he and I began to court;
Two years later I became his wife, and so began our married life;
Two years later I became the mother, of a little fair-haired boy;
And he was surely the love of my life, and he gave me so much joy;
It took us a while to choose a name, but finally we reckoned,
That we would call our firstborn son Arville Travis the second;
Then after two more years had passed, again we were richly blessed,
With a little beautiful brown eyed angel, and I held her to my chest;
It was just a week before Christmas, I remembered with a grin,
And her name was easy to choose, I called her Tracy Lynn;
I thought that I was through having children, but the good Lord said, not yet,
Six years later, another little angel, and we called her Erica Lynette;
And now all three of our children are grown,
And married with children of their own;
We've tried to teach them to shun the wrong,
And always choose the right;
As we grow old together, and sweet Heaven is just in sight!
© 2013 Carolyn Jordan-Jones

## The End of Day

The good Lord thought it good to give me yet another day,
And as the day comes to its close, I wondered what I should say;
All the day long my thoughts have been, how good He's been to me,
How none of His promises have ever failed, and the years I've lived to see;
I've known the love of a Wife and family, and many friends so dear,
And yes my life has known some failures, for which I've shed many a tear;
But my soul has tasted the goodness of God, His truth, His mercy and grace,
And at the end of every day, toward Heaven I turn my face;
He has made me to know the joy of living by a simple faith in Him,
And even though my body is weary, and my eyes are now growing dim;
My heart and soul can rest at ease, knowing I shall never die,
But simply fall asleep in Christ, and rise to my home on high;
My only longing is for those I love to know His love and peace,
And that all the world could have this joy, the joy that will never cease;
He made a way for all of us on a Cross on a hill far away,
And He promised to gather us all together in the Father's house someday;
Oh please consider Him my friend, as life's journey you pursue,
For what He has done for others, He can surely do for you.
© 2014 Arvil Jones

## The Father I Knew

When he was young and handsome and strong,
He rose up early, and stayed up long;
He plowed the fields and planted the seed,
For he had a rather large family to feed;
His hair was dark and his eyes were blue,
His duties were many, his pleasures were few;
All he ever wanted was a simple life,
His greatest joys were his children and wife;
His hands were callused and his back was bent,
From the many hours that he had spent;
Just to see that his family was clothed and fed,
And had a soft place to lay their head;
His bibbed overalls were faded and worn,
His old sweaty hat was tattered and torn;
But he always smiled as he worked all day,
Whether hoeing corn or pitching hay;
He taught his children to live off the land,
To trust in God, and to take a stand;
To cherish the things that mattered the most,
And to do what was right whatever the cost;
As we watched as his dark hair turned to gray,
And the light in his blue eyes faded away;
The time and the toil had taken their toll,
And much pain and sorrow had pierced his soul;
At whatever task he had to do, he always gave his best,
And on Easter Sunday of '73, my Dad was laid to rest.
© Arvil Jones

## The Final Words of a Father

Surely there are many more fathers who have thought about this day,
The day when life on earth is ended, and what words we would have to say;
When our dearest friends and loved ones begin to gather about,
Hoping our words will give them comfort, and not leave any doubt;

Well, I, for one, do not intend to wait until that day,
I will let my life speak for itself, and say what I have to say;
If the life that I live does not speak of God, then God I have not known,
If my neighbor says not that I love him, then no love have I shown;

I have read the last words of other men, but from them I dare not borrow,
Let my daily life be my epithet, for where shall I be tomorrow?
If I gave not of my daily bread to feed the hungry and poor,
The words of my mouth will mean nothing when death shall visit my door;

Hear not so much the sound of my lips, but the deeds of my callused hands,
Or find one prisoner who can testify it was I who loosed his bands;
If my children say not that it was I who led them to the Cross,
Then I myself will testify that my life has been but loss;

And if the Spirit shall bear no witness to the words that I have spoken,
Then my last words shall not suffice, and leave no certain token;
If the works that I do speak not for me, then who to my words shall give heed?

May my works speak louder than my words, that I am a Christian indeed;

If in my footprints others may walk, and find not the way to God,
Then my walk did not match my talk while here on earth I trod;
Oh hear me then my children, as my tired feet press the soil,
Learn from the sweat upon my brow, and the back that bent with toil;

Hear the lessons that can only be learned from the moisture in your father's tears,
And take to your hearts the blessed virtues that come from many years;
Let the lives that I and your Mother have lived be the words of our last refrain,
And may our final words be these - "Until we meet again."
© 2014 Arvil Jones

## The Fool

The fool hath said in his heart, There is no God (Psalm 14:1).

Did you ever really think about the atheistic fool,
Who sits on his philosophical stool;
Convincing himself that he's really cool,
Just living each day by only one rule -
His own?

He's very proud of his genetic pool,
And all the degrees he earned in school;
He spent most of his time in the vestibule,
He doesn't even know he's as dumb as a mule;
Now he's grown!

He's good at dishing out ridicule,
Upon all those of the Christian school;
He employs every vicious tool,
He finds each fault however minuscule;
Then he's gone!

But where Oh where did the poor fool go?
To Heaven above? or to Hell below?
But he didn't believe in either of these,
And he never once fell on his knees;
To pray!

'Tis not my place to tell his fate,
But if he waited one moment too late;

With broken heart, I shudder to state,
He'll never make it to the pearly gate;
No Way!

And although God by His mighty power,
Could have been his fortress and tower;
Upon him many blessings did shower,
Brought him from the womb as a flower,
And he bloomed!

If he called not upon God's Son,
Before his earthly race was run;
Eternity for him has begun,
He'll never see another rising sun;
He is doomed!

© 2014 Arvil Jones

## The God I Know

His timing is always perfect, His way is always best,
Although I try to urge Him to answer my request;
Sometimes He makes me wait a while, and I don't understand,
Sometimes I simply cannot trace the moving of His hand;
Sometimes I fret and worry whether He has heard my prayer,
Sometimes I find myself asking, does He really care;
Then after all my impatience, the answer comes at last,
And once again I thank Him, and hold His promise fast;
And once again I must repent that I ever doubted His grace,
And once again I'm forced to bow and hide the shame of my face;
How could I ever doubt the One who calmed the raging sea,
How could I question His wisdom or His integrity;
I have His Word before me, and not one word can fail,
No weapon formed against me can ever hope to prevail;
No battle has He ever lost, nor any blood-washed soul,
I am His and He is mine while the ceaseless ages roll;
The world and all its treasures, I count them naught but loss,
For the God I know has bought my soul by the blood of Calvary's Cross!
2016 Arvil Jones

## The Good Old Days

How sweet and precious are the memories I have of long ago,
When everything seemed so much simpler, and time passed kind of slow;
Back in those quiet and peaceful hills where every day was filled,
With praying hearts and working hands, as the fruitful land was tilled;
Where hope and love and family ties bound all of us to each other,
Where every child was taught respect, and to care for one another;
A time and place wherein truth abounded, and we feared to tell a lie,
When children honored their family name, and held their heads up high;
When every child knew his Father and Mother, and never had to guess,
When parents taught the Golden Rule, and demanded nothing less;
A time when we believed that our leaders were good and decent men,
And we never heard of an elected official being caught in sexual sin;
We were taught that righteousness exalts a nation, and that crime never pays,
That a man should earn his living by working, and being mindful of his ways;
Our preachers reminded us of a loving God who knows all of our deeds,
And how a young man ought to be careful about sowing too many wild seeds;
A time when Mothers taught their daughters to keep their dresses down,
And walk the aisle on Daddy's arm, in a snow-white wedding gown;
But now it seems hardly anyone remembers those old fashioned ways,
And I guess that's why us country folks still call them the good old days;
It was a time when we didn't have to guess about what was bad or good,
And no one ever locked their doors in our country neighborhood;
A time when a man could count on his neighbor if ever the times got rough,
And no one was ever hungry or homeless, and everyone had enough;
If ever a man was down on his luck, his friends and neighbors would share,

And it seemed that every family had bread enough and to spare;
It was a time when all of us trusted in our God above,
Leaning on the promises of His Word, and resting in His love.

## The Great Beyond

Ever since I was but a lad, down in those Kentucky hills,
I was told of a beautiful country far away;
A land where folks all get along, and never a tear is shed,
Where time gives place to one eternal day;
A place where no storm clouds ever arise, where no pain or sickness come,
Where no sorrow ever dawns upon the soul;
A country where only peace abounds, and no wars are ever fought,
And no homeless person shivers in the cold;
A place where there is room for all, to live, rejoice and sing,
And enjoy the things of which we are so fond;
Where the toils of earth are all forgotten, and no one bends with age,
This blessed Land we call The Great Beyond;
For many years my heart has longed to see that blessed place,
And to join the ranks of those who went before;
But for reasons only known to Him, the Lord still keeps me here,
And He tells me I have just a few days more;
And so each night as I lay my head upon my pillow soft,
And gaze toward the starry sky above;
My longing heart receives His peace, and He bids my soul, be still,
And I fall asleep within His arms of love;
No fear can ever haunt my dreams, no dread of death have I,
For His mighty angels encamp around my bed;
His Word I've hidden in my heart, His promise is mine to claim,
And I rest upon each sacred word He said;
And so if in the morning light, you find that I am gone,
And my lifeless body is all that's left behind;
I hope to see you in The Great Beyond, before the shining Throne,

And rest assured, I won't be hard to find;
I'll be somewhere near my Savior, listening to His words,
And gazing at His blessed, glorious face;
Then you and I can join our loved ones, there in the Heavenly choir,
As we lift our voices, singing Amazing Grace.

## The Joy of Giving

When the morning sun first pierced the sky, and the day began to dawn,
My eyes looked upward, and I greeted the day with a smile;
I could almost see the face of my heavenly Father, smiling down upon me,
As He and I had fellowship for a while;

I first had to thank Him for all the sweet comforts, like a soft pillow for my head,
For the roof above me, a good night's sleep, and a nice big comfortable bed;
And when I arose, there was food on my table, even more than I wanted to eat,
I had a nice home, a loving family, warm clothes, and shoes for my feet;

I clicked on the TV, just casually browsing, when some pictures caught my eye,
They were pictures of hungry, homeless people, and suddenly I wanted to cry;
They had no shoes for their swollen feet, and some had no clothes to wear,
Their bodies were covered with ugly sores, with flies buzzing in their hair;

Both parents and children appeared to be starving, nearly to the point of death,
Many were lying alone on the ground, struggling for just one more breath;
I slowly sat down in my big recliner thinking, this is not what I want to see,
But then I looked closer, and those sunken eyes were looking straight at me;

I thought of that big hardy breakfast I had, and I was overcome with shame,

I shifted my eyes away from the screen, searching for someone to blame;
A still small voice whispered, Mr. Jones, you can no longer look away,
The one to blame is the man you see in the mirror every day;

I fell to my knees there on the floor, and bowed my head in prayer,
Asking, Lord show me what to do, to prove that I really care;
His soft voice whispered to my soul, son, you know what you must do,
You must give of yourself, and share what you have, and to My Word be true;

Give, and it shall be given to you, in an overflowing measure,
Give to the poor, and lay up for yourself in Heaven an eternal treasure;
Give to the hungry, the sick and the lame, to the helpless and homeless one,
Give from you heart, asking nothing back, and when your race is run;
Your Father shall reward you with heavenly treasures untold,
Eternal riches, treasures unseen, and a mansion on a street of gold.
© 2013 Arvil Jones

## The Legacy

The wise old King from long ago said all is vanity,
And a man's whole life is quite like a vain show;
He's born, he lives a little while, he toils all his life,
And then on to his long home he shall go;
What happens to one happens to all, whether rich or poor,
And life is a brief journey at its best;
And what good is all the toil of man, and what good is his wisdom,
If in his soul he never finds sweet rest?
And to whom shall he leave it all at last, when all his work is done,
Will his son be a wise man or a fool?
Has he followed his father's good advice, and lived by his example,
And is his heart inclined to his father's rule?
And so I now examine my life, with all that I have done,
And many a scene I've wished I could no longer see;
Has my life been of any value to God or my fellow man,
Is there anyone who would wish to be like me?
Have I set a good example before the ones I love,
Could they follow in my footsteps without fear?
Have I always been consistent in both my walk and talk,
Have the principles by which I've lived been clear?
And if of my life it cannot be said – He was a godly man,
Then Oh what a miserable servant I have been;
'Twould have been far better that I had not been born,
Than to fall into the ways of ungodly men;
Has my desire always been pure, my motives above reproach,
Has my life been what my Master meant it to be?
But more, much more than all of this, the greatest question of all,
Can anyone see Christ when they look at me?

## The Liberal Lie

It has never been acceptable since the dawn of life,
For one human being to take the life of another;
"But this is America"
Believe it or not, like it or not,
I'm responsible for my brother;
"But this is America"


The proof is overwhelming, life begins at conception,
And to take that life is murder in the first degree;
"But this is America"
It has never been acceptable for men to marry men,
Or women kissing for all the world to see;
"But this is America"
It was never intended for lawmakers to live above the law,
Or for the law to set the guilty free;
"But this is America"
The laws were intended to govern behavior, and secure justice for all,
And the law that applies to you applies to me;
"But this is America"
I wonder if America were to change her name today,
Would our country stop killing the babies then?
If America changed her name today, and called it something else,
Would abortion and same-sex marriage be a sin?
What does the name of our country have to do with right and wrong?
Would wrong be right under any other name?
And if we called her something else other than America,
Would men kissing men suddenly be a shame?
"But this is America", the liberals cry, and we can do as we please,
And neither God nor man can tell us NO!

This is America, This is America, and I can burn her flag,
And America's constitution tells me so!
"But this is America, land of the free", the liberal cries aloud,
And no one can tell me what to do or say;
But I say if changing America's name would stop all the stupidity,
Then by all means, let's change her name today.
Arvil Jones

## The Man in The Mirror - by Arvil Jones

Ahh! That smiling lovely face we see in the mirror each day
A countenance so perfect that we hardly know what to say
Surely there are none in the world
Quite as lovely and perfect as me
Then the Man in the Mirror replied one day
You're nothing but a Pharisee
Oh Heaven forbid, I quickly replied
I'm as righteous as a man can get
But the Man in the Mirror quickly replied
You're nothing but a Hypocrite
But surely my Neighbors are far worse than I
They have drunken and stolen and cursed
The Man in the Mirror said, among them all
You are the very Worst
Then with horror I gazed in the Mirror again
Do I see what I think I see
A poor and miserable deplorable wretch
Staring back at me
And I fell to my knees, and I cried Oh Lord
I have been such a cruel Judge
I've taken so much, and given so little
And I've held onto many a Grudge
Oh Savior forgive my horrible wrongs
And save my poor Soul tonight
Then the Man in the Mirror smiled and said
You finally got it Right.
© Arvil Jones

## The Master Poet

There have been so many men and women
Since the very dawn of time
Who have been given a precious Gift
Of creating lines that rhyme
Their messages have been recorded
Upon many a gilded page
Their rhythmic lines have been preserved
To be read by a future age
But let us not forget the One
Who Created the tongues of men
The One who gave men wisdom
To invent the paper and pen
He takes a life that is ruined and broken
By the ravages of Sin
And His Grace gives Rhyme and Reason
And He makes them whole again
And the tongue that once could only curse
Now only wants to bless
And the heart that once could find no joy
Finds Hope and Happiness
Do you know the Master Poet
Have you read His Blessed Word
The Poet's Name is Jesus
Our Savior and our Lord.
© Arvil Jones

## The Meaning of Life? Or a Life with Meaning?

The greatest minds of all the ages have searched for the meaning of life,
 With microscopes and telescopes, and even with the surgeon's knife;
  Man has reached into the heavens with instruments of every kind,
   With sophisticated cameras to document what he might find;

He digs into the crust of the Earth, searching for fossil remains,
 Forever digging deeper into the past, taking the greatest pains;
  Meticulously recording everything that he can find,
   And all of this in hopes of finding the origin of mankind;

He searches desperately for the meaning of life, as he digs and looks and groans,
Believing the meaning of life can be found in the dust of dinosaur bones;
He searches the depths of the oceans, and the bodies of dead fruit flies,
 And after all his searching is done, he gives up the ghost, and dies;

How sad to have lived, but never learning the meaning of life at all,
 A search that has proven futile since the day of Adam's fall;
  And yet he goes on searching, but is never satisfied,
   The meaning of life still escapes him, no matter how hard he tried;

One day long ago on a lonely hill, an old rugged cross was raised,
 Upon that cross there hung a Man who was both cursed and praised;
  His life was a life full of meaning, not a moment did He waste,
For all whose lives had lost its meaning, the pains of death He must taste;

In His body He bore the sin of all whose purpose in life had been lost,
To give new meaning to life with no meaning, He paid an awful cost;
The meaning of life can never be found by digging in the sands,
But a life with meaning is free to all, through the blood of His nail-pierced
hands.

## The Mighty Conqueror - by Arvil Jones

To all of us who know Him there is no greater Name
Yes we know His Identity and the Place from whence He came
From the Glory of that Heavenly Realm to a sin-cursed world below
There came The Mighty Conqueror, His Sovereign Power to show
The world only saw Him as a lowly carpenter's son
In spite of all the mighty works and Miracles He'd done
But as His fame began to spread throughout all Galilee
Men began to ask each other, "Who might this Man be"
There were only a few who recognized Him both as God and Man
And others who refused to believe 'Til they saw His nail-pierced Hand
He said it was His Father Whom He came to reveal
And there was Something in this Man that flesh could not conceal
Each mighty work that He performed revealed His Father's Love
Then slowly men began to ask- "Is this Man from Above"
But it's been said there's none so blind as those who refuse to see
And some would not be satisfied 'til they nailed Him to a Tree
They watched Him die in agony and spat in the Face of God
A Man who had done naught but Good while here on Earth He trod
In a borrowed tomb three days and nights His wounded Body lay
While Heaven and Earth awaited the dawning of the Day
And on that Appointed Morning our God the Victory gave
The Mighty Conqueror arose with Power over Death, Hell, and the Grave.
© Arvil Jones

## The Minister's Mate, by Arvil Jones

According to the Scriptures, we give honor where honor is due
To all those who labor in the Word, and a Godly vocation pursue
We give double honor to those who rule well
Who endure great hardships and strife
But sometimes I fear we greatly neglect
To honor the Minister's Wife
For in whatever duty he is engaged
She also has a great part
She cooks his meals and washes his clothes
And she prays with all of her heart
And wherever he goes, her prayers go with him
Though she may not be at his side
She prays for his safety and for his success
In his heart she doth ever abide
And when no one else encourages him
He yet knows that she really cares
And with every burden he carries
That burden she also bears
And together they pray and labor
No matter what may be the cost
For they both have but one objective
That they reach out to the lost.
© 2013 Arvil Jones

## The Mother I Knew - Ethel Keene-Jones

She married my Dad when she was fourteen, back in Nineteen-twenty two
And of course there were the usual comments as to how folks thought they would do
Some would say they didn't do so well, but when the whole story is told
How folks do is determined I guess by the standard that you hold
There came from her womb fourteen children, but one was dead in her womb
And as the years passed she watched them bury five more in a hillside tomb
She survived the deaths of her children, the Depression and two World Wars
Then there was Korea, and Vietnam, with all of life's heartaches and scars
She scrubbed the clothes on a washboard, and cooked on a wood burning stove
She read the Bible by a coal oil lamp, and a car she never drove
She never complained about anything, her faith in her God kept her strong
Side by side with Dad and the children, she worked in the fields all day long
She had no flattering figure to show, but whenever my Mother passed by
Men young and old removed their hats with a look of respect in their eye
She had more than enough of love to share for her husband, her children and others
And in my heart she will always be the fairest of all Mothers

And then the day came when her race was run, and we all had to say
goodbye
And now she sings in Heaven's choir, in her mansion in the sky.

## The Mother of My Children

I met her first when we were children
But didn't even get her name
A little blonde haired country girl
With blue eyes and a skinny frame
Then some years passed and we both grew
To that tender age of fifteen
And now she was the most beautiful girl
These eyes had ever seen
And I knew then that I had to try
To make her a part of my life
And so just two years later
I asked her to be my wife
And I love her more now than I ever have
Even after forty-five years
She's been my right arm and my very best friend
Through sickness, pain and tears
She's the Mother of our three children
And what a godly Mother she's been
A kinder, gentler loving woman, this world has never seen
She has a smile and a sense of humor
That can gladden the saddest soul
Though time and troubles of her own
have certainly taken their toll
She is a woman of simple faith
In her God whom she greatly adores
And for many years she has sung from her heart
Of Heaven, and those bright peaceful shores
And since we know not the number of our days

Nor the sum of the years of our life
I just wanted to take this opportunity
To honor my Blessed Wife
To Carolyn Jordan-Jones
From Arvil

## The Next Leader?

Give me the man who can walk our streets without a bodyguard,
A man whose character makes him loved by the humble and the hard;
Give us the man who has no lust for money, sex or power,
A man whose inner strength makes him like a mighty tower;
Give us the man whose only promises are to serve and love,
Give us the man whose only faith is in the God above;
Find us the man whose hands are tough from working hard all day,
Find us the man who is not ashamed to fall on his knees and pray;
Give us the man who is honest enough to say he's made some mistakes,
A man with great discernment who is able to spot the fakes;
Give us the man who surrounds himself with other honest men,
A man who is never afraid to look at sin – and call it sin;
Give us the man whose reputation says he's a man we can trust,
Give us the man whose heart can stand against all pride and lust;
Give us the man who would be willing to carry our flag to the fight,
A man who can have compassion for a nation in a pitiful plight;
Give us the man who will sit and listen to the voice of the common man,
A man who is humble enough to know only God has a perfect plan;
Give us the man who can shed a tear o'er the graves of our honored dead,
A man who loves the homeless and helpless enough to give them a bed;
But where, Oh where can we find such a man? Some patriot might say,
My dear fellow Americans – We can only hope and pray!
2016 Arvil Jones

## The Old Cowboy's Dream

He had done all the things a cowboy must do in order to just survive,
He always made sure he had what he needed in order to stay alive;
He herded the cattle and roped the steers and branded the calves and cows,
And each night as he laid his sore body down, he made some sacred vows;
He vowed someday he would hang up his spurs, and ride the range no more,
He promised himself he'd rest from his labors, and never be saddle sore;
He dreamed of a little farm of his own close by a clear flowing creek,
With a sweet country lady to cook his meals, and kiss his smooth shaven cheek;
A place where there were no rattlesnakes, and no coyotes to howl,
No rustlers to catch, no horse thieves to hang, and no wolves on the prowl;
All he wanted was a simple life, and not a lot of work to do,
Just maybe one horse, one hog and a cow, some chickens and a young un or two;
And maybe if the good Lord would be so kind, he could even put a few dollars back,
To buy his wife something pretty for Christmas, not made from an old feed sack;
Why, he might even settle close to a church, and put the young uns in Sunday school,
And teach them to love and fear the Lord, and to live by the Golden Rule;
Yes every night, at the end of the trail, these thoughts floated through his brain,
As he covered himself with his saddle blanket, just praying that it wouldn't rain;
And then one night in late autumn, 'neath the stars above an old camp site,

As the cold wind blew he knew there was something strange about this night;
Somehow the stars seemed dimmer than he'd ever seen them before,
And that darned wind just pierced his bones and chilled him to the core;
Not even the campfire could get him warm, as his body tossed and turned,
Then suddenly inside his heart, another kind of fire burned;
And then the old cowboy lay quite still, smiling 'neath Heaven's great dome,
He heard a voice from Heaven saying, "Ben, it's time to come home";
Then Old Ben awoke in a beautiful place like his eyes had never seen,
There was a river as clear as crystal, and the grass was tall and green;
The land spread out so far and wide like nothing he'd ever known,
Then like a flash his eyes were drawn toward a shining Throne;
He knew he'd reached the end of the trail, and had seen his last setting sun,
As the Savior beckoned to him saying, Well done cowboy, Well done.
2012 Arvil Jones

## The Ol Left Hander - A Tribute to Joe Nuxhall
## By: Arvil Jones

It was indeed a blessed day,
When this lanky young talent was found;
And the youngest man in the history of the game,
Stepped onto the pitcher's mound;
He was only a lad of fifteen years,
But he was ready for life's best and worst;
He gave his best, and passed the test,
And Joe had rounded first.

Joe played the game for the love of the game,
And not just to make himself a name;
And to all who knew him, the message was clear,
Big Joe was headed for a great career;
The Old left hander was more than a pitcher,
He was also our neighbor and friend;
He brought character to the game of baseball,
And his charity knew no end.

But the game takes its toll on both body and soul,
And when some lines had creased his face;
With unbroken stride and Cincinnati pride,
Joe rounded second base;
He knew there was no stopping now,
For he had home plate in sight;
And with friends and fans all waving him on,
He ran with all of his might;
With one quick glance at the fielder,

Joe knew the throw would come;
With his great heart pounding, Big Joe was rounding,
Third, and heading for home.

And if someday someone should ask,
Where the Old left hander has gone;
Why...didn't you know, He beat the throw,
And they called him....Safe At Home!

## The Poet and his pen...by Arvil Jones

Before he writes a single word he ponders what to say,
Not knowing who will see his lines at last;
Oh, yes, he cares, and contemplates, and tries to do his best,
Not to copy what's been said in the past;
He asks himself how can he be true to himself and everyone else,
Without repeating what others had to say;
But somehow as he puts his pen upon the waiting page,
He says it all, but in a different way;
His motive must be well-examined, his mind put to the test,
That he might pass to others what's on his mind;
And so he searches his heart and soul for proper words to write,
Not wanting to be callous or unkind;
Will what he is about to write be of any value, to others, or to himself
alone?
Will others catch his temperament, his conscience or his soul,
And sense the little errors to which he is prone?
Will the lines upon a single page cause someone to laugh or cry,
Will his story bring a blessing or a curse?
Will every sentence that he writes make any sense at all,
Should he expect reactions to his verse?
And if reactions do ensue, with some not to his liking,
Will he take it like a man, or will he pout?
Will all who read his lines come away with an understanding,
Of what the beleaguered poet is talking about?
If he has cast his heart and soul into each word and line,
Does it matter what subject he chooses to unveil;
Whether politics, religion, or any philosophy,
He knows may succeed, or he may fail;
To reach the hearts and minds of others, some more gifted than he,

Who will scrutinize his words with keen insight;
Some will offer criticism, others a bit or praise,
But in the end, it's his own will he must fight;
In his heart there is compulsion to say a little more,
Than the length of the lines and pages will allow;
He can only pray that when it's done, he's done his very best,
To say what needed saying some way somehow;
And so he writes of many things, of life and love and death,
And his own experience along the passing years;
And each who reads with discernment is able to see his heart,
To know his joys, his sorrows, and his tears;
And many can themselves relate to much that he has written,
For they have also been where he has gone;
As they read the words that take them back to sometime long ago,
When they were loved, embraced, or left alone;
His lines arrest the conscience, and address those inner thoughts,
Kept secret for reasons which only they can know;
But in the silence of their rooms, alone with what he's written,
What's in their hearts and minds begins to show;
In either a bright and happy countenance, or perhaps a deepening frown,
For some perhaps a mixture of both of these;
And so his purpose is accomplished, as he lays down his pen,
And feels the softness of the evening breeze.

## The Politician's Autopsy

I'm just a wee bit puzzled, the seasoned examiner said,
I've examined her from head to toe, and again from toe to head;
I see no signs of injuries, no signs of a heart attack,
And I've performed every possible test from front to back;
The Secretary wasn't poisoned, she didn't die of a stroke,
Her lungs are in perfect condition, so I know she didn't smoke;
There isn't a single lesion, neither a bullet hole,
Her skin is soft and pliable, she hasn't a single mole;
I've taken every X-ray that can possibly be done,
And as for any kind of disease, I haven't found a one;
As for her dental records, I've examined every page,
She wasn't even seventy, she didn't die of old age;
And so with all the tests I've done, I simply must surmise,
The Secretary met an untimely death;
From telling too many lies!
2016 Arvil Jones

## The Power of Prayer

A simple prayer, a heart-felt petition, rising up from the soul of man
Reaches into the throne room of Heaven, bringing back in its grateful
hand
The reality of that for which he asked, the substance for which he had
hoped
Though he lingered long upon his knees, and in the darkness groped
On wings of faith, ascending upward, the power of a simple prayer
Doth lock the jaws of lions, or the gates of the devil's lair
And a holy messenger is sent, dispatched from Jehovah's throne
To tell the humble praying soul that what he asked is done
It may have been a dreaded sickness he had borne for many years
Or a loved one lost in sin for whom he shed many tears
But knowing the heart of the One who cares, and hears his every plea
He returns to his prayer room day by day, and falls on bended knee
And though sometimes his heart is broken, and he knows not what to say
He pours out all his soul and knows the answer is on the way
A man of faith who prays to God, and seeks the Master's face
Shall see his children's children blessed with mercy and with grace
Though men may boast of power and might, while here on earth they
trod
There is no greater power than prayer that can touch the Throne of God.
2012 Arvil Jones

## The Prodigal

Have you, like the Prodigal, wandered afar, to a land so strange and unknown;

Are you, like the Prodigal, reaping the harvest, of the bitter seeds you have sown;

Have you, like the Prodigal, wasted it all, and found that you have not a friend;

Have you, like the Prodigal, spent all you have, and facing a road with no end;

Are you, like the Prodigal, wallowing now, in the muck and mire with the swine;

Do you, like the Prodigal now recall, your Father's table so fine;

Do you, like the Prodigal, now realize how much your Father loves you,

Will you, like the Prodigal, make up your mind, as to what you're going to do;

Will you, like the Prodigal, rise up and come back home to your Father so dear;

Do you not see Him running toward you, is that not His voice you hear;

Yes, dear Prodigal, it is He, who welcomes you home again;

He cares not what you may have done, but He sees, and He feels your pain;

Come now my child, and let us dress you in garments fit for a king,

Let all my servants dance with gladness, and let all the maidens sing;

For this my child was lost and undone, but now he is safe and whole,

Rejoice, Rejoice, and praise ye the Lord, Bless the Lord , Oh my soul!

## The real crisis – what is it?

Harry S. Truman was President when I was born. That means, of course, that I have now lived to see twelve different administrations – some Republican and some Democrat sit in Washington, DC, doing all those wonderful things politicians do for their, and our, country. Most of the men who occupied the Oval Office were, in my opinion, sufficiently qualified for the position. But can we all at least agree that none of them were perfect? Not one of those men did everything exactly right, and none of them did everything wrong. None of them pleased everyone during their tenure in office. But America survived the wars, the Depression, the recessions, and everything else she had to face, from either real or imagined threats from several other countries who, for one reason or another, do not like our way of life, to every natural (or supernatural) disaster that came upon her.

During every presidential campaign that I have witnessed in my sixty-five years, the campaign rhetoric has, for the most part, been virtually the same. Some, of course, were more bitterly fought than others, and some were downright disgusting on the part of both candidates and their supporters. In recent years, I have written some pretty sarcastic and/or humorous articles and poems (all in good fun) about some of the more recent candidates for the office of President. I have discovered that in my lifetime, every other candidate who lived before my time experienced this same sort of political sarcasm to some degree before, during, and after his campaign.

But today America is faced with something quite different. Our country is not the same country she was in the eighteenth and nineteenth centuries. America has always found a way to survive, bounce back, and even prosper under seemingly impossible conditions which would seem to render it impossible for her to do so. But America has lost her focus.

America has forgotten and forsaken her very foundational principles upon which she was built, and upon which she has thrived as a nation, which brings me to the main point of this article.

In the Bible we read of a young man – Esau, the twin brother of Jacob, who, for all intents and purposes, sold his soul...for a mess of pottage! And this is, in a very real sense, what America has done with her soul. America would rather have money than morals. America demands rights without righteousness. America boasts of civic pride, but belittles civic principles. America condemns genocide, but legalizes murder, calling it by another name, of course.

And now look at who we have vying for the highest office in our land. My heart breaks at the very thought of the choices we have in this election. With the possible exception of Jimmy Carter, we have, in this upcoming election, the poorest two choices this country has ever had for the office of President. I will probably lose some close friends by what I am about to write, but so be it – it must be written. I am a conservative Republican, and have been for many years, and have, for the most part, strongly supported the ideas and ideals set forth and followed by my Republican ancestors. But as far as qualifications go for the office of President, I have to say that Hillary Clinton is probably the best qualified person. But Hillary Clinton is a proven liar, careless, a crook, and a spineless liberal who would, in my opinion, sell her very soul in order to obtain the office of President. I sincerely hope that I am wrong.

Donald Trump, in my opinion, has very few, if any qualifications for the office of President, and yet he is the chosen candidate of the Republican Party. He is, no doubt, a highly motivated, successful business man, depending upon your definition of success. According to prevailing business principles and practices, there are few men who surpass Mr.

Trump in business acumen. But in the office of President of the United States, Mr. Trump would, in my opinion, have to surround himself with scores of individuals who are far more competent than himself in order to function in that office.

These are our choices! And we must choose one! And yet I haven't said what I really wanted to say. It is not the fault of the candidates themselves that they are our only choices in this election. It is our own fault – yours and mine that they are our only choices. We have brought the situation upon ourselves. There was a time when we Americans demanded that our leaders have strong moral and spiritual convictions, coupled with proven track records which indicated they were both capable and worthy of being considered for their respective offices. But we have lowered our own standards, and as a result are now reaping the bitter harvest of the seeds we have sown. We are, in a sense, getting what we asked for, but not necessarily what we are paying for.

So if you are looking for someone to blame – blame me. I have failed to pray as I ought to have prayed, and I have failed to pray as often as I could and should have prayed for the leadership of my country. I have neglected my God-given duty to be the best citizen I could be. I have spoken when I should have remained silent, and I have remained silent when I knew I should have spoken. I have, far too many times, taken my rights and privileges for granted, while neglecting my responsibilities, forgetting the unspeakable cost at which my liberty came to me.

And now I can only bow my head and ask God to forgive me, and make me more cognizant of my responsibilities, and perhaps a bit less demanding of my rights.

## The Recipe

I'm sure that all of us could name our very favorite food,
The dish that makes our mouths water and puts us in the right mood;
But do we ever stop and think of how that dish came to be,
And how many of us could recite from memory that very recipe;

And are we ever aware at all of the carefulness it took,
And all the tedious time and toil of the lady we call the cook;
These tasty nourishing recipes do not happen by accident,
In order for us to enjoy them, a lot of time and effort was spent;

And if any ingredient should be missing, or not in proper measure,
The taste just simply isn't the same, and neither is the pleasure;
We want our food to please our taste, and pleasant to our sight,
And in order for this, the mixing and measures and the timing must be
right;

The hands of the chef must always be clean, the food must be properly
seasoned,
The chef must stick to the recipe with clarity and reason;
To ensure the proper texture and taste, no shortcuts can be taken,
The oil must be spread just right, the salt and pepper shaken;

And so it is with our spiritual food, if it is to please our taste,
To feed the spiritually hungry soul, we must never proceed in haste;
Every ingredient must holy, the preacher's heart must be clean,
He must be anointed with holy Oil, and upon His God he must lean;

His words must be seasoned with the Holy Spirit, and mixed with
Heavenly Love,

He must always be as wise as a serpent, but harmless as a Dove;
He cannot allow any mixture of error in this recipe Divine,
In proper measure the Holy Spirit and the Word must always combine;

And when the Spirit and Word combine, the sheep will be well fed,
The hypocrites will run and hide, and tremble in their bed;
The lost will be convicted, the backslider will be ashamed,
The drunkard will be made sober, and the wild man will be tamed;

When all the holy ingredients are right, the people will be awakened,
The politicians will all take notice, and the nation will be shaken;
The church will be a bright shining beacon for all the world to see,
But only when the preachers stick to God's great Recipe.
© Arvil Jones, Ph.D.

## The Redneck Philosopher – on evolution.

Now look here son the professor demanded,
I'm the one teaching this class;
How dare you challenge my wisdom,
You sure have a lot of brass;
Well I don't believe in evolution,
The country boy replied;
I believe in a Divine Creator,
And I'm quite satisfied;
Well if you don't believe in evolution,
You cannot pass my course;
Well Sir, then I'll just have to fail,
And I have no remorse;
But let me tell you professor,
Your theory cannot prevail;
Some of my ancestors swung by their neck,
But none of them swung by the tail.
Arvil Jones

## The Ship, The Storm, The Anchor
By Arvil Jones

The old ship didn't look like much, quite unworthy to sail,
Her boards were loose, her sails all rent and torn;
For many years she'd sailed the seas through every kind of gale,
Her crew and captain all so weary and worn;
Many said it was too dangerous to sail the ship again,
They said she'd never make it across the tide;
But the faithful captain and his crew would not be persuaded,
There were treasures waiting on the other side;
The ship sat creaking in the harbor, as the crew prepared to sail,
Patching the sails, securing the tackle and ropes;
The dark clouds hovered overhead, as thunder shook the timbers,
But nothing could destroy the sailors' hopes;
The treasures that lay waiting far across the sea,
Were worth far more than what they were leaving here;
They'd bravely face the hurricanes, and all the pirate's cannons,
Just to catch a glimpse of what was over there;
The storm bore down in all its fury, straining at the sails,
As the captain fought the wheel with all his might;
With not a star to guide him, nor sextant in his hand,
He sailed the old ship through the stormy night;
'Twas hard to tell whether day or night as the dark clouds hovered,
But now the raging sea had calmed a bit;
The hands of every crewman were bloody on the ropes,
And a few announced they were ready to quit;
But the aged sea-worn captain encouraged all the crew,
As he stood alone upon the old ship's bow;
His piercing eyes looked to the skies, for any ray of sunshine,
He said it's time to drop the anchor now;

With not a twinkle of a star, nor moonbeam up above,
And not a sight of land either near or far;
The trusted rusted anchor was lowered 'neath the waves,
As the Captain cried, "Now tell me what ye are;"
Are ye men of faith, or no, do ye believe in God?
Do ye rely upon His strength alone?
Do ye not know that this old ship has sailed the seven seas?
She's gone where greater ships have never gone;
'Twas never any strength of mine, nor yet my sailing skill,
That brought her into harbor safe and sound;
'Twas not my courage nor my crew that guided her along,
Had it not been for God, we'd all have drowned;
Look not to the rusty anchor that lies beneath us now,
To hold us fast throughout this stormy night;
But look to Him who made the sea and the boundaries thereof,
In Him alone we'll find our guiding light;
Fear not the mighty gale my mates, nor yet the lightning flash,
Fear not although the waves around you roll;
Let the rusty anchor hold the feeble ship,
But let Christ be the anchor of your soul.

## *The Stranger*

*I took a stroll in the woods one evening*
*With so many things on my mind*
*I had so many unanswered questions*
*Many answers I needed to find*
*I guess I wanted to just get away*
*From the hustle and bustle of life*
*To hear a bird singing, a babbling brook*
*No hurry, no worry, no strife*
*I wanted the answers to all of life's questions*
*The how, the why, and the when*
*And where did all the sorrow come from*
*And why does God allow Sin*
*Then off in the distance a Stranger approached*
*Very slowly He walked toward me*
*And the nearer He came, and the closer I looked*
*A soft light in His eyes I could see*
*He spoke with a voice so gentle and kind*
*Each word sank deep in my heart*
*But when I tried to talk to Him*
*I didn't know quite where to start*
*It seemed all my questions were already answered*
*So I asked if His Name He would tell*
*Then just before He disappeared, He whispered...Emmanuel*
*© Arvil Jones*

## The Treasures Of The Snow

Hast thou entered into the treasures of the snow (Job 39:22)?
So softly it landed among the others, so many billions untold,
It made no sound, but it made a difference, or so I've been told;
The difference was – the snowflake was different,
Distinct from all the rest;
Neither better nor worse than any other,
None could boast it was best;
And yet no two are exactly alike,
Yet together all of them dwell;
Whatever difference one snowflake makes,
The others make as well;
The value of a snowflake? You ask,
Do you care to calculate?
A tiny speck of frozen crystal,
That knows neither love nor hate;
Its form is Oh so delicate,
Yet intricate beyond compare;
Seemingly insignificant, yet causing men to stare,
For they cannot know all its mystery,
For so its Designer planned;
Yet the snowflake will instantly perish,
If touched by a human hand;
Ahh! There it is, the secret lesson,
Learned by so very few;
That men ought to ponder more carefully,
The things they say and do;
How many things which God has made,
Intended for the good of men;
Are desecrated by the human touch,

**Tainted by human sin;**
Men are not happy with knowing just a little,
They want to know it all;
Yet he can't understand the snowflake,
A thing so fragile and small;
The snowflake is a testimony to the wisdom of the Lord,
A symbol of His purity described in His living Word;
Men cannot be as wise as God, no matter how hard they try,
They can never know all that He knows;
And they do not understand why,
And so they make themselves their god;
And demonstrate how much they know,
They peer and ponder, and at last discover, artificial snow;
Artificial! How appropriate to describe the creations of men,
But whatever they make, they first must take;
From that which has already been,
For after man has strained his mind, and all his plans are laid;
He must begin with something which the Lord has already made,
How sad that men can know so much, and yet so little they know;
For as yet no man has entered into the treasures of the snow.

## The Value of His Blood - by Arvil Jones

As this old world moves swiftly toward its Destiny
A Rendezvous with Judgement for all Eternity
A Day when the secret things of men will be brought into the Light
When the strongest of men will tremble
And will mourn their awful plight
But there is a Remedy for Man, A mighty Cleansing Flood
Yes, It is still relevant today, that Precious Sacred Blood
The Blood that will never lose It's Power
To Cleanse and to Sanctify
The Blood from the veins of Emmanuel
Who hears each Sinner's Cry
And though it's been two thousand years
Since He died in Agony
His Blood still Saves and Justifies
His Blood still sets men Free
There is no other Source of Hope
Where men may rest Secure
It is still the Blood of Jesus
That makes the Sinner Pure.
© Arvil Jones

## The View From The Cross

We all have read and heard the story
Of His death upon the Cross
And how the crowd scorned and mocked Him
As He suffered such pain and loss
The Gospel writers have painted a picture
For all the world to see
But have you ever wondered
What His view from the Cross might be
Although His blood and tears filled His eyes
Yet He could still see it all
A multitude of broken lives, all ruined by the Fall
He saw the self-righteous Pharisees
Who denied His every claim
He saw the unbelieving Jews
Who scorned and mocked His Name
He saw the Roman soldiers
Who had beaten Him in His face
And a handful of faithful followers
Who had been saved by His Grace
He saw His loving Mother whose soul was pierced with grief
And He saw the face and heard the cry
Of one repentant thief
He saw a rebellious nation with eyes that could not see
But aren't you glad that through His eyes
He could also see you and me
© Arvil Jones

## The voice of reason, or the choice of faith?

On and on the rhetoric goes, and nothing changes for the better! Words will not, because they cannot, change the hearts and minds of men and women. Everyone has a comment and an opinion about what happened and why it happened, but no one has a reasonable, concrete solution that will work, and bring the hate and resultant violence and crime to a desired end. When will men learn, and finally believe, and conclude that they are incapable of saving themselves from themselves? That is a rhetorical question – it answers itself:

The wholesale slaughter of innocent lives among all races, colors, creeds, religions and all other ethnic groups and individuals has a cause behind it, and I know those of you who are reading this now are waiting for the writer to express his own "opinion" as to what that cause is, and I also know you are waiting for me to offer a solution. All of us, of course, know how much opinions are worth, and how far opinions go toward bringing about lasting change – not very far at all! And yet we have to listen to the media, the public, the leadership of cities, counties, states and nations, and other secular groups express their opinions, reasons, and propositions day after day, week after week, month after month, year after year, on and on, endlessly proposing solutions which, if and when they are ever implemented, seem to work for a short time, temporarily calming nerves, cooling tempers, and soothing hurt feelings.

And then another attack happens, and another, and another...one is a "radicalized Muslim" who hates all Americans for one reason or another; another is a Muslim officer in the U.S Military; another is an honorably discharged black male, claiming he is simply retaliating against police brutality. And we wonder what the ethnic background of the next killer/terrorist/murderer is going to be? And then some brilliant, civic-minded, patriotic politician hits upon the answer...we must take all the guns away from all American citizens, and that will end all the violence and murders on our streets! Yes, that would do it alright – for a short time! And a very short time it would be, because then those who want a gun badly enough will find a way to get one, and when they do, they will kill with it, because the rest of us will be helpless and defenseless against them.

The cause of all killings – every one of them, from the killing of Abel at the hand of his brother Cain, to the latest killing in Michigan, is sin in the human heart. Sin is not just the *opposite* of righteousness, it is the *absence* of righteousness. Hatred, which is a by-product of sin, is not just the *opposite* of love – it is the *absence* of love. Evil is not just the *opposite* of good, it is the *absence* of God, because where God is, evil cannot abide. The violence we are seeing is the out-working of the sin and hatred rooted deep in the hearts of those who pull the triggers.

I have been a minister for about 40 years now, and have met thousands of born-again Christian men, women, boys and girls of all races and nearly every nationality, and not once have I ever heard one of them express a desire to kill another human being. Why? Because they know Jesus Christ as Lord and Savior, and having been indwelt by His Holy Spirit, and being made partakers of His divine nature, we have no desire, no inclination to take another human life by any means. The president often cites the atrocities committed in The Crusades by the "Christians" of that time as justification for the Muslims of today to hate and kill Christians of today. But has it ever occurred to anyone that those who fought and killed Muslims in the Crusades may not have been Christian men at all? Yes, they wore crosses on their clothing and upon their shields and banners, but wearing crosses on ones garments does make him or her a Christian any more than wearing an American flag lapel pin makes you an American!

For centuries Christians and Christianity have borne the blame for many such atrocities as those committed during the Crusades, the torture and plundering of the Aztecs, and countless other atrocities, simply because the atrocities were committed by men wearing crosses on their banner and shields, and hardly anyone has ever had the courage to counter those accusations because it has been assumed and accepted that if a man wears a cross, he is therefore a Christian. Let me emphatically proclaim – NOT SO! Neither wearing nor carrying a cross or crosses upon one's person makes him or her a Christian. Calling oneself a Christian does not make you a Christian.

Being born again by a simple childlike faith in the crucified and risen Savior, Jesus Christ, and that alone, makes one a Christian. But how and when does this childlike faith come into being? It comes by hearing the unadulterated, anointed preaching of the Gospel, being convicted of our own sins and sinfulness by the working of the Holy Spirit upon the soul, being drawn to a heartfelt repentance, and a personal faith in the death, burial and resurrection of Jesus Christ, and receiving Him and His forgiveness – and it is done!

## The Whispering Rose
By Arvil Jones, Ph.D.

The aged but gifted poet
From a far and distant time
Strolled sad and slow through flowering fields
He was searching for a rhyme
The words will surely come he mused
Yet many years had passed
And not one line had he composed
Is my gift quite gone? He asked.

Perhaps if I but pause and rest
Sweet words my mind shall fill
I must not worry, fret nor groan
But bid my soul be still
So there amidst wildflowers bright
No other soul around
With prayerful heart and hope renewed
He lay upon the ground.

Soft breezes made the blades of grass
To dance with joyful grace
They played among the flowers fair
And swept across his face
In quiet slumber long He'd lay
And rest his weary frame

But wait! What's this? His heart replied
Did someone call his name?

Nay, but it cannot be, he said
For no one else is near
'Tis but the sound of rustling leaves
That fall upon my ear
But now the soft voice came again
And many voices more
From whence they came he could not tell
And yet could not ignore.

The breeze had now ceased blowing
Not a leaf moved on the trees
Then at his feet he beheld a sight
That made him bend his knees
It could not be true, and yet it was
Down there among the clover
The lilies and the daffodils
We're laughing with each other

I've gone quite mad, the poet cried
It's just a childish dream
I'm wise enough to know that things
Aren't always what they seem
Surely God would not allow
That mindless flowers should talk

If it were so, then rocks might grow
And the great Sequoias walk.

# 293

Have all my senses grown so dull
Or am I so racked with fear
That I'd mistake one drop of dew
On this tulip for a tear?
Again I must lie down and rest
And sleep in sweet repose
But before his eyelids closed he spied
One tiny, blood-red rose.

Ah yes, he laughed, could not be wrong
To gaze on this a while
And then he saw its petals move
As if to form a smile
He leaned a little closer now
With trembling hand, and weak
Then soft as a timid angels sigh
The rose began to speak.

I know your troubled thoughts, it said
And how its been so long
Your soul has searched for words that rhyme
For the lines of some sweet song
Your prayers have all been heard above
Your quest is nearly done
You'll have your very heart's desire
Ere the set of tomorrow's sun.

Fear not, kind Sir, reach down your hand
And pluck with gentle care
For the one you cherish waits to fix

My petals in her hair
The journey we must make today
Is treacherous and long
Please tarry not a moment more
Arise, let us be gone
Oh hasten now and stop for naught
Except it be to pray
For my fragrance will but last until
The dawn of one more day.

So with lightened heart and quickened step
And his treasure newly found
To him it seemed his tired old feet
Now barely brushed the ground
The Eastern sky was greying now
Faint shadows crept along
He caught the sound of a whip-poor-will
Then the larks began their song.

The distance mattered not at all
Nor yet the evening's chill
O'er mountains steep, 'cross meadows wide
Though tired, he journeyed still
The sun was hastening westward now
And he had yet miles to go
He dared not stop to ponder now
For his steps were getting slow.

But yonder in the distance
At long last now he sees

# 295

And old familiar cottage
Nestled under tall oak trees
And now across the narrow stream
A hundred paces more
Then up the little winding path
He stood in her open door.

In the candle's glow he viewed her face
Sweet countenance bathed in Heaven's grace
Now in her tender hand he'll place
The tiny rose, and plead his case
The rhyming words for which he'd searched
Now came with greatest ease
And gathering all his courage up
He bowed there at her knees.

Accept this tiny gift, my love
I pray, refuse it not
To bring it here has taken nearly
All the life I've got
This rose I offer with my heart
With not a blush of shame
I know God grew this rose for you
For I heard it speak your name.

And then with stars all smiling down
Beneath the pale moon's crest
She smelled and kissed the tiny rose
And drew him to her breast
Content at last, all strength now gone

His soul in rapture's deep
One soft embrace, one gentle kiss
And the poet went to sleep.

Then quick the shining Seraphs flew
To bear his soul up high
Above the clouds and far beyond
The realm of Earth and sky
On through the garnished gates he passed
As silver bells did ring
He knelt before the throne to touch
The scepter of the King.

And then a whisper, soft but near
Who's this? Ah yes, he knows
For fixed in the braids of her golden hair
Are the petals of a rose.

Arvil Jones

## The World's Greatest Book
By Arvil Jones, Th.M.,Ph.D.

If someone were to ask you, "What's the world's greatest Book"
Then where in the whole wide world would you begin to look
Would your first answer be the Library, with a thousand shelves or more
Or would you hope to find It down at the corner store
Would you think of all the so-called Classics that you have ever read
Would the names of famous authors go running through your head
Could you recite from memory a famous quote or two
And could you remember those precious lines
That once meant so much to you
And of all the books that you have read
Is there One that you still hold dear
The One that gave you hope and courage
Or relieved some dreaded fear
Do you remember that Title now
And the famous Author's name
Do you know about His heritage
And the Place from whence He came
Oh yes, I do remember now
It's the Bible of which you speak
The Book that always gave me strength
When I was sad and weak
It's the Book that gave me comfort
In times of sorrow and pain
Yes, It's the world's Greatest Book
I think I'll read It again.
© 2012 Arvil Jones

## Then Came The Burger

Now down in the hills where I was raised
There's a lot of stuff we honored and praised
We raised our own hogs and chickens too
And watermelons and honeydew
But things kept changing at a rapid pace
And we found new ways to feed our face
We had never heard of such a thing
But somebody called it Burger King
A big chunk of meat on a fancy bun
And they hauled that stuff in by the ton
And we never dreamed that family ties
Would someday revolve around burgers and fries
We watched each other get big and round
From eating this newfangled burger we found
Then we started buying em by the sack
'Til some of us had a heart attack
Now we had a dilemma with which to wrestle
So we switched our business to the new White Castle
Then they built a McDonalds just down the road
And we wuz gettin as fat as a toad
So we finally decided we'd had enough
Of all that fancy greasy stuff
So we went back to killin our own fresh meat
And now we can all fit back in our seat
Yeah, we're all done with them burgers and fries
And back to the table and our family ties
Cornbread and buttermilk, taters and pie
'Cause we're all just too young to die.
© 2012 Arvil Jones

## Things I Know for Certain (and so can you).

As the world becomes more modern, with technology and such,
Compared to those around me, I guess I don't know much;
No one ever called me a genius, and I've never claimed to be,
But before I leave this fast-paced world,
There are some things you should know about me;
The best teaching I ever received was from my Mom and Dad,
Who taught me that some things were good, and other things were bad;
I learned from the calluses on my Daddy's hands,
And the melody in my Mama's song;
My Mama who read to me from the Bible, which taught me right from
wrong,
And if there's ever a question about what, or what not to do;
The answers are all in that Holy Book, the only Book that's true,
I know for certain that the Holy Bible is indeed the Word of God;
And I hope to die with it in my hand, when my last mile I have trod,
I know for certain that there was a Cross, upon which Jesus died;
And I know for certain that faith in Him is what makes me justified,
I know for certain there's an empty tomb from which my Lord arose;
And having committed my soul to Him, I sleep in sweet repose,
I am certain that if I never awaken on Earth again to roam;
I have a mansion not made with hands up there in my Heavenly home,
I know for certain that there are others who made the crossing before;
Who are now awaiting my arrival upon that peaceful shore,
I know for certain that it won't be long till I meet my loved ones again;
Where God shall wipe away all tears, and there's no more sorrow or pain,
I know for certain that there's another place - a bubbling burning Hell;
A place of eternal suffering that no mortal tongue can tell,
I know for certain that if anyone would escape that awful place;

He must rely upon Jesus' blood, and God's amazing Grace,
I know for certain that I am saved for all Eternity;
And I wish that I could be as certain, that you will follow me.

## This Day Will be Different

This day will be different, for I will make a difference,
In the life of some precious soul;
I will visit the widow and fatherless on whom fate has taken its toll,
This day will be different, because today I refuse to whine or complain,
No matter how heavy my burden, or how deep may be my pain;
Today will be different, because today I will not accuse nor judge,
But I choose to forgive all trespasses, and I will not hold any grudge;
Today will be different because the dawning found me on my knees,
Instead of folding my hands in sleep, or doing as I please;
Today will be different because I claimed a promise from God's Word,
And He inclined His ear to me, and my feeble prayer was heard;
Today will be different, for I have determined that my lips shall speak no guile,
My tongue shall not curse another man, whether virtuous or vile;
For he was made in the image of God as well as you and I,
And my mouth shall bless him as best I can, for both of us shall die;
Today will be different, for I will be different, and the world looks better now,
Though evil is rampant on every hand, I can see some good somehow;
Today will be different from yesterday, and when it comes to its end,
Again my knees will bow in reverence to my very dearest Friend.
Arvil Jones

## Three men, Three Crosses, Three Testimonies - by Arvil Jones

Three men walked slowly up the hill, each one condemned to die,
And each man knew without a doubt that his end was very nigh;
The shouts and cries of the howling mob fell upon each man's ear,
As the hearts of two of those guilty ones were gripped with morbid fear;

Two of the three were thieves by trade, and deserving of their fate,
And if for them there was any hope, it was surely getting late;
And could there be any hope at all, as the hammer drove the nails,
As men of earth and Heaven's angels heard their dying wails;

One of the three was arrogant and prideful, although so near to death,
He clung to his hate and foolish pride, even to his final breath;
How sad to die in such a state, with God hanging by his side,
And sadder still to know his fate the moment that he died;

But there was something about that third man, something so noble and
strong,
Condemned to die as the other two, although He did nothing wrong;
Hanging there in the blazing sun, His life quickly slipping away,
The heart of a dying thief rejoiced to hear the Savior say;

With Me this day in Paradise, your soul shall surely be,
And for no other reason than the fact that you believed in Me;
Three men, three crosses, three testimonies, to which do you now hold,
Your answer tells where you will be, after your life's story is told.
© 2013 Arvil Jones

## Three Righteous Men

Old Noah was righteous, and he walked with the Lord,
He preached and he labored, and trusted God's word;
He sailed o'er the flood, and he suffered no loss,
But Noah didn't carry the old rugged cross;

Now Daniel found favor in the eyes of the king,
And told him the secrets of all of his dreams;
His faith brought him out of the old lion's den,
But Daniel could not pay the price for my sin;

Now Job was a man whom God richly blessed,
Tormented by Satan, his faith stood the test;
In sorrow he cursed the day he was born,
But Job didn't wear a crown made of thorns;

Only my Savior could pay the great price,
To save a lost soul from sin and from strife;
Though we love the old Prophets, and honor their name,
No one but Jesus could bear all my shame.
  2013 Arvil Jones

## Thy Word, Oh Lord

Thy Word Oh Lord is a Fountain, with Living Waters deep
Throughout the passing ages It has watered many Sheep
Thy Word, Oh Lord is a burning Lamp unto my stumbling feet
Lighting my way unto the place where You and I can meet
Thy Word Oh Lord is Pardon from all my sin and shame
Thy Word that Thou hast magnified even above Thy Name
Thy Word Oh Lord each passing day brings such sweet Peace to me
Thy Word Oh Lord is full of Grace and Power and Purity
Thy Word Oh Lord is my daily Bread
And Thy Spirit the Oil that anoints my head
Thy Word is my shelter from life's raging storm
Thy Word is the fire that keeps me warm
Thy Word is the Sword with which I must fight
Thy Word puts all my foes to flight
Thy Word is my Fortress that keeps me from fear
And my Guardian Angel that hovers so near
Thy Word is my Comfort when I am weak
Thy Word is Thy Voice with which Thou dost speak
Thy Word is a Friend in whom I confide
A Friend Who is always close by my side
Thy Word It begat me when I was lost
Thy Word did guide me straight to the Cross
And when all the words and works of men
And the world itself is gone
Thy Word Oh Lord shall yet endure
And lead us safely Home.
2012 Arvil Jones

## Time – Are there not twelve hours in a day (John 11:9)?


Time, like so many other gifts our Creator gave to man,
Is such a precious and intricate part of His great master plan;
But time is also a God-given tool, and we must learn how to use it,
And what a pity if we should ever squander or abuse it;
We have a choice concerning time, as to how we will employ it,
Some folks seem to only endure it, while others choose to enjoy it;
And how much of this precious gift is often wasted away,
In foolish thoughts and selfish deeds, and unkind words we say;
How much of time is spent each day in learning how to measure it,
'Twould be more fun and practical if we'd only learn to treasure it;
Time, after all, is a borrowed thing, from God it has been lent,
And to Him we all shall give account as to how it was all spent;
So what about our waking hour, was it spent upon our knees?
Or did we make the conscious choice to spend it as we please?
This morning I awakened to the light of another day,
Determined I would spend one hour upon my knees to pray;
But then I was distracted by the ringing of the phone,
And before I even realized, my hour of prayer was gone;
Oh, but I have eleven more, and my prayers can surely wait,
And fluttering about the house, I heard the clock strike eight;
I bowed my head and hurried through a quick and silent prayer,
Then glancing at the coffee table, my Bible was lying there;
I knew I should search its pages for the truths that lie within,
So I quickly scanned some verses as I heard the clock strike ten;
I have so many chores to do, I simply cannot study,
Oh yes, I remember now, I must call my golfing buddy;
But what about the folks who are sick, I know I should visit them,
But then there's my golfing buddy, and I can't break a promise to him;

306

So instead of going to visit them, I'll simply give them a call,
The clock struck twelve, and the gently chimes echoed down the hall;
Half the day had slipped away, and nothing had I done,
As I just stood and wondered where all the time had gone;
And yet I have six hours more, and there's so much to do,
Let's see now, what shall I do first? And then the clock struck two;
Oh my, I must get busy now, there's no more time to waste,
Places to go and people to see, and so I must make haste;
And so I quickly donned my coat and hurried to the store,
Then on to the doctor's office, and now it was nearing four;
Then driving home I texted my friend to see if he was alive,
I got no answer, so I hurried home, just as the clock struck five;
Dear God, I prayed, please help me, for I'm in an awful fix,
If only I had a little more time, then I heard the clock strike six;
Twelve hours quickly came and went- I had wasted another day,
Then down upon my bended knees, I found the time to pray;
Dear God, I asked, forgive me please, for all I left undone,
For neglecting you, neglecting your Word, and neglecting your precious
Son;
I let twelve hours slip away, time I can never retrieve,
And how my conscience screams at me, and how my heart does grieve;
And now the night is falling Lord, and I must lie down to rest,
And through my tears I realize how richly I've been blessed;
My aching heart now longs for You, draw near me Lord, I pray,
And if I wake to see the dawning of another day;

Dear God I make this promise now, I know what I shall do,
I vow that I will spend tomorrow, all alone with You.
2015 Arvil Jones

## Tired, Weary and Worn

.........Jesus therefore, being wearied with his journey....(John 4:6b)

All who have ever worked hard for a living know what tiredness and
weariness mean,
When every part of the body hurts, and wants something on which to
lean;
When you barely have enough strength left to turn the knob on the door,
And you body tells your mind that you cannot take one step more;

When the toil of the day has taken its toll, and you long for the day to
end,
It's a tiredness that only a good hot meal, and a good night's rest will
mend;
And it helps to know there are loving arms that wait at the end of the day,
And the smiles of an understanding family seems to help take the
tiredness away;

But as tiredness affects the body and mind, and you long for a place to sit,
Weariness affects the soul and spirit, and says you ought to just quit;
A tired man knows with a little rest, he can work again tomorrow,
But weariness often overwhelms a man with grief or sorrow;

Grief and sorrow were things with which our Lord was well acquainted,
He often grew so tired and weary, and yet He never fainted;
He spent much of His younger days working in a carpenter's shop,
But when about His Father's business, He found no place to stop;

No human pen could tell nor measure His suffering and loss,

Even from childhood He always knew, His journey would end on a Cross;
Such weariness and grief of soul, no other man has known,
And yet such Love for all mankind, no other man has shown;

Some days when I have worked so hard, and I'm tempted to complain,
I bow my head and am reminded of His unspeakable pain;
Sometimes when I grow weary, and I just want to give up,
I see Him sweating drops of blood, Oh what a bitter cup!

And when I think of the weight of each burden I have borne,
I see Him hanging on the Cross, His body rent and torn;
And when I am so weary, no hope at the end I can see,
I hear Him gently say -Take up thy cross, and follow Me;

But  Lord, I am so weary, must I go another mile?
May I not lay this cross aside for just a little while?
I promise You tomorrow I will take it up again,
But Lord right now I'm just too tired, and my body aches with pain;

And then I hear His gentle voice, the sweetest I've ever heard,
As my body gains new strength as I listen to His Word;
He says, Dear child I've known you even from your Mother's womb,
Do you not remember that beyond the Cross, there is an empty tomb?

One more step, and then another, My weary child go on,
For I will not forsake you when it seems your strength is gone;
It was for you upon the Cross My life I freely gave,
And by My blood you have the victory;
Over death, Hell, and the grave!
© 2014 Arvil Jones

## A Blessed Memorial Day

We just want all of you to know we are grateful for all that you do,
We know it is not a glamorous life you have chosen to pursue;
And although you may be here at Home, or someplace far away,
You will never be forgotten on this blessed Memorial Day;

Some of us know deep in our hearts the loneliness you feel,
And we also know the dangers you face each day are very real;
We know the safety and comfort we have are neither cheap nor free,
And we know there are many other places you would rather be;

We wish we could bring you all home today, and the world would be alright,
We wish there were no political differences, no reason for men to fight;
But as long as you are away from us, the flame of hope will burn,
As we bow our heads in fervent prayer, and ask for your safe return;

We know that most of you have families who are missing you so much,
A wife, a husband, a child or parent who longs to feel your touch;
We pray this Memorial Day will a safe one for you all,
That not a single shot will be fired, and none of you shall fall;

We know that freedom is not free, it comes at an awful cost,
And we want you to know that we, like you, remember the ones we lost;

And if our words mean anything, these few we'd like to say,
May Christ Himself be near you all on this Memorial Day.
God bless you every one!
Arvil and Carolyn Jones

## To Doris

Simply amazing! What more can I say?
A lady in every respect;
She loves, she laughs, she makes others smile,
And yet I dare not neglect;
Her God-given beauty, her character, her genuine concern,
And from her shining example, all of us could learn;
Always giving of herself, asking nothing in return,
As in her heart God's flame of love never ceases to burn;
She leaves behind her seeds of kindness, wherever she may go,
Simply amazing, a cherished friend that I am proud to know.

## *To Laura, from Grandpa*

There are so many things in life with which I have been blessed,
I doubt that I could count them one by one;
A good long life, a loving wife, a marriage of forty-eight years,
Two lovely daughters, and a tall and handsome son;
And as if these were not enough to show me His great love,
Seven grandchildren have now come along;
How gracious God has been to me, and I thank Him every day,
For all the children and grandchildren are healthy and strong;
Dear Laura, as I see you now, and turn back the pages of time,
Reflecting on that day I first saw your face;
Holding you, and your little twin brother, passing you around,
I couldn't help but thank God for His grace;
I said a silent prayer for you, holding you in my arms,
As I have for all these years continued to do;
I asked for you to be happy and healthy, and grow up to be a lady,
And that God Himself would always watch over you;
And yes, my prayers have surely been answered, looking at you now,
So radiant, so beautiful, so loving, gentle and kind;
All too quickly becoming a woman, a lady in every respect,
As the time slips away, and you leave your childhood behind;
I pray you set your goals up high, your standards even higher,
High enough that others must strive to reach;
But always remember to remain humble, reaching out to others,
And if there is only one other lesson I'd teach;
Put your trust in God above, for He will never fail you,
If you have no other friend, He will be there;
He gave His Son to die for you, upon a cruel cross,
And one more thing dear Laura I must share;
Our love for you will follow you wherever you may go,

And we want you to know we're very proud of you;
You will always have our love and support, along with our daily prayers,
No matter where you go, or what you do.
With all my love
Grandpa Jones

## To Legislate or not to Legislate - That is the Question!

As we the American voters sit around MEDITATING,
Hoping our elected leaders will do some LEGISLATING;
It seems the situation just keeps DETERIORATING,
And some of us are sick and tired of WAITING, WAITING, WAITING.

The two parties of DC dummies keep meeting and HESITATING,
While the tempers of the American people are now ESCALATING;
As the Democrats and Republicans keep staring and CASTIGATING,
And all the President knows how to do is to keep EXACERBATING;

It's time they got off their sorry butts and stop the childish DEBATING,
And employ a little bit of common sense, and do some DELIBERATING;
I wonder if the whole bunch of crooks aren't secretly COLLABORATING,
Maybe we should go to the Oval office, and do some INVESTIGATING;

But I know that some deluded souls will just keep on DONATING,
While the egos of our elected official's just keep on INFLATING;
And it seems none of you realize the disaster you're CREATING,
While you keep pretending to be Congressmen, but we know you're just
IMITATING.
A.J. Ph.D.

## To Make a Grown Man Cry

I've heard so many of the sayings of old, sayings like - What's in a name,
And spare the rod and spoil the child, and for a man to cry is a shame;
And don't take any wooden nickels, and where there's breath, there's life,
And the vanity of beating a dead horse, and where there's a tongue,
there's strife;

I grew up thinking that as a man, I'd let no one see me cry,
And if someone happened to see me crying, I'd never tell them why;
But the longer I lived, and the more I learned, some things just didn't
seem right,
Things that broke my heart in two, and made me cry at night;

And now I am not ashamed to admit, many tears have streaked my face,
Many of which were just from being a member of the human race;
In my younger days some of my tears were just the tears of a child,
From being over-confident, or being reckless and wild;

I've cried at the loss of many loved ones who I had known so long,
I've cried remembering my Mother, and the words of her favorite song;
She loved to sing - The Old Country Church, still one if my favorites today,
And Oh how my heart was broken the day she passed away;

I've cried remembering my dear old Dad who loved to hunt so well,
And I often miss his radiant smile, and the stories he loved to tell;
I've cried remembering a family of fourteen, now reduced to three,
For now all the family is gone except two sisters and me;

But as the years pass, there are other things that now bring a tear to my
eye,

As I see the direction our nation is headed, and so few seem to know
why;
It breaks my heart to see our country so deeply engrossed in sin,
Where women can now marry women, and men can marry men;

I cry at night just knowing that today so many have died,
At the hands of an abortionist, and the liberals who take their side;
I weep for the families whose children were murdered in the halls of a
school,
Where God and the Bible have been expelled, along with the Golden
Rule;
God help the man who cannot cry, who will not shed a tear,
Who can murder an innocent baby without an ounce of fear;
God help the eyes that cannot weep for a nation engulfed in shame,
Where men feel no remorse at all to curse God's Holy name;

Those of us who still hold dear the values we were taught,
Still reverence the men who gave their lives, and the freedom for which
they fought;
We weep when we see that freedom being slowly swept away,
And only those who agree with the government are allowed to have their
say;

But our voices will not be silenced till we take our final breath,
And we will cry and we will pray till our eyes shall close in death;
God help me if I ever cease to cry for my fellow man,
God help me if I fail to tell him of God's salvation plan;

There is hope for our nation in Christ alone, for He alone can save,
'Twas He who died upon the Cross, and rose up from the grave;

## 316

The One who cried Forgive them, for they know not what they do,
The One who freely gave His life for men like me and you;

Yes, I can cry, for Jesus cried, when He saw a world that was lost,
The tears from His eyes and His broken heart were only part of the cost;
His very life's blood had to be shed to save the world from sin,
No, I am not ashamed at all to cry for the souls of men.
© 2014 Arvil Jones

## To Mary

In the dawn of her youth the fair young maiden was virtually unknown,
And no one even suspected the grace that God had already
shown;
His mighty hand o'er shadowing her from the day she was conceived,
To perform a work within her womb that most would not believe;
But her kindness, beauty, charm and grace would soon be manifest,
And all the nations of the world would someday call her blest;
No other of her gender had a calling such as she,
To be the Mother of the Blessed Lamb of Galilee;
The fairest of all women gazed into His cherub face,
As She held Him there in Bethlehem, the Giver of all grace;
Worshiped by the holy angels, scorned by men of Earth,
Yet loved beyond all human words by the one who gave Him birth;
Knowing that the day would come that she would suffer loss,
And yet she followed her blessed Son, even to the cross;
No poet's pen could ere describe the horror of that sight,
So terrible the sun itself refused to give it's light;
In His suffering she suffered as she heard His mournful cries,
As thunders rumbled, rending rocks, and darkness clothed the skies;
But death could not constrain Him long, nor yet the cold dark tomb,
For He was God incarnate from the blessed Virgin's womb;
We give her honor for the life she lived while here she trod,
The lovely maiden who became the Mother of our God;
And when someday in Heaven we all gather 'round  the throne,
We'll meet the fairest Lady the world has ever known.
　Arvil Jones

## To My Beautiful Wife

Since you already know that I'm not very good at poetry and such,
Just allow me to tell you in my own quaint way just why I love you so much;
It goes without saying you're very beautiful in every way a woman can be,
But when I look at you there is so much more than beauty and grace that I see;
You were loving and radiant the day we first met, and even more so today,
And what your sweet loving smile does to me, I can't find the words to say;
If I had searched the whole world over, I know I could never find,
A woman more loving and caring and gentle, and gracious and cheerful and kind;
For forty-six years, some smiles and some tears, you're always my very best friend,
And no matter what happens I know you're the one on whom I can always depend;
You've given me courage in the hardest of times, when it seemed that all was lost,
And you've given your all for me and your family while never counting the cost;
You've been by my side for better or worse, forever faithful and true,
And when I can't count on anyone else, I can always count on you;
Oh, yes we've had our share of troubles and trials and stormy weather,
But I've always known that I'm never alone, for we've faced them all together;
I'm a better man because you are my wife, and yes, you bring out my best,
And I often stop to wonder how one man could be so blessed;
And beside all this you've given me three children to adore,
How gracious God has been to me! What man could ask for more?

*And although I cherish your beauty and grace, and all the little things that you do,*
*The greatest reason I love you so much, is simply because you're you!*

*With all my love, now and forever*
*Arvil*

### `To My Family
### from Dad
### "The Seasons of My Life"

Not every man in this old world is nearly as blessed as I,
And if you should ask how I make such a claim;
Well, I'll tell you the reason why,
But before I can tell you why I'm so blessed;
I'll have to go back a few years,
For before I became so richly blessed;
There were many heartaches and tears,
And for every heartache, and for every tear,
There is no one to blame but me;
And I often wonder why it takes so long,
For some men to finally see;
That the place in which we now find ourselves,
Is determined by the roads that we take;
And happiness, or the loss thereof, is by the choices we make,
And as I sit here now, writing these words
Reflecting on the years that have passed,
I ask myself as each season goes by; "will this season be my last?"
I recall the days when I was so young, and it seemed life would never
end,
And it really didn't matter at all, what waited around the next bend;
I never dreamed there might come a day, when life would come to a
close;
But the Spring was all too quickly gone, like the fading of a beautiful Rose;
And the Spring was soon forgotten, as the warm Summer took it's place;
And I realized that time was passing at an awfully rapid pace,
And before I could enjoy it all, the Summer was nearly gone;
And all the things I had planned to do had mostly gone undone,

And the few little things that I did accomplish, now seemed so very small;
And it seemed that in the blink of an eye, Summer gave way to Fall,
And Fall has a way of reminding the soul, "You have only one season more";
Whatever you're going to do, do it now,
Before Winter closes the door;
And now the cold blast of Winter has come, and I cannot turn it back,
And I feel the pain of it's chilling wind, as it howls at my crumbling shack;
But through it all, the snow and the cold, the wind and freezing rain,
My heart still gazes upward, and I dare not to complain;
For though the harsh storm lingers long, and I feel it's bitter sting,
I hear a sweet voice from Heaven say; "I'll give you another Spring";

Another Spring? My heart replied – another Season of joy?
To romp and play among the hills as when I was a boy?
Oh No, the still small voice replied, You'll play on Earth no more,
You have far greater things to do, and better things in store;
I've granted you this precious time to go and make amends,
To spend more time, and share more love with family and friends;
To say the things you should have said, and to do what you left undone,
So use this Season wisely my child, for it will soon be gone;
And then a soft serenity came over my soul at last,
As I reflected once again on the Seasons that have passed;
And one by one I began to count the blessings I have known,
With all the tender mercies, and love that God has shown;
He gave me a loving family to cherish and adore,
And as I think of them each day, I can ask for nothing more;
So let us cherish every day, to laugh, to love, and sing,
'Til the Father finally calls us Home, to the Land of Eternal Spring.
© 2011 Arvil Jones

## *To my Friend*

Each time a poet takes his pen in hand,
To express what's on his mind;
It may be to tell his own life's story,
Or that of a friend true and kind;
He slowly ponders each face he has seen,
All along his journey of life;
He thinks of all those who brought him great joy,
In the midst of his trouble and strife;
He remembers all the love and laughter,
But he also remembers the tears;
He recalls those times when someone was willing,
To listen to his deepest fears;
And there is always that special person,
Who stands out above all the rest;
Not because of their looks or possessions,
Or because they're the biggest or best;
His mind runs back to that special one,
Who simply cared from the heart;
The one who loved him as much at the end,
As she did from the very start;
The one who stood by him when no one else would,
With sweet words of comfort and hope;
The one who always understood, while in the darkness he'd grope,
Yes, friends of this sort are hard to find,
They are far between and few;
And the life of this poet has been richly blessed,
For He found such a Friend in You!

## To Our Illustrious Politicians
By Dr. Arvil Jones, Th.M., Ph.D.

To those of you on Capitol Hill, and to those in my own hometown,
To all of those politicians, from the President, and right on down;
I've been told since I was a lad, that every dog has its day,
And I was told that here in this land, everyone can have his say;
Well all of you fellows have had your say, with your polished words so fine,
Yes, you've had your say, and you'll have your day, but now it's time I had mine.
I guess I should warn you Washington boys, my blood's been boiling a while,
And some of what you're about to read ain't apt to make you smile;
Oh, I know all of you have a way with words, and your high and haughty looks,
Just remember that all of us common folks know that you're all a bunch of crooks;
And with only these few lines I've written, my blood is already cooled,
We just want you to know that - say what you will;
You don't have all of us fooled


They say that plain English is easily understood, so let's just see if that's true,
I don't believe that you got where you are by the number of votes cast for you;
Now if you're thinking the words you're reading are both unkind and uncouth,
There are still a few of us here in this land who believe in the simple truth;

It is my contention that you got where you are through politics, money and lies,
With some powerful "connections", and some liberal news media ties;

Yes, you all sit and live quite well up there on Capitol Hill,
While you fleece your fellow Americans, with both your hands in the till;
You take from us and give to yourselves, and tell us it's all for our good,
Well, not all of us have lost our marbles, here in the neighborhood;
No, dear sirs, we won't go hungry, for our great God will supply,
And just in case you've all forgotten, it's Him you will face by-and-by;

We will all still fervently pray for you, and we refuse to hold a grudge,
We just want you to know that it won't be us, but God who will be your Judge;
We do not intend to whine or complain, or point the finger of blame,
We just wonder how you can sleep at night, and never blush with shame;
While millions of little babies die, and thousands of soldiers too,
And all for the sake of expediency, and the policies that you pursue;
And don't bother to answer this poem dear sirs, with your fancy twisted words,
Ya really want to know what we think of you?  Well, you're all a bunch of t---ds!
Your humble constituent, Dr. Arvil Jones

## To Our New First Lady,

Melania Trump
Dear First Lady, I search for the words to say how thankful I am,
That you and your family will soon be on Capitol Hill;
Such beauty as your's, such charm and grace, along with your character,
Is enough to make America's heart stand still;

May I be the first to welcome you, along with the rest of your family,
I assure you, all of us welcome the change;
And I guess you and Mr. Trump are going to be quite busy,
Getting ready to decorate and re-arrange;

So I'll keep this poem short and sweet, and just say that we love you,
And we stand behind you in whatever you do;
But may I say before I go – of all who came before you,
We've never had a First Lady as lovely as You!
Arvil Jones

## To Prince William and Kate – In honor of their Royal Wedding

'Tis with the utmost honor, sincerity and pride,
That I offer these few words of praise to the Prince and his lovely Bride;
May Great Britain and all the world rejoice at what you do today,
You could not have made a better choice, and may I humbly say;
That we loved your precious Mother Diana, there were none so fair as she,
And as she watches from Heaven today, how proud that she must be;
To see her wise and handsome son as he stands with his Lady fair,
One whose beauty shall grace the Realm with her charm and modest air;
And though we know not what the future holds, we know not when or how,
We pray that God will grant to you the Crown to grace your brow;
Long live the Royal Couple, and blessed may their union be,
May the joy of this occasion be felt across the widest sea;
And may the glad and golden bells of Earth and Heaven ring,
For the Princess and her handsome Prince, who will someday be The King.

With all my love and blessing,
Arvil Jones, Ph.D.

## To The Preacher

How beautiful are the feet of those who preach the Word of God,
Who sow good seed and meet each need while here on Earth they trod;
Who many times must go forth weeping, yet sowing all the while,
Who even though he is tired and weak, must go another mile;
His love for Christ compels him to find the soul that's lost,
And lead the erring one toward home, and bring him to the Cross;
And when one wayward soul is won, he goes to find another,
To give him faith and love and hope, to call him friend and brother;
And if he finds a wandering sheep who somehow lost his way,
He prays that God will give him the proper words to say;
And it matters not to him how far the wandering sheep has gone,
He follows Christ''s example, and leads him gently home;
And when all his Earthly work is done, and as this world he leaves,
He goes to Heaven rejoicing, bringing in His sheaves;
And as he enters the pearly gates, knowing his race is run,
He hears his loving Father say, Well done my child, Well done.@
© Arvil Jones

## To The President – Mr. Trump

I offer my congratulations to you and all your team,
You've proven conclusively, things aren't always as they seem;
Though I may never meet you, Sir, I just want you to know,
I pray that all you've said and done was not all just for show;
One thing I know about America, we know when we're fed up,
And we're fed up with Washington, now can you fix it up?
Are you determined, Mr. Trump, to end the political fighting?
And how long till we can expect to see our country uniting?
The problems are many, as you well know, and they won't just go away,
And we're all waiting to see and hear what you will do and say;
Remember, Sir, who put you there, please don't ever forget,
Lest you, someday, are forced to bow your own head in regret;
We've put our trust and confidence in the promises you've made,
And we're expecting more from you than a victory parade;
And when you take that oath, dear Sir, all of us will hear,
And pray that you will always uphold the values we hold dear;
You have four years, Mr. President, to prove that you are true,
And I give you my promise, Sir, each day I'll pray for you;
And now we all look forward with hope and anticipation,
As we pray for peace and unity in the new administration.
Arvil Jones

## To The Troopers

Their job is like no other, and they all deserve respect,
They must enforce the law without prejudice or neglect;
Each day they don the uniform their lives are on the line,
They must remember every law and discern every sign;
No two days are exactly the same, they never know what's next,
It may be a drunken driver, or a teen sending a text;
They may confront a terrorist with a bomb strapped to his chest,
Or help a stranded citizen, or respond to a simple request;
Whatever the situation, the Trooper must be alert,
He knows his main objective is to help and not to hurt;
The Trooper honors all the law and the country for which it stands,
The fate of a county or the country may be in his hands;
Sometimes he quells a riot that's gotten out of control,
Or he may simply have a stretch of highway to patrol;
He knows the badge upon his chest is bigger than himself,
He sighs a sigh of relief each time he lays his gun on the shelf;
He faced each situation that happened to come his way,
Thankful that he can rest tonight, and serve another day;
He's more than just an emblem of our country's law and order,
What he does affects us all, from border to border;
His job is often dangerous, and yet he serves with pride,
And with all our nation's finest the Trooper stands side by side;
So if in your rear view mirror you see the flashing blue,
Remember he or she is an American just like you.

## To The Woman I Love, by Arvil Jones

As I study your picture hanging there on the wall,
Your beautiful blue eyes just light up the hall;
Then I start to dreaming of our younger days,
When you won my heart with your sweet loving ways;

I always brought flowers on our special day,
The day we were married, and I heard you say;
I'll be your's forever, and we'll never part,
Even till death dear, you'll live in my heart;

Yes, we've had some good times, and we've shed some tears,
And I've cherished each moment all down through the years;
It was always your sweet love that carried us through,
What I'm trying to say dear, is that I love you;

So darling draw closer, for now I must go,
To that land filled with flowers, where tears never flow;
Just remember your promise, that we'd never part,
Yes, even in death dear, you'll live in my heart.
© 2013 Arvil Jones

## Today I met...

Today I met an aged man, sitting all alone,
I cautiously sat beside him, hearing his somber tone;
It seemed he only needed a friend to listen for a while,
And at least once I looked and thought I saw the old man smile;
I couldn't help but notice the well-worn suit he wore,
He said "the children just don't seem to love me anymore;
I lost my dear beloved wife to cancer long ago,
And why the children don't come by, I simply just don't know;
It seems the only time they call is when they have a need,
And sometimes, sir, it hurts so bad, I think my heart will bleed;
I'm sure they know I love them, and all the grandkids too,
I want to see them all so much I don't know what to do;
I leaned a little closer, hoping he could hear,
Then he took out his handkerchief and wiped away a tear;
I tried to speak, but couldn't, my own heart ached so bad,
I threw my arms around him, crying, I love you Dad!
2016 Arvil Jones

## Today went...

I really must say today went quite well,
I have nothing of which to complain;
But tell me, one dear friend asked me,
Did you not have any pain?
Oh yes, I replied, I had some pain,
But you see, the pain keeps me humble;
For there are so many with much more pain than I,
And so I dare not groan or grumble;
Yes, today went very well, I can honestly say,
Even though there were a few tears;
I had to wipe away,
Those tears were just a reminder,
That my heart can still be touched;
By the sorrows and suffering of others,
Who I've come to love so much;
My ears heard the sound of a choir singing,
Such a spiritual melody;
I felt the touch of the hand of a friend,
Who offered sweet comfort to me;
Today went quite well, for I found in God's Word,
Another promise to claim;
And Oh how my heart is always reminded,
There's just something about that Name;
How is it your day was filled with blessings,
My friend asked – Tell me please?

# 333

The answer is really quite simple my friend,
I began this day on my knees.
2016 Arvil Jones

## Today's Greatest Tragedy

I saw the news, it troubled me, and yes, I did complain,
I heard many overdosed on heroin and died;
Many young people were killed in the cities and towns of the world,
Some gays got married, and another politician lied;
Families are worried about their safety, others about their next meal,
And others about Greece defaulting on her loans;
In several third world countries, children are starving to death,
As their helpless parents listen to their dying moans;
It seems nearly every nation on Earth is poised for a fight,
As on the horizon World War III seems to loom;
For many millions around the world there seems to be little hope,
And all their hearts can foresee is utter doom;
Racial tension is escalating, no one trusts in their government,
To the voice of the people the government pays no heed;
Crime grows more rampant every day, murders are on the rise,
And the nation is consumed with lust, power and greed;
I could mention many more tragic things that happened here today,
And some would no doubt agree with my every word;
But the greatest tragedy in the world today, was none of the above,
But that I led not a single soul to my Lord!
Arvil Jones

## Tomorrow

The day is quickly waning, soon night will take its place,
How quickly the days are flying, as if they are in a race;
It seems like only a few hours ago, I gazed on the rising sun,
Then all too quickly the shadows fall, and soon the day is done;
But there's always tomorrow I've told myself along these passing years,
It seems the hope of tomorrow somehow stifles many fears;
And so we take for granted that the sun again will rise,
And perhaps tomorrow no dark clouds will hover in the skies;
Ahh, yes, tomorrow, how sweet the thought, another opportunity,
And perhaps tomorrow nothing will disrupt my serenity;
Perhaps tomorrow I may forget the pain I felt today,
Perhaps something tomorrow holds will sweep it all away;
Perhaps tomorrow not one child will have a hunger pain,
Perhaps tomorrow not one child will have to die in vain;
Perhaps tomorrow everyone will have a place to sleep,
Perhaps tomorrow each promise I made, I will endeavor to keep;
Of tomorrow I can only dream, and fashion what might be,
For if there is a tomorrow, it is not left to me;
As these old eyes and this old heart now ponder the days gone by,
I dimly watch today a fading, and breathe a heavy sign;
Tomorrow is not promised me, nor to any man alive,
That ghostlike dream we call tomorrow, for some will not arrive;
Today I live, today I breathe, today I know my lot,
Tomorrow is a phantom, today is all I've got;
So what shall I do with this day, this gift my Maker gave?
Shall I sow the fertile furrows, or dig tomorrow's grave?
Shall I languish in self-pity as the hours swiftly fly?
Or shall I render kindness ere the sun slips from the sky?

Shall I wait until tomorrow to say what I must say?

And run the risk of never seeing the light of another day?

Too much, too much is already wasted to waste a moment more,

For what man knows but that the reaper stands before his door;

'Tis late, 'tis late the sweeping hands of time now cry aloud,

How then shall I boast of tomorrow, as one who is overmuch proud?

And so I rise from ease and comfort, and cast all fears away,

To do all that must now be done, ere tomorrow becomes today.

2015 Arvil Jones

## Too near Home

As soon as some folks hear me speak they ask me where I'm from,
But I really believe most of them already know;
But being the nice polite folks they are, they ask me anyway,
I guess it's sort of a courtesy they show;
And yes, I have a distinctive accent, most folks call it hillbilly,
And you'll find it spoken in several southern states;
Kentucky's the place where I was born, along with my lovely wife,
You'll have to excuse me if I don't give you the dates;
And if you're wondering – Yes sir, we were raised kinda poor,
But so were all our neighbors, so we didn't know it;
But we were richer than a lot of folks in things that really mattered,
We had some morals, and weren't afraid to show it;
Now I'm not saying we were better than anybody else,
But we all knew the difference between right and wrong;
Our parents taught us a thing called respect, and love for one another,
And "you're gonna get fleas if you lie with dogs too long."
The preachers in our country church preached from The Holy Bible,
And they taught us – You must be born again!
All the preaching and singing was done with the Holy Spirit,
And every sinner was convicted of his sin;
Now a lot of years have come and gone since I was a little boy,
And I keep hearing that this world sure has changed;
A lot of folks keep telling me I'm just an old diehard,
And I need to have my thinking re-arranged;
I'm often told that I should pause, and consider a compromise,
And maybe just bend a little now and then;
For after all, they ask me now – What could be the harm,

If once in a while I indulge in a little sin?
But believing the Bible as I do, and knowing what sin has done,
To the bodies and souls of men, including mine;
I quickly and reverently refer them to the Sacred Holy Scriptures,
"It's the little foxes that destroy the vine."
I'm told that I should change with the times, and just try to blend in,
Like all the politicians in Washington do;
I'm told I should accept whatever the majority is doing,
Like casual sex, or a glass of champagne or two;
Well sirs, if that's how you want to live, I know I cannot stop you,
And you may never heed a word I say;
But with all the love I have in my heart, I have to remind you,
There is surely coming a Judgment Day;
I've lived too long to be flattered by the siren voice I hear,
Enticing me to forsake the God of my soul;
I'm too near home to turn back now, too close to my reward,
Just a few more days till I reach Heaven's goal;
My soul has felt His Spirit, my heart has heard His Word,
My feet are about to tread where angels roam;
So do not waste your time dear sirs in trying to dissuade me,
I can hear the sweet old hymn – I'm too near Home.
2016 Arvil Jones

## Two Trees

Look there my love, in the midst of the garden, two trees stand side by
side,
But may we eat of both of them, and under their shade abide?
Nay my love, of this one tree, we may neither eat nor touch,
Do you not remember just today, our Maker said as much?

But dear, 'tis such a lovely tree, and pleasant to my eyes,
But dear the Master said who eats of this tree surely dies;
Then came a quiet whisper floating softly on the breeze,
Hath not your Master said that ye may eat of all the trees?

Why should you not partake of this, for is it not your right?
And didn't your Maker make you ruler of all that's in your sight?
I say dear lady, be not afraid, for the fruit shall make you wise,
And you shall know the secrets of the seas and of the skies;

The two of you shall be as gods, with the world at your feet,
With only one small taste of this delicious treat;
Oh linger not dear lady, eat it now, and do not fear,
For as you can see my lovely one, your Master is nowhere near;

And why would He restrain you from a single fruit as this?
Could it be that in His counsel something is amiss?
"Tis I and I alone whose words are honest and true,
And why should one fruit be withheld from one as lovely as you?

But sir how may I know that your word is not a lie,
For God has said that if I eat it, that day I'll surely die;
Oh lovely one, the choice is your's, which way your mind shall go,
But if you eat not of this fruit, then you will never know;

I see dear sir, and with your words I cannot disagree,
And all the angels in Heaven watched, as she reached toward the tree;
A single choice, one decision, based on the words of a stranger,
Questioning the Word of her own Maker, she brushed aside the danger;

See now my love, I have eaten the fruit, and I am living still,
I beg of you, come eat with me, do not oppose my will;
My dear is the fruit as sweet to the taste as your voice is to me?
Take it my love, taste for yourself, and surely you will agree;

As she raised the fruit to Adam's lips, he gave in to her smile,
Looking deep into her eyes, trembling all the while;
The serpent's voice whispered again, you shall not surely die,
But once the fruit had touched his tongue, he knew it was a lie;

Their eyes now met in horror at their nakedness and shame,
As hastily the man and wife now sought someone to blame;
Now each of them was certain that the crooked serpent had lied,
As quickly each of them now ran to find a place to hide;

With trembling hearts and trembling hands, and tears upon their face,
Among the trees they hid themselves in terror and disgrace;
Upon each other's nakedness they were ashamed to look,

Turning their backs to each other, some fig leaves each now took;

It was the best that they could do to hide their shame for now,
They'd simply make the best of it, and carry on somehow;
Would God come looking for them? And would He love them still?
Or could they bear to face Him, having disobeyed His will?

And then they heard a familiar voice, it seemed not far away,
It was the voice of God Himself, walking in the cool of the day;
They held onto each other, cringing in dread and fear,
Where art thou Adam? The voice rang, and they knew that He was near;

I am over here my Lord, hidden among the trees,
And again the voice of God resounded upon the evening breeze;
Why must you hide from Me my child, tell Me what hast thou done?
I was naked Lord, and hid myself, and from Thee I have run;

Who told thee thou wast naked? Have you eaten of the tree?
My Lord, my heart was overcome by the Woman You made for me;
Oh Woman what is this I hear? Are you both now defiled?
I listened to the serpent Lord, and so I was beguiled;

Oh vile and crooked serpent, on thy belly shalt thou go,
Till the Seed of the Woman bruise thy head, and all the world shall know;
That I am True and thou a Liar, and that I am God alone,
And the Woman's Seed, My beloved Son shall rule upon His Throne;

And cursed be the Earth itself, for thorns and thistles shall grow,
And you my son shall till the fields, in sorrow shalt thou sow;

# 342

Thy brow shall sweat, thy back shall bend, thy heart shall sorely yearn,
For from the dust were ye taken, and to dust shall ye return;

In sorrow shall the Woman conceive, and the man shall be her head,
In the sweat of his face the man shall toil, and earn his daily bread;
And now before your very eyes, another deed I must do,
Innocent blood must now be shed, so that I may cover you;

Your aprons of leaves that you have made can never hide your sins,
The Lord Himself then slew the Lambs, and made them coats of skins;
And so the two were driven from the garden at God's word,
Looking back they saw the Tree of Life and a flaming sword;

Now banished from the Garden, they faced a life of toil,
As each day Adam bent his back turning up the soil;
He grieved with every painful step, sweating beneath the sun,
As thorns and thistles cut his legs till the weary day was done;

And then one day while in the field, he heard a horrible scream,
He dropped his plow, ran through the thorns, and leaped across the
stream,
Inside the tent he saw his wife, holding a baby boy,
And for a while they forgot their troubles, and shared a bundle of joy;

Oh Adam, God has given a son, I have even forgotten my pain,
And dear he looks so much like you, I think I'll call him Cain;
Here in my arms I hold the Seed, just as the Lord has said,
Perhaps he'll be the very one to smite the serpent's head;

Oh may the good Lord hasten the day when sin shall be no more,
For since the day we ate the fruit, it surely has vexed us sore;
Oh yes my dear, I share your thoughts, I too remember that day,
When all the bliss of Paradise was suddenly taken away;

Yet in my heart I have a hope that God will prevail somehow,
And make the life of all mankind much better than it is now;
I still recall the solemn words our Master said that day,
About the shedding of innocent blood, to take our sin away;

I do not understand it all, but I believe it still,
Though we have sinned, He yet forgives, and keeps us in His will;
And though my sin bring me to death, and cause me grief and pain,
Somehow I know that innocent blood will bring me life again;

And so the couple raised their son, and taught him all they knew,
They watched him play among the clover, wet with the morning dew;
And though they had their troubles and trials, they also shared some joy,
And a few years later Eve gave birth to another baby boy;

Now Cain learned quickly from his father, how to sow and reap,
But Abel very soon became a keeper of the sheep;
His heart was set on being a shepherd, and Cain loved tilling the sod,
Then one day both of them brought offerings to their God;

In reverent faith Abel brought the firstlings of his sheep,
And Cain brought of the fruit of the ground, a large and goodly heap;
Each of them was certain he was doing what was right,
And surely both the offerings would be pleasing in God's sight;

Upon Abel and his offering, God smiled with acceptance and favor,
The blood and body of the lamb sent up a sweet-smelling savor;
And Cain was sure that God would accept his offering as well,
But when God refused him and his offering, then Cain's countenance fell;

His anger was kindled against the Lord, and against his brother too,
And in his wicked heart he then decided what he'd do;
He plotted to take his brother's life, he'd find a time and place,
And in the field his brother saw the hatred in his face;

And there Cain slew his brother while no one was around,
But God saw the innocent blood as it soaked into the ground;
Adam and Eve saw their son's dead body, and screamed with a mournful
cry,
As again the words of God echoed - Ye shall surely die!

Ye shall surely die!
Ye shall surely die!
Ye shall surely die!
Arvil Jones

## Waiting

Oh how much time we spend waiting, for people, for answers, for things,
We wait for trains, we wait for planes, for cabs and wedding rings;
We wait for buses, we wait for bosses, we wait for the alarm,
We wait for our children's footsteps, to know they are safe from harm;
We wait for the teacher to teach us the things we do not know,
We wait for the precious fruit from the tiny seeds we sow;
We wait with anticipation for the little baby's first breath,
We wait for the doctor to inform us of a loved one's death;
We wait for the ones we love to tell us that they love us too,
We wait for the supervisor to tell us what to do;
We wait for all the good things of life to somehow come our way,
We wait for the words of the politicians, to see what they have to say;
We wait to see the outcome of our favorite sporting event,
We wait to receive a fair return from the money we have spent;
We wait for our wives to finally find their very favorite dress,
We wait for the slothful teenager to clean up his or her mess;
We wait for the preacher to tell us we're really not that bad,
We wait for relief from the night before, and all the fun we had;
We wait for our daughters to find a faithful man to wed,
We wait for our parents to tell us, it's time to go to bed;
We wait for the teacher to tell us we finally passed the test,
We wait for the judges to give us a ribbon, proving we are the best;
Yes, we wait for a lot of things while here on earth we trod,
But how much time do we ever spend, simply waiting on God?
2016 Arvil Jones

## Watching

When we were small, they watched us intently, watching us play and grow,
They watched us get hurt, and kissed our wounds, and ahh how they loved us so;
They made many a sacrifice just to see that we were clothed and fed,
And they prayed for us with fervent heart, and tucked us into bed;
They laughed at all the silly things we often said and did,
And they always knew those secret things we tried hard to keep hid;
They watched us develop our character, as they taught us day by day,
And we were so often careless as the time slipped quickly away;
And it seemed we hardly noticed that their eyes were growing dim,
And suddenly we realize that we are watching them;
We watch them as their aching bodies slowly bend with age,
And the cruel years of time pass by as the turning of a page;
We watch them now and see they cannot do what they used to do,
As the brilliant smile they used to show now has a more somber hue;
We watch them and we recognize their steps are getting slow,
And their voice that once was strong and clear is now so soft and low;
We watch as the deepening lines of age begin to crease their face,
And yet somehow they bear it all with dignity and grace;
We watch them as they trust their God, as they have for many years,
The One who has sustained them through all their grief and tears;
How long we have to watch them, we really cannot tell,
But yet we'll keep on watching 'til they bid us all farewell.

## We sure miss you Joe

A few men I have met in life have left an indelible mark,
The life they lived was like a candle, lighting up the dark;
Some who left a legacy that will forever endure,
Men whose word could be trusted, their steps steady and sure;
Men who saw their calling in life, and followed it to the end,
Men who everyone was proud to call a neighbor and friend;
I'm proud to say I knew such a man from many years ago,
They called him The 'Ol Left Hander, better known as Joe;
A man of integrity and character, ever so gentle and kind,
And if Joe was your friend, no better friend could you find;
I can still hear him in the booth, sitting close to the mic,
Beside his close friend Marty, calling each ball and strike;
I often wonder what Joe would think about the game today,
Things have changed a lot since Joe had to go away;
So Joe, if you can see us, just say a little prayer,
For there are still some in MLB who seem to really care;
Father's Day is coming up, and we wanted you to know,
We'll always love and remember you, and we all miss you Joe;
We'll never forget your famous line, no matter what may come,
"The 'Ol Left Hander, rounding third, and heading for home."
2015 Arvil Jones

## *We want to get married...*

We want to get married, the young couple laughed, without giving it
much thought,
The young girl gazed at the golden ring and the beautiful gown he'd
bought;
The young man gazed upon her beauty, and that's about all he could see,
He was thinking-"in a few more minutes, you'll belong to me;"

Their young minds filled with anticipation of a wonderful honeymoon,
As each of them was thinking it couldn't some too soon;
The wedding and the honeymoon were all that they could see,
She whispered-"in a few more minutes, you'll belong to me;"

But suddenly there was a change in the whole atmosphere,
As they heard the wise old preacher man say-"please, come, sit here;"
"I'd like to talk to the two of you, that is, if you don't mind,"
And don't take me wrong, but I guess you're both thinking- "love is blind?"

Now I know you're in a hurry to become man and wife,
But tell me sir, how much do you know about married life?
Yes, I understand you'd like the ceremony soon,
But tell me Miss, have you even thought beyond the honeymoon?

May I say to you that marriage is far more than just a vow,
And I hope you understand it goes beyond the here-and-now;
You say you love each other, but is that really true?
Love isn't something that you have, it's something that you do;

The couple sat in silence as the wise old preacher spoke,

*He asked-"young lady, will you love him, even when he's broke?"*
*"And young man, will you love her when her hair has turned to gray?"*
*"And will you love her just as much if her beauty fades away?"*

*The couple squirmed a little as he continued on,*
*And before they even realized, a whole hour had gone;*
*But the preacher man was patient, his voice soft a low,*
*He said-"dear friends, I think there are some things you ought to know;"*

*"I'll tell you of three marriages, one of them my own,*
*We were married sixty years, but now my wife is gone;*
*She was my only woman, and I her only man,*
*I know you're in a hurry, but bear with me if you can;*

*Our love survived disasters, disease and world wars,*
*We endured the great Depression, we gathered many scars;*
*We loved each other through it all until her final breath,*
*The only thing that could part us was the chilly hand of death;*

*And then there was my Mom and Dad, married for seventy years,*
*Their love survived fourteen children, and many bitter tears;*
*Through happiness or heartache their devotion carried on,*
*And Mother held my Daddy's hand till his final breath was gone;*

*And yet there's one more marriage, I pray you'll recognize,*
*A marriage that is yet to come, beyond the starry skies;*
*A marriage with a love so deep the Bridegroom bled and died,*
*Who laid His life down freely for His spotless Bride;*

*Now, how much do you love this girl? He asked the man again,*
*Will you defend her with your life, in sorrow and in pain?*
*Young lady, Is there any man you love as much as him?*
*And will you love him just as much when his eyes are growing dim?*

*The couple thought it over as they saw the preacher smile,*
*He asked-"Now would you rather think on this a while?"*
*The preacher's smile grew broader as the young man held her hand,*
*His old heart pounded with delight as he watched them stand;*
*They said-"We'll love each other with every breath of life,"*
*The preacher smiled and said-"I now pronounce you Man-and Wife."*
*2016 Arvil Jones*

## Welcome to America, Land of the Me, Home of the Slave

Wherefore God also gave them up to uncleanness through the lusts of their own hearts, to dishonor their own bodies between themselves: Who changed the truth of God into a lie, and worshiped and served the creature more than the Creator, who is blessed forever. Amen. For this cause God gave them up unto vile affections: for even their women did change the natural use into that which is against nature: And likewise also the men, leaving the natural use of the woman, burned in their lust one toward another; men with men, working that which is unseemly, and receiving in themselves that recompense of their error, which was meet. And even as they did not like to retain God in their knowledge, God gave them over to a reprobate mind, to do those things which are not convenient: Being filled with all unrighteousness, fornication, wickedness, covetousness, maliciousness; full of envy, murder, debate, deceit, malignity; whisperers, Backbiters, haters of God, despiteful, proud, boasters, inventors of evil things, disobedient to parents, Without understanding, covenant breakers, without natural affection, implacable, unmerciful: Who knowing the judgment of God, that they which do such things are worthy of death, not only do the same, but have pleasure in the that do them (Romans 1:24-32).

When it's all about Me...then I am my own slave,
When it's all about Christ, then, and only then, am I truly free.
Arvil Jones

## What Christmas Means to Me

When I was much younger, carefree and wild,
Just being myself like any other child;
There were many things I looked forward to,
For the things I could get, and the things I could do;
And Christmas was all about tinsel and toys,
And candy and presents for the girls and boys;
It was sledding and sleigh rides and snowball fights,
And singing carols, and flickering lights;
A season of joy filled with laughter and glee,
And decorating the most beautiful tree;
But as I grew older, more mature and wise,
Slowly I began to realize;
That Christmas is more than just a season,
It has a purpose, a meaning, and reason;
I learned that Christmas is not about me,
Nor finding presents under a tree;
It's about how God has dealt with our sin,
By coming to Earth to dwell among men;
It's all about Him, God's gift to mankind,
The greatest gift we could ever find;
Christmas is all about Jesus our Lord,
Who gave us a gift that no man could afford;
The babe to whom the angels did sing,
Is Christ our Savior, our Lord and our King.
© 2012 Arvil Jones

## What Have I Done?

Today I sit and ponder the hours that have gone by,
As the sun keeps hastening quickly toward the western sky;
And as I reflect I reach to brush another tear from my eye,
And ask myself – how many more little babies had to die?
The little ones who never got to see the light of day,
Who never got the chance to crawl, or walk, or talk, or play;
Because of those in power, who say they had no rights,
No right to birth, no right to live, or see earth's many sights;
They say the law must, at all cost, protect the mother's rights,
While the child is robbed of all its tomorrows, of all its days and nights;
Days and nights he could have been loved, and held so tenderly,
But because the mother demands her rights, the baby cannot be;
That little boy or little girl will never ride a bike,
He or she will never be taken out for a mountain hike;
They will never sit at the supper table, or break a piece of bread,
For someone decided that they must live, and the little child be dead;
And as I reach toward my eyes and brush another tear away,
My heart is broken as I search for the proper words to say;
What have I done in my lifetime to stop the holocaust,
The wholesale slaughter of the innocent ones whose lives should mean
the most?
If I have but one way to fight, and if it be my pen,
May God give power to my words – let me write, and then;
If He may grant that my few words may at last do some good,
At least I may lie down in death, and say I did what I could;
If only one small life is saved, then shall my soul rejoice,
That God would choose to use my pen to give the world my voice;
No longer can I remain complacent, no longer silent be,

For I was once a baby, bounced on my Mother's knee;
Along with thirteen others, she loved us one and all,
Ahh, how I remember responding to her call;
The call to come to supper, when the family gathered 'round,
How often now I wish I could again hear that sweet sound;
The sound of love and laughter, as the children were all fed,
The gentle good night kisses as we scurried off to bed;
Abortion was never an option where I was born and raised,
My Mom loved all her children, as her God she daily praised;
And to those of you who kill the babies, this question I ask of you,
How would you feel if your own mother believed in abortion too?
And to those of you who sat on that bench, and as your gavel fell,
Creating that first murderous law, spawned in the pits of Hell;
Aren't you glad your mother didn't choose to murder you?
And if you are, then please take time to consider what you do;
What have I done? What will you do, to stop this awful thing?
I pray as you lie down tonight, these words will loudly ring;
That little one in his mother's womb has just as much right as I,
To live, to love, to work and play, and then, when he must die;
Let his death be from old age, and not from a butcher's knife,
For in the sight of God you have no right to take his life.
2016 Arvil Jones

## What I Have Written I Have Written...

These fateful words from long ago, from the lips of a Roman governor,
Spoke volumes about what was then upon his mind;
After he had brutally scourged the Man from Galilee,
Mercilessly beaten, and treated so unkind;
The words read – Jesus of Nazareth, King of the Jews,
And truly Jesus was their rightful King;
But now they had rejected Him, and gave Him over to die,
The world has never seen such a horrible thing;
The words that Pilate had inscribed, and placed above His head,
Offended the very ones He came to save;
But now that they were written, they could not be changed,
Those words would follow Pilate to his grave;
What I have written I have written, how solemn the words he spoke,
And their meaning has a lesson for us all;
For we, like Pilate are also writing, and like his words of old,
Our written words will either stand or fall;
As each day of our lives gives way to the shadows of the night,
You and I have written another page;
Perhaps not either with pen or ink, but still it is all written,
And how will it be read in a coming age?
Today we wrote another page in another chapter of life,
And what we wrote today cannot be changed;
The words we spoke, the deeds we did, the things we left undone,
And none of it can now be re-arranged;
Another day in our history has now been written down,
Are we willing to let others read it all?
Or would we change it if we could, maybe a sentence or two?
A deed or two we'd rather not recall?

What I have written I have written, and now the ink is dried,
Indelibly it will forever stand;
The day is gone, but not forgotten, for Heaven saw it all,
Another page produced by my own hand;
What I have written I have written, by others to be read,
And when they read it, will they smile or frown?
When all the pages and the chapters come to be a book,
What kind of story have I written down?
And as I read my own life's story, one page at a time,
How many pages would I love to erase?
If only I had written better, I often tell myself,
But now it's written, and the writing I must face;
But in my heart there is a hope that if tomorrow comes,
Tomorrow's page may have a brighter tone;
Perhaps I yet may leave behind a better page or two,
For others to read whenever I am gone;
And if you are the one who reads the story of my life,
When that little book is closed at last;
May it be said – He did his best, at least with what he had,
He was no judge, and had no stones to cast;
What I have written I have written, and now the day is done,
As I let the pen fall from my weary hand;
My witness is in Heaven, my record is on high,
And now I go before the bar to stand;
And now I hear Him reading my record back to me,
He has recorded every idle word;
What I have written I have written, and He has read it all,
And every word I spoke His ear has heard;
And now I see Him look at me, as He takes me by the hand,

Should I be glad, or bow my head in shame?
What I have written I have written, He says to me at last,
As in His Book He points to my name!
2016 Arvil Jones

## What Lies Ahead?

Ever so quickly another year has now come to its close,
And what lies ahead in the coming year, not one of us really knows;
But as I reflect upon the year that has gone, I simply have to say,
I have the Lord above to thank for each and every day;

God does not give to us the knowledge of what tomorrow holds,
But He gave us two eyes to watch whatever He unfolds;
Tomorrow has not yet been born, and from it we cannot borrow,
We know not what tomorrow holds, but we know who holds tomorrow;

Can each of us reflect upon the year that has now gone,
And say that we have no regrets, and are ready to move on;
Or did we make a few mistakes, and wish we could call them back,
If only God would grant that we could somehow erase our track;

But we know that is impossible, for the past cannot be changed,
The things that we did yesterday cannot be re-arranged;
But there is something we can do, we can learn from yesterday,
And shun those things that caused us to stumble on our way;

What lies ahead? What fear or dread? What test, what trial or shock?
And what if before tomorrow comes, death at our door shall knock?
There are so many unknown things that catch us unawares,
But the wise man knows that he shall die, and for that he prepares;

Trusting in Jesus Christ alone, tomorrow holds no fear,
For the One who holds tomorrow is always very near;
He who holds the keys of death, of time and eternity,

Has sworn that with His children, He shall forever be;

What lies ahead in this brief life matters not much at all,
When once the soul has heeded to the Master's gentle call;
What lies ahead for the child of God, no mortal tongue can tell,
We rest assured in His grace alone, knowing that all is well.
Arvil Jones

## What Makes You Special

What if someday we would take the time
To tell our dear friends all our heart
And tell them the things that make them so special
Would we really know just where to start
If we look only at the outward appearance
How much can we really see
No, there is far more than the outside
That makes you so special to me
The very first thing that I noticed about you
Was a smile that could melt a cold heart
And a light that shone through your radiant eyes
And somehow I knew from the start
That you were filled with a goodness of character
And integrity so real and sincere
And that I could trust you with unfailing faith
And that I had nothing to fear
I saw in you a deep compassion, and a love for all of mankind
The good things that dwell down deep in your heart
Are things that aren't easy to find
My life has been blessed for just knowing you
If only for just a short time
To a life that really needed a friend
You have brought some reason and rhyme
And I will always cherish you with the fondest kind of love
And if we never meet down here, I'm sure we'll meet above.
Arvil Jones

## What Matters Most of All

Quite recently an election was held here on American soil,
We all saw and heard the candidates, and watched their labor and toil;
We heard all the polished speeches they made, about how much they cared,
We patiently listened day by day, as their political views they shared;
Of course all of this is nothing new, it happens every four years,
And much of what they had to say bored many of us to tears;
And yet we listened again and again, from dawn till setting sun,
As each man told us what he could do, and a little of what he had done;
We heard a great deal about how these men would bring about great change,
And yet it seems nothing changes, now don't you think that's strange?
These men keep saying that they have the answers to all that is wrong in the world,
While face to face upon a stage, slanderous accusations were hurled;
They pitted Americans against each other in a bitter political fight,
And all the while they were telling us that all of us should unite;
Now I ask you, What's wrong with this picture? Do they take us all to be fools?
Do they think that because they are who they are, that we must bend to their rules?
Now don't get me wrong, I greatly respect the office of the President,
But as of today no one in that office can convince me that he's Heaven-sent;
It matters not at all to me, the name of the man in that chair,
For I know a Man far greater than he, Who has promised all my burdens to bear;

I care not at all about power, nor wealth or worldly fame,
And I'd rather die than to tell a lie in order to have a great name;
May I ask the reader who reads these lines - What matters most to you?
Do you know that God keeps a record of all that we say and do?
Do our leaders know that God Himself causes Kings to rise and fall?
And that someday He will require an account, and each man will answer that call;
And so I leave it to other men to curse and to kill and to fight,
What matters to me is to stand before Christ in a robe of spotless white.
© 2012 Arvil Jones

## What shall I write?

What shall I write, the puzzled poet asked himself one day,
What can a man such as myself possibly have to say;
What can I write to other men which has not already been said?
Or shall I copy the sacred lines of men both living and dead?
Something which deserves to be written, that other eyes may see,
And if when written will cause other men to know that it was me?
For I've learned the lesson that our words can cause men to laugh or cry,
As the Sacred Word teaches – our words have the power to cause men to
live or die;
Or does it matter what is written in this pretentious age?
Does anyone really pay attention to what's on the printed page?
And does that which is written reveal its author's heart?
Can the reader read between the lines, and pick the story apart?
What truth, what message, what great ideal does the author intend?
And will the reader be enlightened at the story's end?
Ahh! But there lies the very essence of the writer's call,
That whatever he has written shall have no end at all;
But that his words, his own ideals might live on and on,
That men might be made to ponder, even when he is gone;
Men of earth, drawn from the clay, knowing that we are vain,
Yet strain our souls in a futile attempt to write in a sweeter strain;
Like a helpless ship in raging waters, having not a sail,
We yet pretend that all is well, and struggle to no avail;
To fill each line with greater worth than the line that came before,
Yet with each line keep drifting ever farther from the shore;
Again I ask, What shall I write? Or should I write at all?
For the day will come when all I have written will either stand or fall,
And how will all my writing fare when finally put to the test?

Will most men say it was worthless, and few say it was the best?
And does it really matter when all is said and done?
What puny men have written ere that final setting sun?
Then let the matter be settled – if it is our gift to write,
Then write we must, whether good or bad, contrary or contrite;
But let us be assured of this – we will give an account someday,
For every word and sentence written, and every word we say;
For man must face his Maker, and behold the open Book,
To view his earthly record upon which he must look;
And by that Standard all is measured, and in that Balance weighed,
Where all accounts will be settled, and every debt be paid;
Oh tremble all ye mortals before you write again,
Lest your words shall be found faulty, and finally bring you pain;
For that which has been written upon the Sacred page,
Will try the words of every scribe and poet of every age;
When all our words and works will be tested by the living Word,
And each shall hear his sentence read before the living Lord.
2016 Arvil Jones

## What to Expect?

Well, now we know for certain who are the candidates,
We've heard a lot of rhetoric, and now it's time for debates;
We can expect to watch them as they cover all the states,
And now the media will scrutinize both their running mates;
So it's Donal Trump versus Hillary Clinton, and now the race is on,
And I know we can expect to hear about all the good they've done;
Of course we'll also hear about all the good they will do,
And how they're surely going to make things better for me and you;
And of course each side will soon collide in heated conversation,
And try to convince the rest of us that they can save our nation;
They'll dig up dirt on each other, of course, and spread it across the
screen,
As the media scrambles to try to keep up with each and every scene;
We can expect a lot of mud-slinging, with a lot of tempers flaring,
There will be some violent protests, and the sound of sirens blaring;
We can expect the liberal media to smile and prognosticate,
And some will argue vehemently over who won each debate;
And as sure as a snake crawls on its belly, and as sure as the eagle flies,
We can without a doubt expect to hear some flagrant lies;
And all the lies we hear, of course, will pretend to be the truth,
I just hope we all remember this when we enter the voting booth;
But then, when all is said and done, I guess we must choose one,
But again I fear that afterward we will weep for what we've done;
Neither candidate can save America from herself,
For America has forsaken her God, and put Him on a shelf;
Which candidate is the better one? Does anyone really know?
Well, there's one thing I know for sure - we'll reap just what we sow!
2016 Arvil Jones

## When I am Gone

There is a Book that I have read, and cherished for many years,
It speaks of life, and warns of death, It speaks of pain and tears;
The Book tells us that our days are numbered, and even the hairs or our head,
It tells of a coming Day of Judgment, a Day that so many men dread;
It tells of a Day when all the secrets of men will be made known,
When all of us must give an account of the seed that we have sown;
The Eternal truths within this Book are infallible, inerrant and true,
Truths that were given from God to men, to lighten the paths they pursue;
These truths are the written laws of God, to govern the ways of men,
To guide them in the ways of God, and to steer them away from sin;
Great peace have they who love God's law, and in it meditate,
To love God's law is to have no fear of a coming future state;
Oh! What then shall we leave behind, when all of life is done,
And what then shall be said of us when finally we are gone;
When our loved ones view the lifeless corpse, what words will they then speak,
Will I be remembered as a man of strength, or one who was fearful and weak;
Will I be remembered as a godly man, who tried to do his best,
Will others say that by my life their own was somehow blessed;
But no matter what is said of me, Let this be the final word,
Let them look into my pallid face, and say - He loved the Lord!
For if I should leave nothing else behind me when I go,
This truth and this truth alone is all you need to know;
For if my life has somehow failed to glorify my God,
Nothing else will matter when I sleep beneath the sod;

Then haste the day my Blessed Lord when Thy glorious face I'll see,
For You know that I love You Lord, because You first loved me.

## When I See a Cross

I have traveled so many roads in Life
And so many things I have seen
I cannot number the miles I have driven
Nor the places that I have been
And sometimes I yearned just to have a friend
To help me carry my load
And then I saw three Crosses
Standing by the side of the road
The "C" in the Cross stands for the Curse
That Jesus bore for me
For Cursed is everyone that hangeth on a Tree
The "R" stands for Redemption bought by His precious blood
Redeemed from Satan, Sin and Self
By that mighty cleansing flood
The "O" stands for Omnipotence
For there is no greater Power
The One who holds the sparrow
And Created every flower
The first "S" means Salvation, forever, full and free
And the last "S" is my Savior
Who gave His life for me.
© Arvil Jones

## When That Day Comes

'Tis a day which no one can postpone and no one can evade,
A day when men will face the earthly record they have made;
How recklessly we spend our days, as if there is no end,
Not knowing what awaits us just around the bend;
How proudly men avail themselves of pleasures here below,
Their lust, their greed, their aspirations, putting on a show;
Ever desiring to increase and improve his lot on earth,
In an endless futile struggle even from his lowly birth;
For after all he is but dust, and to that he shall return,
And yet he never ceases to covet and to yearn;
He disregards his immortal soul in search of wealth and fame,
To gain the applause of others, to make himself a name;
Somewhere in the deep recesses of his distracted mind,
He longs for peace and happiness, but no peace can he find;
And happiness eludes him, and so he must pretend,
That all is well, and that his earthly life will have no end;
And so he gathers all he can to fill the void within,
Yet nothing can fill the void nor alleviate his sin;
He tells himself he has no need except himself alone,
He needs no God and no forgiveness, he will make it on his own;
Then suddenly the days and months have now turned into years,
And he has kept his fears inside, and hidden many tears;
He lets no one see his pain, still he must play his part,
He acts as if there's nothing wrong, while horror grips his heart;
He knows that day is swiftly approaching when he must breathe his last,
And now he realizes his life has gone so fast;
His wealth, his fame, his friends applause have all been but in vain,
Oh how he wishes he could go back and do it all again;

He tells himself that he would change his life in many ways,
He'd strive to be more careful as to how he spent his days;
He vows he'd be more sensitive to others and their needs,
And surely he'd restrain himself from sowing so many wild seeds;
He sees the wrinkles and the scars that have all taken their toll,
And now he's looking inward at his immortal soul;
So long he has neglected that, and now he feels the sting,
As somewhere in the distance a bell begins to ring;
He hears a voice from within which says – it tolls for thee,
And someone is approaching - he asks- Who could it be?
And now he sees the sickle and the reaper's ghastly grin,
He tells himself perhaps I should repent of all my sin;
But then before his tongue can speak, or ere his head can bow,
His soul has left his body, and we ask – Where is he now?
2016 Arvil Jones, Ph.D.

## When Words Just Aren't Enough

As we once again as Americans face yet another tragedy
There are some who say we should all hang our heads in shame
That something as horrible as what we have seen could happen here in this land
And it seems that all of us are searching for someone to blame
While the hearts and homes of so many families have been broken beyond repair
And no one seems to have an answer anymore
We ask ourselves what will happen next, and how many more must die
And should we add yet another deadbolt to our door
Can any of us feel safe in our homes, in our schools, or the shopping mall
Or is there safety anywhere we might go
Can anyone be safe where sin is rampant, in a land where God is insulted
Surely you must agree that the answer is NO
Men are not safe from their fellow men, and neither can they be
As long as there is sin in the human heart
It is a fact so sad but true, since Cain killed his brother Abel
Men have been killing their brothers from the start
And the killing will continue for as long as men shall live
In a fallen world that has long been cursed by sin
Time cannot cure it, words cannot slay it, and men can find no answer
There must be a transformation wrought within
Until the hearts of men are changed by the grace of the risen Lord
There will be no safety for them anywhere
For He alone has the power to save, to cleanse and sanctify
And on a cross He proved His love and care
To the dear families who are grieving today, I can only offer you this

That there is safety in Jesus Christ alone
In Him there is comfort, peace and hope, and consolation sweet
And the deepest love this world has ever known

## When

When the mountain is too steep to climb,
And the summit seems too far away;
When the dark storm clouds blot out the sun,
And I cannot see the light of day;
I pray.

When the pain is just too much to bear,
And nothing takes the pain away;
When my heart is loaded down with care,
And no one knows just what to say;
I pray.

When the doctors hang their heads,
And tell me there is no more hope;
When life is hanging by slender threads,
And it seems I can no longer cope;
I pray.

When it seems each breath will be the last,
And the loved one can no longer speak;
When it seems that life is ebbing fast,
And my own faith is growing weak;
I pray.

I pray to Him though it may seem,
There's no more reason to pray;

Though some may say 'tis but a dream,
I call on Him anyway;
By faith I call, and call again,
Though the answer may not come;
Till I've exhausted all my strength,
And though my knees are numb;
My Lord has never failed me,
And this I surely know;
Sometimes He answers – Yes,
Sometimes He answers – No;
Sometimes He tells me just to wait,
And trust His perfect will;
Though I may wait a lifetime,
Yet I will trust Him still.
2016 Arvil Jones

## Whenever I See A Rainbow - by Arvil Jones

I can never forget the very first time I saw a rainbow in the sky,
Of all the things I could have seen, it was the rainbow that caught my eye;
Back then I still had the heart, the mind, and the eyes of a little child,
And the sight of that many-colored arch above made my imagination run wild;
The beauty of that shining rainbow surpassed everything else around,
And I strained my neck just trying to see where each end touched the ground;

I had no knowledge of science or nature, just the imagination of a little boy,
But nothing else in my young life had brought me so much joy;
I needed no explanations how the rainbow came to be,
I only knew it was a beautiful sight for a young boy's eyes to see;
Those who were with me laughed to see the wonder in my eyes,
At my first sight of that gorgeous arc stretching across the skies;

We slowly lost sight of that rainbow as we quickly sped along,
But its beauty lingered in my heart like the melody of a song;
Somewhere deep inside my soul that image would forever remain,
And my young mind wondered if I would ever see something that lovely again;
There were so many things about that rainbow my young heart yearned to know,
And when I asked, someone replied, "Son it's just a rainbow";

But somehow I knew there was more to that rainbow than just what meets the eye,

There had to be something, or someone above who placed it in the sky;
Then as I began to get older, and started going to school,
Where we learned to read and write and spell, and abide by The Golden Rule;
One day right after a frightening storm, another rainbow appeared,
And again its beauty greatly surpassed the storm that we had feared;

I asked my teacher to tell me how the rainbow came to be,
He said, "Son, open your Bible, and in it you will see";
He smiled as I opened my Bible, laying all other books aside,
And my heart began to pound with wonder as I read what was inside;
I read of God's awful judgment upon the sin of all mankind,
Because when He looked for righteousness, no righteousness could He find;

And yet He saw one faithful man who still believed in His Word,
While everyone else just did as they pleased, not listening to what they had heard;
God gave to Noah a master plan for an ark in which to sail,
And when the Flood came, those left behind began to weep and wail;
But Noah and his family landed safely, and a whole new life began,
Because he believed in the Word of God, and followed the Master's plan;
If not for the mercy and grace of God, the ark would have been their shroud,
But God, in His infinite wisdom and love, set a rainbow in the cloud;
A bright and shining token of His covenant with man and the earth,
A glorious symbol of how much the Lord thought the souls of men were worth;
He made an everlasting covenant for all the world to see,

A thing of rarest beauty that says He still loves you and me;

And now when I see a rainbow, right after the storm has passed,
I know how the rainbow came to be, and I have no questions to ask;
And after all the storms of life, and the winds of judgment have blown,
Again I will see the shining rainbow, like an emerald around His Throne.
© 2013 Arvil Jones

## Where Angels Roam - by Arvil Jones

Who are these bright and Holy Ones whose forms are seldom seen
Who sometimes come in flaming fire, and sometimes come as men
They are the Faithful agents who are sent from God on High
Sometimes to bring us comfort when our heart just wants to cry
Sometimes they come to guard us when the foe would do us harm
Sometimes they give us shelter from the wind and raging storm
Sometimes they simply follow us to catch us when we fall
Then sometimes they defend us when our back's against the wall
Sometimes they go before us to make sure the path is clear
Sometimes they stop us in our tracks, so the Master's voice we'll hear
Sometimes they gently whisper a sweet message to our soul
When it seems that all the storms of life, like mighty thunders roll
And no matter where we go in life, no matter how great our fear
We can always calmly rest assured, an Angel is always near
And when all of life is over and on Earth we cease to roam
Again He'll send the Angels, and they'll carry us safely Home.
2012 Arvil Jones

## Whispers

The day was ending like most other days had ended the past few years,
My tired old body was aching, and desperately needed sleep;
My wife had cooked a wonderful supper of all my favorite things,
I just wanted to close my eyes and not hear a peep;
I was very thankful for another safe trip of more than a thousand miles,
So I looked up and thanked the good Lord one more time;
My bed looked so inviting as I made my way toward it,
Then I could have sworn I heard the sweetest chime;
But I just simply ignored it, for my hearing isn't so good,
And the chimes are outside, beside our old porch swing;
I told myself it was just a bit of ringing in my ears,
So I listened closely, and didn't hear a thing;
Besides, I thought, there is no wind, and all is quiet and still,
So again I attributed the sound to my old age;
I smiled and sat on the side of the bed, almost falling asleep,
When I heard a soft whisper, like the turning of a page;
The whisper was like no other I'd heard from any human voice,
As gentle as the brush of an angel's wing;
And now I knew there was someone else inside the room with me,
So I closed my eyes and didn't say a thing;
I bowed my head and waited for the voice to speak again,
But my heart was saying softly – Lord here am I;
I haven't forgotten your voice Lord, I still know it quite well,
Then I felt His touch, and breathed a gentle sigh;
Although I couldn't see Him, I felt Him take my hand,
And I knew that He was sitting by my side;
It was as if time had stood still, His voice was silent now,
As my life flashed before me, and I almost cried;

But then He gripped my hand again, and whispered, Look at Me,
I turned and saw my Savior sitting there;
There was such a softness in His eyes, my heart began to throb,
As I heard ten thousand voices in the air;
He stood and lifted me from the bed, then threw His arms around me,
And I knew exactly why the Lord had come;
As I began to sing – Swing low sweet chariot,
Coming for to carry me Home.
2015 Arvil Jones

## Why God gave us two feet!

God did not give man two feet so that he could kick the dog,
Neither to kick his children or his wife;
His feet were not made to kick other men, neither to kick his neighbor,
But without his feet he would have a miserable life;
'Tis sad but true that some never learn why God gave them their feet,
And so they go through life without a clue,
Using their feet, their hands, their mouths, their eyes, their ears, their noses;
Doing with them whatever they choose to do;
Man's feet were designed to be a foundation upon which he could stand,
And be a man in the face of doubt and fear;
And so that he could ambulate from one place to the other,
To walk or run to places far and near;
Some men choose to walk circumspectly, being careful how they walk,
Shunning the evil and running to the good;
Some men stand for what is right, immoveable and strong,
Standing firm where men of honor stood;
Never backing up or down, no matter what the cost,
Because there was a principle involved;
They stand their ground undaunted by the slanderous words of others,
Whenever there's a problem to be solved;
'Tis sad but true that many cower, and never take a stand,
Unwilling to offend the liberal crowd;
Their feet are swift to join in, rather than stand alone,
Not having a thing of which they can be proud;
They live and die without a cause, no substance can they show,
For a life that was spent without a solid creed;
They live and die without any honor, no lasting legacy,

Never knowing whether to follow or to lead;
The feet of man were made to walk, never backward, but straight on,
And to stand whenever a stand is to be made;
His feet were made to run a race, or climb the highest mountain,
Pressing forward no matter how steep the grade;
And then, when the race is finally over, and the mountain has been conquered,
When his feet have gone that last long weary mile;
At last he sees the summit of Zion's sunny slope,
To meet his Maker with a beaming smile!
2016 Arvil Jones

## Why God gave us two hands...By Arvil Jones

Have you ever seen a man with no hands, and pitied him?
Did you wonder how it was he lost his hands?
Did it take your thoughts to the sights you've seen, maybe on TV,
Of the poor, the sick, the homeless of many lands?
Does it make you wonder what you would do if that man were you?
If in his condition you had to live each day?
How does he live, how does he eat, how does he dress himself?
How would he react to whatever you might say?
And what do you say to such a man? Do you offer pity or love?
And which do you think he would want the most?
Did he catch your reaction the moment you first saw him?
Looking as if you had seen a ghost?
So how do we use our God-given hands? For evil or for good?
Do we employ them to meet our need?
Or do we use our hands for the benefit of others?
Or do our hands sustain our lust and greed?
Have my hands been employed in the work my Maker gave?
Have my hands fulfilled the purpose He ordained?
Have my hands built anything that's good, that will stand the test of time?
Or have my hands with filthiness been stained?
Can my neighbor say it was my hands that helped him in his need?
Or did I hide my hands behind my back?
Did my hands reach out to the poor, whether near or far away?
Did I question if the needy were white or black?
And when someday before the seat of judgment we arrive,
When each man before his Maker stands;
How will it be with you and me when we hear Him ask,
How many sheaves do you have in your hands?

'Twould be far better for a man to have no hands at all,
Than to fail to use the hands his Maker gave;
How much good he could have done for himself and others,
But now his hands lie lifeless in the grave;
The hands of some men strum the harp, and make a joyful sound,
While the hands of others take a human life;
The hands of some men help a child come from its Mother's womb,
While the hands of others wield the butcher's knife;
A loving Mother takes her hands and rocks the little cradle,
Then rises up to cook and mend and sew;
While other hands hang idle, till they find something to steal,
And have never used a shovel or a hoe;
So why did God give us two hands? The answer is quite simple,
To serve the Master and our fellow man;
To work, to play, to help someone, to write, to strum, to reach,
To do whatever good we possibly can.
2016 Arvil Jones

## Windows of the soul

Ever had a friend or foe with a secret they couldn't tell?
Something you knew they were trying to hide?
And though you wanted an honest answer, when they walked away,
You wondered if they'd told the truth, or lied?
Ever had a husband, a boyfriend or a child,
Who somehow couldn't look you in the eye?
No matter how sweet might be the words, or how many excuses,
You somehow knew they were telling you a lie?
If ever it has happened to you, then you know what I mean,
Each time the honest truth is being evaded;
When a man can't look you in the eye, and give an honest answer,
Then you know the truth is being shaded;
The eyes are the windows of the soul, and God designed it so,
To let us know when something isn't quite right;
But somewhere in the great beyond, when all accounts are given,
All will be brought out into the light;
Every idle word we speak, with every twisted truth,
Before the universe will be exposed;
Every secret, here unknown, there will be unfolded,
Those things which in our hearts we have enclosed;
The piercing eyes of God Himself will cause each heart to tremble,
Before whose throne no sin can hope to hide;
Where all our records will be read, broadcast for all to hear,
Where nothing but the truth can 'ere abide.

## Words

A soft answer turneth away wrath: but grievous words stir up anger (Prov.15:1).

Pleasant words are as an honeycomb, sweet to the soul and health to the bones (Prov. 16:24).

For by thy words thou shalt be justified, and by thy words thou shalt be condemned (Matt.12:37).

My Mother said "son folks will judge you by your words, and how you treat them,

So let all your words be sweet, for someday you may have to eat them;

The One Who invented the spoken word tells us how to use them,

But like everything the Maker gave us, we sometimes tend to abuse them;

Words were originally designed to give praise to God above,

Sometimes through prayer, sometimes through song, or just to express our love;

Loving words spring from the heart, and bless the one who hears,

But when the heart is bitter, our words may bring forth tears;

A word of wisdom in due season can strengthen and instill,

While a single word of hatred can maim, or even kill;

A word of vengeance, a word of strife, I ask you which is worse,

We're told to guard the gates of our mouth, lest our neighbor hear a curse;

The tongue holds the power of life and death, then shall we not restrain it?

The damage done by a single tongue – Hell cannot contain it!

Shall my mouth utter that which is wrong when it knows to utter right?

Shall I bless God with my tongue today, and curse my neighbor tonight?

Shall I rejoice in the time of plenty, and give my thanks to Him?
Then mourn and weep in the evening as the light begins to dim?
Oh let my words be sweet and few, and let me bless my friend,

If my tongue speaks not truth and wisdom then cut it out I pray,
For what good will a bitter tongue do me at the end of day?
Better to have no tongue at all, no mouth with which to speak,
Unless my tongue shall bless the poor, and strengthen him that's weak;
And if my tongue gives no glory to the One who gave me life,
'Twould be far better for my tongue to feel the sharpest knife;
Oh let my tongue rejoice in Him, let my heart retain His Word,
But let my tongue be silent if it honors not my Lord.

www.ingramcontent.com/pod-product-compliance
Lightning Source LLC
Chambersburg PA
CBHW071403090426
42737CB00011B/1333